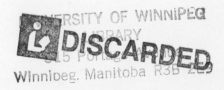

Medieval English Domestic Life and Amusements in the Works Of Chaucer

THE CATHOLIC UNIVERSITY OF AMERICA

1.

Medieval English Domestic Life and Amusements in the Works of Chaucer

A DISSERTATION

BY

SISTER MARY ERNESTINE WHITMORE, A.M.

NEW YORK
COOPER SQUARE PUBLISHERS, INC.
1972

Originally Published 1937
Published 1972 by Cooper Square Publishers, Inc.
59 Fourth Avenue, New York, N. Y. 10003
International Standard Book No. 0-8154-0382-8
Library of Congress Catalog Card No. 77-145877

TABLE OF CONTENTS

PAGE

ABBREVIATIONS _____ vii

PREFACE _____ ix

CHAPTER

I. THE HOUSE AND ITS FURNISHINGS IN CHAUCER _____ 1
    A. Houses in General _____ 2
    B. Types of Houses in Detail _____ 2
        a. Castle _____ 2
        b. Manor _____ 9
        c. Town House _____ 12
        d. Cottage _____ 18
    C. Furnishings in General _____ 21
    D. The Hall and its Furnishings _____ 22
    E. The Solar and its Furnishings _____ 30
    F. Lodging Houses _____ 46

II. THE GARDEN IN CHAUCER _____ 53
    A. Gardens in General _____ 55
    B. The Kinds of Gardens _____ 56
    C. Size and Location of Gardens _____ 66
    D. Trees, Fruits, Flowers, and Herbs _____ 68
    E. Social Significance of the Garden _____ 82

III. MEALS AND TABLE MANNERS IN CHAUCER _____ 91
    A. Meals in General _____ 91
    B. Number of Meals and Time of Eating _____ 92
    C. Place of Eating _____ 97
    D. Menus for Feasts and Meals _____ 98
    E. Cookery _____ 113
    F. The Dining Hall and Service at Table _____ 119
    G. Table Manners and Miscellaneous Matters _____ 129

TABLE OF CONTENTS

CHAPTER   PAGE

IV.   DRESS AND PERSONAL ADORNMENT IN CHAUCER 139
     A.   Dress in General 140
     B.   Masculine Dress and Accessories 140
        a.   Civil 141
        b.   Military 155
        c.   Religious 161
     C.   Feminine Dress and Accessories 171
        a.   Civil 172
        b.   Religious 181
     D.   Attitude of Moralists and Preachers toward Dress 186

V.   SPORTS AND PASTIMES IN CHAUCER 192
     A.   Sports and Pastimes in General 192
     B.   Hunting and Hounds 193
     C.   Hawking 204
     D.   The Tournament 208
     E.   Dancing 219
     F.   Archery 226
     G.   Wrestling 227
     H.   Chess and Tables 230
     I.   Gambling 234
     J.   Music and Reading 236

GENERAL SUMMARY AND CONCLUSIONS 248

APPENDIX 254

BIBLIOGRAPHY 262

INDEX ....

ABBREVIATIONS

1. CHAUCER'S WORKS

BD	The Book of the Duchess
Cl. T.	The Clerk's Tale
CYT	The Canon's Yeoman's Tale
Fkl. T.	The Franklin's Tale
Gen. Prol.	The General Prologue of the Canterbury Tales
HF	The House of Fame
Kn. T.	The Knight's Tale
LGW	The Legend of Good Women
Mcpl. T.	The Manciple's Tale
Mer. T.	The Merchant's Tale
Mil. T.	The Miller's Tale
Mk. T.	The Monk's Tale
MLT	The Man of Law's Tale
NPT	The Nun's Priest's Tale
Pard. T.	The Pardoner's Tale
Pars. T.	The Parson's Tale
PF	The Parlement of Foules
RR	The Romaunt de la Rose
Rv. T.	The Reeve's Tale
Sh. T.	The Shipman's Tale
Sq. T.	The Squire's Tale
Sum. T.	The Summoner's Tale
Sir Thop.	The Tale of Sir Thopas
TC	Troilus and Criseyde
WBT	The Wife of Bath's Tale

The letters A, B, C, D, E, F, G, H, and I, used before certain of the above abbreviations, indicate the section or group to which each tale belongs according to Skeat's arrangement.

2. Journals, Publications, Etc.

EETS	Publications of the Early English Text Society
JEGP	Journal of English and Germanic Philology
MLN	Modern Language Notes
MLR	Modern Language Review
MP	Modern Philology
NED	New English Dictionary
PMLA	Publications of the Modern Language Association
RHS	Publications of the Royal Historical Society

PREFACE

This investigation has been undertaken with the avowed purpose of presenting a composite view of English medieval social life as seen in the numerous, scattered allusions made by Chaucer in his literary works to the manners and customs of his times. By means of classifying the references and a comparative study of them in relation to other medieval sources, the social background is reconstructed in various of its phases and is seen to be in large part characteristically English, even in poems influenced by other literature and those having, at least nominally, foreign settings.

That a study of this nature would be helpful to Chaucerian students was first evident to me when in giving some thought to the treatment of social manners and customs in the *Troilus and Criseyde* I learned that little had been written on such a subject except in occasional papers dealing with only one or two of the poet's allusions, or in works of unusually wide scope in which social life is only a small part of the investigations. One dissertation, Maria Koellreuter's *Das Privatleben in England nach den Dichtungen von Chaucer, Gower und Langland,* submitted in 1908 at Halle, bears in some respects remarkable likeness to the subject as I have treated it. Yet this work, as the title suggests, is not confined to Chaucer's treatment of manners and customs. Furthermore, it is of very wide scope, considering numerous topics in addition to the ones dealt with in the present work, and is not complete in that it can be concerned only with the most obvious of Chaucer's references and hardly at all with the incidental, often merely suggestive ones. There is likewise little effort made by Miss Koellreuter to study the allusions in relation to those of other sources than those mentioned in her title.

Among specialized studies, in which references made by Chaucer to but one or two aspects of social history are treated, may be mentioned Stuart Robinson's "Elements of Realism in 'The Knight's Tale';"[1] Oliver F. Emerson's "Chaucer and Medieval

---

[1] *Journal of English and Germanic Philology,* 14 (April, 1915), 226-256.

Hunting,"[2] Albert S. Cook's "Beginning the Board in Prussia,"[3] Gordon H. Gerould's "The Social Status of Chaucer's Franklin,"[4] and so on. Works dealing with English medieval civilization and treating of Chaucer's allusions in a general way include George G. Coulton's *Social Life in Britain* and *Chaucer and His England;* Edward L. Cutts' *Scenes and Characters of the Middle Ages;* William B. Rands' *Chaucer's England,* and Frederick Tupper's *Types of Society in Medieval Literature.* Still other works, treating of particular aspects of civilization and referring occasionally to Chaucer, prove valuable for a study of this type. Among them may be cited as representative, Thomas Wright's *The Homes of Other Days;* the anonymous *Our English Home;* William E. Mead's *The English Medieval Feast;* Sir Frank Crisp's *Medieval Gardens;* Joseph Strutt's *A Complete View of the Dress and Habits of the People of England* and *Sports and Pastimes of the Middle Ages.* All of the foregoing works, special and general, together with the notes given in Chaucer texts, particularly those of Skeat, Manly, and Robinson have been helpful in the preparation of this dissertation and I acknowledge with gratitude the assistance they have rendered.

In the hope of presenting an intensive rather than a comprehensive treatment of English medieval domestic life and amusements, I have limited my investigation to but relatively few topics. Trivial as they may seem in relation to the broader scheme of life, they are yet significant. Information concerning the medieval house and its furnishings, the garden, meals and table manners, dress and adornment, and sports and pastimes is valuable insofar as it indicates the principal externals of domestic life and consequently allows one to participate vicariously in the activities which occupied the medieval person from day to day. Along with the study of customs the collection of Chaucer's references to the subject has entailed the consideration of their relative value as sources of information. Some of them, for instance, are

---

[2] *Romanic Review,* 13 (April-June, 1922), 115-150.
[3] *Journal of English and Germanic Philology,* 14 (July, 1915), 375-389.
[4] *Publications of the Modern Language Association,* 41 (June, 1926), 262-279.

strongly dependent on other works and follow the literary conventions of the times; hence, the phases of social life which they present are likely to be less realistic than those phases which are based on descriptive details of greater originality. Where it has been possible I have showed the distinction between the two types of allusions, namely the conventional and the realistic, suggesting at the same time that all the references are generally based on actual fourteenth century life.

In limiting the problem in the foregoing manner, it has been necessary to omit many aspects of society which are of importance. This study does not treat of religious ceremonies and practices, of education, of daily occupations, of social classes, except incidentally, of economic factors, or of human relationships, all of which are frequently alluded to by Chaucer. Probably too, there is some omission of references to the topics considered; anyone familiar with Chaucer's works knows that each re-reading discovers something new, either in a direct statement or, what is more likely, in a hidden or incidental comment made by the author. However, my intention has been to record as many as possible of the allusions to English medieval domestic life that the conclusions reached might be at least reasonably accurate.

It is with pleasure that I acknowledge my indebtedness to all who have in any way made this work possible. Particularly am I grateful for the opportunity afforded me by Mother M. Josepha and the Sisters of the Congregation to pursue my studies in the graduate school of the Catholic University of America. To the Reverend Speer Strahan, of the Department of English, I am indebted for his assistance in the selection of my subject and the encouragement and aid he rendered while the work was in progress. I am also grateful to Doctor Paul J. Ketrick, of the Department of English, and to Doctor Martin R. P. McGuire, Associate Professor of Greek and Latin, for their careful reading and helpful criticism of the manuscript; and to the Staffs of the Library of Congress and Mullen Library for their gracious courtesy and service.

SISTER MARY ERNESTINE

June, 1937.

CHAPTER I

THE HOUSE AND ITS FURNISHINGS

His woning was ful fair up-on an heeth,
With grene trees shadwed was his place.
—A Gen. Prol., 606-607.

The house of Chaucer's England is significant in the development of English domestic history. Prior to the fourteenth century the construction of houses had been governed largely by the necessity of defence;[1] now the principles of beauty and comfort were

---

[1] The earliest houses in England of which we have record in literature appear to have been great banqueting halls, with sleeping quarters for the lord's family built apart from them, all within an enclosing wall. There is little evidence of the home as a center of family life. See *Beowulf,* trans. by Francis B. Gummere (New York, 1909), 25-78, *passim;* "The Wanderer," in *Anglo-Saxon and Norse Poems,* ed. and trans. by Nora K. Chadwick (Cambridge, 1922), 11-13; "The Seafarer," *ibid.,* 21-23; and "The Ruin," *ibid.,* 55-56. For evidence of the type of home occupied by the humbler and the very poor people, see the Venerable Bede's *Ecclesiastical History,* ed. and trans. by Thomas Miller, EETS, OS 95 and 96 (London, 1890-1891), Part I, bk. 3, 181 ff., and his "Vita S. Cuthberti," Migne, *Patrologia Latina,* XCIV.

It was because these homes were undefended that the Normans so easily captured them. Realizing that they would be in danger of being similarly conquered, the Normans constructed well fortified castles to replace the Anglo-Saxon homes. The main feature of these castles was the great keep, a massive wooden or stone structure, roughly rectangular in form, with rampart walks at the summit of its walls. It was generally of two or three stories in height, with the living quarters in the upper story and supply rooms, housing for soldiers, and shelter for cattle in the lower. It was a dismal habitation, having only narrow windows or arrow slits for light and air, and was often damp and very cold.

Gradually these castles were modified by the successors of William the Conqueror. The outside walls of the site, rather than the keep, were strongly fortified; the buildings, including a hall for living quarters, a chapel, stores for men and arms, and shelters for cattle, were grouped in orderly fashion within the surrounding walls. Sometimes the old keep survived as a tower or prison, but it was no longer used as a dwelling for the lord and his family. The castle as a whole was very strongly defended, especially by virtue of the fortified walls around the site.

being combined with that of security, and the modern home was beginning to take shape.[2]   It may be said that domestic architecture, as well as house furnishing, was developing into an art. Chaucer's literary works offer much information on the dwellings of the period.   Interpreted in the light of other sources his allusions to this aspect of domestic life appear important.

Houses in General in Chaucer

Many of Chaucer's references to houses are necessarily fragmentary and often almost accidental.   There is no complete view of any single dwelling or of any one room.   In several cases the descriptions are based on literary models rather than on actual observation and are so enhanced by the poet's imagination as to appear singularly unreal.   Yet even in view of these limitations it is possible to reconstruct fairly well nearly every type of fourteenth century house.   Architectural details, the immediate surroundings, such as walls, gates, and the like, the general arrangement and juxtaposition of the rooms, furnishings and decorations are more or less fully described.

Types of Houses in Detail: Castle, Manor, Town House, Cottage

I

The castle is more specifically described than any other type of dwelling in Chaucer's works.   Yet because it is generally of an imaginary character it seems strangely unreal.   The descriptions of it depend often on literary sources and follow closely the traditions established by romance literature; they show, however, most of the characteristic architectural features of the actual fourteenth century castle.

One of the most completely outlined of Chaucer's castles is that which the poet presents in his translation of the *Romaunt de la*

See John A. Gotch, *The Growth of the English House* (London, 1928), 4-7; Edmund B. F. D'Auvergne, *The English Castles* (New York, 1926), 7 ff.; John J. Stevenson, *House Architecture*, 2 vols. (London, 1880), II, 7 ff.; E. Viollet-le-Duc, *Dictionnaire raisonné de l'architecture française du XI-XVI siècle,* 9 vols. (Paris, 18—), III, 75-105, *passim.*

[2] *Our English Home* (London, 1860), 17.

Rose.[3] Less significant than if it had been of his own creation, it is nevertheless not to be disregarded in a study of his allusions to medieval dwellings. Whether or not the original description was modelled on the actually existing Louvre of Philippe-Auguste, as has been suggested by Viollet-le-Duc,[4] Chaucer's use of the details is such as to make the castle appear singularly real.

In true fourteenth century fashion the castle is surrounded by a deep ditch, or moat, which is

> Right wondir large, and also brood.[5]

Upon the banks of this moat is a sturdy wall, made of squared stones and of great thickness, which is a hundred fathoms square. The wall is well fortified:

> Lest any tyme it were assayled,
> Ful wel aboute it was batayled;
> And rounde environ eek were set
> Ful many a riche and fair touret.
> At every corner of this wal
> Was set a tour ful principal;
> And everich hadde, withoute fable,
> A porte-colys defensable[6]
> To kepe of enemies, and to greve,
> That there hir force wolde preve.[7]

Within the enclosure of this wall is a tower, the survival of the great keep of Norman times. This is "large and wyde, and of gret might."[8] It is made of stone "hard as ademant," reinforced with

---

[3] In spite of many discussions as to whether the translation of the *Romaunt de la Rose* is really to be accredited to Chaucer, it seems safe to assume here that it is. In most points the particular passages relating to the Castle of Jealousy are similar to those in the French version.

[4] *Dict. Arch.*, III, 122-128, *passim*.

[5] *RR* Frag. B, 4152-4153.

[6] The portcullis was an iron gate at the entrance to the castle yard. It was operated from a guard room above it. Sometimes this room was sufficiently large and commodious for a family residence. Chaucer, himself, lived in such lodgings above the Gate of Aldgate in London. See D'Auvergne, *op. cit.*, 212-213; Stevenson, *op. cit.*, II, 7; Henry T. Riley, ed., *Memorials of London and London Life* (London, 1868), 377-378.

[7] *RR* Frag. B, 4154-4170, *passim*.

[8] *Ibid.*, 4175.

mortar made of quick lime and acid, tempered, Chaucer tells us, with vinegar.[9] Immediately surrounding the tower is another wall, protected by machines and by men with crossbows.[10]

Four huge gates, one on each side of the great square wall surrounding the castle, are carefully guarded. Wikked-Tunge, keeper of one of the gates, keeps his night watch by walking atop the walls, playing various musical instruments while he is on the lookout for approaching enemies.[11]

In this description one notes particularly the defence features of the castle.[12] Although there are many details missing for the complete view of the buildings, still the essentials—the moat, the surrounding wall with its towers and gates, the principal tower within the enclosure, and the means of protection against enemies—are given accurately.[13]

A far more elaborate castle is found in the *House of Fame.* Although it is obviously an imaginary dwelling and described in an extremely exaggerated fashion, it is significant in the study of Chaucer's references to castles because of its basic elements of reality. Undoubtedly no such dwelling ever existed in England or indeed in any country; still, Chaucer must have described many of the details from actual observation.

The buildings of the castle, tower, hall, and bowers, are "of stone of beryle," rather than of the traditional "lyme and stone" or marble so often referred to in the romances.[14] This reference

---

[9] It is improbable that vinegar was actually so used. Frederick N. Robinson, *The Complete Works of Geoffrey Chaucer* (Cambridge, 1933), 995.

[10] *RR* Frag. B, 4177-4196, *passim.*

[11] *Ibid.,* 4207-4265, *passim.*

[12] Cf. *supra,* f.n. 1, for comparison with this.

[13] Such a castle as here described is apparently of twelfth or early thirteenth century construction. The later castle had more buildings—a great hall for living quarters, a chapel, houses of office and the like—arranged around the three sides of a court. The tower was usually not the principal, although probably the most conspicuous building. Cf. Viollet-le-Duc. *Dict. Arch.,* III, 139; 154-155; Hudson Turner, *Domestic Architecture of the Middle Ages,* 2 vols. (Oxford, 1853), II, 4 ff.; D'Auvergne, *op. cit.,* 212 ff.; Ross W. Collins, *A History of Medieval Civilization* (Boston, 1936), 230 ff.

[14] See the descriptions of the castles in "The Earl of Toulouse," *Middle English Metrical Romances,* ed. by Walter H. French and C. H. B. Hale (London, 1930); "The Vows of the Heron," *Political Poems and Songs,* ed.

to the gem as building material at once gives the description an air of unreality. However, the architectural details—"the babewinnes[15] and pinnacles,"[16] the numerous carvings, and the little niches in the pinnacles filled with figures of jesters, harpers, and the like[17] —bespeak those of the fourteenth century,[18] even though they appear to be excessive in number and over-elaborated.

The gate at the entrance of the castle bailey shows the same combination of the unreal and the possibly actual. It is of gold,[19] which seems to indicate its imaginary quality; but is decorated with florid ornaments and carvings as the great gates probably were in this period.[20] It is interesting to observe the poet's use of architectural language in his description of the gate:

> Hit nedeth noght yow for to tellen,
> To make yow to longe dwellen,
> Of this yates florisshinges,
> Ne of compasses, ne of kervinges,
> Ne how they hatte in masoneries,
> As, corbets fulle of imageries.[21]

On the whole this castle is vague in general outline. In comparison with that in the *Romaunt de la Rose* it offers but little information as to the layout of the buildings and merely suggests an enclosing wall. Such vagueness emphasizes the imaginary quality. On the other hand, the minute details of the decorations of the

---

Thos. Wright (London, 1859), I; and *The Tale of Beryn,* ed. F. J. Furnivall and W. G. Stone, EETS, ES 105 (London, 1909); *Sir Gawayne and the Green Knight,* ed. R. Morris, EETS, OS 4 (London, 1864).

[15] Lit. "baboons;" grotesque figures in architecture, gargoyles. Robinson, *op. cit.,* gloss.

[16] *HF,* III, 1189.

[17] *Ibid.,* III, 1190-1282, *passim.*

[18] The fourteenth century has been styled "the decorated period of architecture," by virtue of its profuse ornamentation. Cf. Collins, *op. cit.,* 562; Viollet-le-Duc, *Dict. Arch.,* VII, 182; Turner, *Domestic Arch.,* II, 2 ff.; Marjorie and C. H. B. Quennell, *A History of Everyday Things in England* (New York, 1922), 145.

[19] Gold was commonly used in medieval descriptions of imaginary buildings and their parts. See Wilbur O. Sypherd, *Studies in Chaucer's Hous of Fame,* Chaucer Soc. Pub. (London, 1907), 111 ff.

[20] Quennell, *op. cit.,* 145.

[21] *HF,* III, 1299-1304.

structures—enhanced by the poet's imagination though they are— testify to the actuality and furnish some information concerning the contemporary trends in the ornamentation of buildings of this type.

Other somewhat significant allusions of Chaucer to the castle show the tower as the focal point of interest. In "The Legend of Ariadne," in the *Legend of Good Women,* the tower seems to serve a dual purpose; in the lower part of it Theseus is imprisoned, and in the upper story the daughters of King Minos have their living apartments. The location of the tower in respect to the whole castle is described in part:

> The tour, ther as this Theseus is throwe
> Doun in the botom derke and wonder lowe,
> Was joyning in the walle to a foreyne;[22]
> And hit was longing to the doghtren tweyne
> Of King Minos, that in hir chambres grete
> Dwelten above, toward the maister strete,
> In mochel mirthe, in joye and in solas.[23]

The tower probably stood at an angle of the wall surrounding the bailey, for the two young women sometimes walked out upon this wall to look "upon the brighte mone."[24]

In the *Knight's Tale* is a tower which corresponds in most respects to the foregoing. Again it is apparently important, but this time principally as a prison:

> The grete tour, that was so thikke and strong,
> Which of the castel was the chief dongeoun,
> (Ther-as the knightes weren in prisoun,
> Of whiche I tolde yow, and tellen shal)
> Was evene joynant to the gardin-wal,
> Theras this Emelye hadde hir pleyinge.[25]

Although the prisoners were evidently confined to the lower story of the tower, their jailer often gave them leave to ascend to the

---

[22] The "foreyne" is defined by Skeat as an outer chamber; it appears to me that it is in the thickness of the tower wall.

[23] *LGW,* VI, 1960-1965.

[24] *Ibid.,* VI, 1972.

[25] A 1056-1061.

upper level[26] and there "thurgh a window, thikke of many a barre,"[27] they could gaze down upon Emelye as she walked in the garden.

In the *Squire's Tale,* too, there is a tower. Its chief use is as a hiding place for King Cambinskan's valuable gifts:

> The presents ben royally y-fet,
>
> .   .   .   .   .
>
> And born anon in-to the heighe tour
> With certeine officers ordeyned therfore.[28]

There is no indication that this tower had been used as living apartments or even as a prison; yet it may have served as both.[29]

In addition to the references cited here, Chaucer alludes in several instances to the castle. However, no further information is offered, for such allusions are so casual as to be almost unnoticed. In the *Book of the Duchess* the poet mentions

> A long castel with walles whyte,
> . . . on a riche hil.[30]

In the *Franklin's Tale* he tells us that

> Now stood hir castel fast by the see.[31]

And in the *Man of Law's Tale* he records that

> Alla the king comth hoom, sone after this,
> Unto his castel . . .[32]

---

[26] *Ibid.,* 1063-1069.

[27] *Ibid.,* 1075.

[28] F 174-177.

[29] See Stevenson, *House Architecture,* I, 12-14, for the description of the tower of a fourteenth century castle, namely, the South Tower of Stokesay Castle. This tower adjoined the great hall, from which a door led into it. The hall was one story in height, but the tower was three, containing bed chambers and other private apartments. Stairs in the thickness of the wall ascended to the upper rooms. This tower seems to have been chiefly for domestic purposes, furnishing additional rooms.

[30] *Minor Poems,* III, 1318-1319. For a discussion of the hidden allusions made by Chaucer in these lines, see Robinson, *op. cit.,* 886.

[31] F 847.

[32] B 877-878.

Any other references to the castle are merely mention of it or are made through suggestions of the rooms within it.

That Chaucer's use of this type of dwelling follows the literary traditions established by his predecessors or contemporaries is evidenced by the fact that the castles he describes with any degree of thoroughness are found in those works belonging to his earlier period, when he was most under the influence of other sources.

Something of the relationship of Chaucer to the conventions of the romances may also be seen by a cursory view of several poems popular in his time. In practically all of these poems the castle is the most popular, if not the only, type of dwelling selected as the scene of action. The castle which Sir Gawayne visits when seeking the Green Knight is one familiar to most readers. It has battlemented walls, watch towers, and "chalk whyt chymnees."[33] Likewise a broad view of the castle is supplied in *Ywaine and Gawin*. Sir Colgrevance tells of having seen it:

> Than com i sone into a playn,
> Whar i gan se a bretise brade[34]
> And thederward ful fast i rade.
> I saw the walles and the dyke,
> And on the draw-brig saw i stand,
> A knight with fawkon on his hand.[35]

Here one misses the fine details of architecture, but discovers the general features.

There is no need of multiplying illustrations; they are plentiful, although often of little real significance, in the romance literature of the times.[36] They are on the whole markedly similar one to another in their most prominent features and often vaguely outlined. It must be remarked, however, that generally these castles are basically modelled on actually existing ones of contemporary England.[37] The tall chimneys and various architectural decora-

---

[33] *Sir Gawayne and the Green Knight*, 25-26.

[34] The gateway or portal of defence in castle or town.

[35] Joseph Ritson, *Ancient English Metrical Romances*, 3 vols. (Edinburgh, 1884), I, 125, ll. 162-168.

[36] Cf. *supra*, f.n. 14.

[37] Viollet-le-Duc, Turner, D'Auvergne, Stevenson, and others give illustrations of such castles as Oakham Castle in Rutland, Yanwath Hall, Westmoreland, the Tower of London, and the like.

tions are witness to the fact that they belong to the fourteenth century rather than to earlier times; the elaborate gateway, the tower, and the drawbridge likewise are characteristic of this later castle.[38]

Like his contemporaries, then, Chaucer represents the castle which he must have known. With true poetic imagination he enlarges and enriches his views of it to accord with his purpose.

II

It has been seen that Chaucer's early works have allusions to the castle and that only incidentally do the later ones mention it. The *Romaunt de la Rose,* the *House of Fame,* and the *Legend of Good Women,* with their dreamlike qualities, all show such a dwelling. *Troilus and Criseyde* and the *Canterbury Tales,*[39] which are on the whole realistic in their treatment, are concerned with other types. Sometimes it is difficult to know exactly what the poet has in mind in his suggestions as to houses; his failure to mention habitations by name and his disregard of presenting any complete exterior views of either manor or town-house as such, means that much of the information must be obtained by implication or inference.

What is evidently Chaucer's one direct allusion to the manor[40] is

---

[38] Contemporary illustrations of manuscripts often show castles in backgrounds. Some excellent views may be seen in *Le Bréviaire Grimani,* ed. Ferd. Ongania (Venice, 1906), for example.

[39] I have pointed out a few allusions in the *Canterbury Tales,* but it will be noted that they occur in poems based on other sources primarily, and that the references are of no great completeness or significance. Cf. *supra,* 6, 7.

[40] The term "manor" is somewhat confusing at times. The difference between the manor house and the castle is explained by Viollet-le-Duc as follows:

Le manoir, bien que ce nom désigne parfois un château, est l'habitation d'un propriétaire de fief, noble ou non, mais qui ne possède pas les droits seigneuriaux permettant d'élever un château avec tours et donjon. Le manoir est fermé cependant; et peut-être clos de murs et entouré de fosses, mais non défendu par des tours, hautes courtines crenelées et réduit formidable. Le manoir est la maison des champs placée, au point de vue architectonique, entre le château féodal et la maison du vavasseur, degré supérieur de la classe attachée à la terre segnieuriale, homme libre. *Dict. Arch.,* VI, 300.

found in the *Summoner's Tale*. The Friar of the tale, after having suffered unmentionable indignities in the home of Thomas and ∨ his wife, seeks another of his friends:

> A sturdy pas doun to the court he gooth,
> Wher-as ther woned a man of greet honour,
> To whom that he was alwey confessour;
> This worthy man was lord of that village.[41]

The term "court" is here used to mean manor house, according to Robinson.[42]   Besides, the social prestige of the lord, indicated here, further suggests this type of dwelling.

Similarly, in the *Merchant's Tale* are casual references to what appears to have been a manor.   January is a knight and

> In honest wyse, as longeth to a knight,
> Shoop him to live ful deliciously.
> His housinge, his array, as honestly
> To his degree was maked as a kinges.[43]

He suggests to May that if she remains faithful to him he will bequeath to her all his heritage, "toun and tour,"[44] so evidently he holds a social position equal to that of the lord in the *Summoner's Tale*.   The allusion to his dwelling as a "halle," in a way distinguishing it from other houses,[45] further points to its being a manor.   A later reference to it as a "paleys"—a term which in Chaucer's general usage seems to be applied to any spacious house

---

The manor as a whole was usually a group of buildings surrounded by a moat; the principal dwelling was the lord's living quarters.   Sometimes the manor consisted of only one large house, surrounded by walls and having a garden. *Ibid.*, VI, 301.

[41] D 2162-2165.

[42] *Chaucer's Complete Works,* 813.   Note that the Friar alludes to the manor house as a "large halle." (D 2188.)   It is generally understood that he means the whole house, not merely the great hall which served as dining room.

[43] E 2024-2027.

[44] *Ibid.*, 2170-2172.

[45] *Ibid.*, 2089.   "That neither in hall, n'in noon other hous."   Cf. *supra,* f.n. 42.

belonging to persons of high rank[46]—does not affect the interpretation of it as such.

The home of the marquis, Walter, in the *Clerk's Tale* is also probably a manor, although it again is not specifically called such. Walter's position of authority over the townspeople,[47] as well as the casual designation of his dwelling as a "paleys"[48] and a "court,"[49] testify to the fact that at least this house is like the two of the foregoing discussion. Some slight additional information regarding the manor is offered in the lines cited here:

> And al the paleys put was in array,
> Both halle and chambres, ech in his degree;
> Houses of office stuffed with plentee.[50]

It will be noted that there is really no exterior view of the manor in Chaucer's allusions. Likewise, no mention is made of the surrounding wall or the moat. The garden in the yard of January's home,[51] references to certain interior scenes in all three of the manors,[52] and the listing of hall, chambers, and houses of office as part of the establishment, as seen above, are the scanty details offered. Whether it was because the manor had as yet failed to become fashionable as a setting in literature or merely because with the development of his artistic powers Chaucer consciously omitted descriptive details of this sort, it is interesting to observe the difference between his views of the castle and of the more domestic manor.

---

[46] Maria Koellreuter, *Das Privatleben in England nach den Dichtungen von Chaucer, Gower und Langland* (Halle, a.S., 1908), 3, distinguishes between "paleys" and manor on the basis of relative spaciousness and imposing appearance, but I believe the terms to have been practically synonymous in some cases. That is, a spacious manor-house might still be called a "paleys," as is done here by Chaucer. Duke Theseus' castle and several town houses (A *Kn. T.*, 2199; *TC*, I, 324, II, 76, 508, 1537; V, 201. etc.) are also called "paleys."

[47] Cf. E 63-69; 190-195; 270; etc.

[48] *Ibid.*, 262; 389; 875.

[49] *Ibid.*, 1133.

[50] *Ibid.*, 262-264.

[51] Cf. E *Mer. T.*, 2029 ff., and the discussion of it, *supra*, 10.

[52] Cf. *supra*, 10, 11.

English domestic history offers much information concerning the manor, often supplying details not referred to by Chaucer. In visualizing the "court" or "hall" to which the poet alludes, this historical material is almost invaluable.

Specifications for a manor house which Sir John Bishopsden of Lapworth, in the County of Warwick, ordered built in 1314, show particularly well the interior plan of such a dwelling. It was to be forty feet in length within the walls, and eighteen feet in width. The end walls were to be three and one-half feet in thickness; the front and back ones, two and one-half each. The doorway was to be in the middle of the house; on one side of it were to be constructed a base chamber with a fireplace and a wardrobe extending out of the said chamber, with proper windows and doors. On the other side of the doorway there was to be a chamber without a fireplace and a wardrobe, but with fitting doors and windows.

Above the doorway and the two base chambers was to be an upper chamber the length and width of the house, with two fireplaces, two wardrobes projecting out of the same chamber, and with fitting doors and windows. This sovereign chamber was to be nine feet high from the floor to the rafters, and parapets of stone two and one-half feet in height were to be raised above the roof timbers. The principal doorway was to be so constructed that a drawbridge might be fitted to it.[53]

III

The line of distinction between the manor and the town house is often barely discernible. The difference in the terms used here is based on the assumption that the town house was stripped of the last vestiges of defence features—namely, the moat, the drawbridge, and generally the great wall—and that it was situated within the city, often very close to other houses. Further, the town house was the dwelling of the professional and merchant classes—that great bourgeois group which was rapidly becoming more important in English society. In a sense, the town house was more than any other type the predecessor of the modern home.

[53] Turner, *Domestic Arch.*, II, 5-7.

Chaucer does not designate the town house as such. Yet by a careful study of his allusions one can classify certain dwellings he presents under this heading. They are found to have some characteristics in common, although no single house is completely outlined.

Criseyde's house is an example of one that is perhaps more spacious than that of the average citizen of medieval England. In his use of the term "paleys"[54] to designate it, as well as in his numerous allusions to the various rooms within it, Chaucer indicates that it is not an ordinary dwelling, but rather that of a person of wealth. On the other hand, he has several suggestions which seem to prove beyond a doubt that this was not a manor, but rather a home within the city[55] and close to other homes.[56]

Troilus' house, repeatedly referred to as a "paleys," may also have been a town house. Not much information is given concerning it, except an occasional allusion to the owner's chamber. Pandarus' dwelling, not called a "paleys," is rather fully described as to the number of rooms in the main part;[57] it also appears to be a fairly spacious town house. There is no description of the exterior, and only suggestions of the interior of any of these dwellings.

Less spacious, probably, than the foregoing are the town houses alluded to indirectly in the *Miller's, Reeve's,* and *Shipman's* tales.

---

[54] Robinson notes the fact that "Chaucer's use of the term *palais* for Criseyde's house, which Boccaccio calls simply 'la casa' or 'la magione' is striking." *Chaucer's Complete Works,* 946. If, as it has been suggested in this dissertation, the term as Chaucer uses it means merely "spacious house," it seems not unusual for him to so translate "la casa."

[55] Cf. *TC,* V, 527-528:

A cause he fond in toune for to go,
And to Criseydes hous they gonnen wende.

[56] Cf. *Ibid.,* II, 1185-1190:

And after noon ful sleyly Pandarus
Gan drawe him to the window next the strete,
And seyde, 'nece, who hath arayed thus
The yonder hous, that stant afor-yeyn us?'
'Which hous?' quod she, and gan for to biholde,
And knew it wel, and whos it was him tolde.

Chaucer's own house, he tells us, is near to neighboring ones. Cf. *HF,* II, 649-651.

[57] Cf. *infra, 32.*

Although there is again no description of the exterior of the house, it is possible to reconstruct the general interior plan from the numerous allusions to the rooms.

The dwelling of the carpenter in the *Miller's Tale* is the most completely drawn by Chaucer.   It has a great hall, open to the roof, as indicated in the following lines :

> But whan thou hast, for hir and thee and me,
> Y-geten us thise kneding-tubbes three,
> Than shaltow hange hem in the roof ful hye.[58]

There seems to have been at one end of this hall an entrance leading into the bower[59] where the carpenter and his wife slept, and above the bower the solar,[60] where Nicholas lived.   Opposite the bower and solar, at the other end of the hall, the stable seems to have been attached.   Nicholas suggests to the carpenter that they break a hole in the gable end of the hall, above the stable, so that when the water rises within the hall they may go

> Unto the gardin-ward, over the stable.[61]

Chaucer mentions no kitchen as part of this town house, but probably it was next the stable, with separate entrances from the great hall for each.[62]

The foregoing shows the typical plan of the interior of the English medieval house, namely, a great hall with rooms at each end.   Variations depended largely upon the wealth of the owner and consisted usually in the addition of rooms.   Criseyde's house

---

[58] A 3563-3565.

[59] This is inferred from the fact that the "shot window" in the bower overlooks the street and is low enough to have been entered from the ground level ; both bower and hall must have been on the ground level.

[60] Cf. *infra*, 34.   Note that the carpenter goes upstairs to enter this room.

[61] A *Mil. T.*, 3567-3572.

[62] For examples of such houses as this, see John H. Parker, *Some Account of Domestic Architecture*, 2 vols.   (London, 1859), II, 24 ff. ; Thomas Wright, *The Homes of Other Days* (London, 1871), 152-154 ; *Our English Home*, 17-75, *passim;* Annie Abrams, *English Life and Manners in the Later Middle Ages* (New York, 1913), 173-178 ; Edward L. Cutts, *Scenes and Characters of the Middle Ages* (London, 1925), 534-535.

has, so far as Chaucer suggests, the hall[63] and a "paved parlour,"[64] with an adjoining small room or closet,[65] which may have been a kind of oratory or "oriel." A chamber[66] is also mentioned, but this may be synonymous with the paved parlour.[67] Houses of office, such as kitchen, pantry, cellars and the like, are not so much as suggested.

The house of Simkin in the *Reeve's Tale* is apparently similar in plan to that of the carpenter, but only one room—the chamber—is actually mentioned. This room is called Simkin's "owne chambre"[68] and is probably the solar. It is of fairly large size, for it provides space for at least three beds and a child's cradle.[69]

The merchant in the *Shipman's Tale* "heeld a worthy hous,"[70] but again the allusions to it are chiefly indirect. Among the rooms is one where the master attends to his financial accounts; it is termed the "countour-hous."[71] All Chaucer says of its location is what is implied in:

> And up in-to his countour-hous goth he.[72]

An allusion in this tale to a room for chapel purposes is of

---

[63] *TC,* II, 1170; IV, 732. The latter reference is significant in that it shows the relation of the hall to the chamber, i. e.,

"In-to hir chaumbre up wente out of the halle."

[64] *Ibid.,* II, 82. This is the only reference of Chaucer to a parlour, and it is probable that it is the solar or chamber to which he alludes. The solar (cf. *infra*) or parlour was not necessarily the lady's chamber, although it often was. See Turner, *Domestic Arch.,* II, 87-88 ff.

[65] *Ibid.,* II, 599-600; 1214 ff. This seems to have been more private than the larger chamber.

[66] *Ibid.,* II, 919; 1117; 1173; IV, 732. Note that the stairs lead down from the chamber (solar? parlour?) into the garden.

[67] The first visit of Pandarus is in the "paved parlour"; other times the chamber is referred to. It seems quite certain they are one and the same room.

[68] A 4139.

[69] *Ibid.,* 4139-4143, *passim;* 4156-4157.

[70] B 1210.

[71] *Ibid.,* 1266 ff.

[72] *Ibid.,* 1267. It is interesting to note that in the *Franklin's Tale* (F 1207-1208) Chaucer refers to a "studie," which may have been a room similar to the merchant's counting house.

significance in the consideration of the medieval house.   Implied in the words,

What! lat us here a messe, and go we dyne,[73]

is the fact that a private mass for the members of the household was celebrated right there in the house, which suggests either a chapel[74] or the license to say mass in the great hall.[75]   The only

[73] B *Sh.T.*, 1413.

[74] Noble or other wealthy persons of the Middle Ages often had private chapels in their homes.   The room varied in size and situation according to the wealth of the owner.   Generally it was near the hall and connected to it by a short passage leading from the upper end of the hall.   The chapel was sometimes divided into two stories by a floor, both parts of which were open at one end or were separated from the rest of the chapel by a screen.

Sometimes the chapel was very small and was separated from the hall by a door with a window on each side of it, the latter being closed with wooden shutters when not in use.   In some cases the chapel was in a projecting wing of the house and was of marked ecclesiastical character on the exterior.   Or again, it was a detached building in the courtyard.   Turner, *Dom. Arch.*, II, 79-81.

Lady Alice West of Hampshire, in her will made in 1395, included many of the effects of her chapel.   To her son Thomas she bequeathed a pair of "Matin's books," and to her son's wife, Johane,

a masse book, and alle the bokes that I haue of latyn, englisch, and frensch, out-tak the forsayd matyns bookis that is bequethe to Thomas my sone.   Also, . . . to the same Johane alle my tapites whit and rede paled, and blue and red paled, with alle my grene tapites that longeth to my chapell forsayd, and with the frontels of the forsayd auter, and with alle the rydelles (curtains or cloth-screens) and trussynge cofres (packing chests) and alle other apparaile that longeth to my chapelle forsayd.   Also . . . a chales and a paxbred, and an haliwater pot, with sprengle, twey cruetis, twey chaundelers, twey siluer basyns for the auter, with scochons of myn auncestres armes, and a sacrynge belle, and alle of seluer.   Also a tablet depeynt of tre.

See *The Fifty Earliest English Wills*, ed. F. J. Furnivall, EETS, OS 78 (London, 1882), 5.   Also, 49, 56-58, 76, etc., for other wills making similar bequests.   A list of heirlooms in the chapel belonging to the Stonors, a prominent family in the fourteenth and fifteenth centuries, is given in *Stonor Letters and Papers*, ed. by C. L. Kingsford (London, 1919), no. 140, 146-147.   It includes vestments of various kinds, particularly.

[75] Such licenses are said to have been given by the Bishops for a just cause and "so that it be done without prejudice to the right of another."

evidence given by Chaucer is that which may be taken to signify the use of the hall.

> But hastily a messe was ther seyd,
> And spedily the tables were ther y-leyd,
> And to the diner faste they hem spedde.[76]

The suggestion that mass was said before the tables were laid may indicate that the hall served as chapel. Then as soon as mass was ended, the tables had to be placed on their trestles and set for dinner.

The foregoing allusions, incidental though they may be, show Chaucer's increasing skillful use of realistic details. He no longer depends on literary tradition to the extent that he finds it necessary to present elaborate castles, minutely described. Rather, he weaves his allusions to the house into the story so that they are unobtrusive, yet significant factors in the medieval background. In the use especially of the town house Chaucer is ahead of his age.

Undoubtedly many of the newer homes in the fourteenth century were of the types which appear in the tales just considered. One has only to note the specifications of a town-house built by a certain Simon de Canterbury in 1308 for William Hanigtone, pelterer, to be assured of this fact:

> . . . a hall and a room with a chimney, and one larder between the said hall and room; and one solar over the room and larder; also one oriole (recess with a bay window) at one end of the hall, beyond the high bench, and one step with an oriole (porch) from the ground to the door of the hall aforesaid, outside the hall; and two enclosures as cellars, opposite each other, beneath the hall; and one enclosure for a sewer, with two pipes leading to the said sewer; and one stable . . . between the hall and the old kitchen . . . with a solar above such stable,

---

John Britton, *A Dictionary of the Architecture and Archeology of the Middle Ages* (London, 1838), 139. Usually it was required that the "owner and his family attend their parish church on the greater festivals and the day of dedication, and that no private offerings should be made at home." Turner, *op. cit.*, 79, f.n. (a).

[76] B *Sh. T.*, 1441-1443.

> and a garret above the solar aforesaid; and at one end is
> to be an oriole (room with a bay window) between the
> said hall and the old chamber. . . .[77]

Another town house which was probably constructed about the
same time was that of Richard Toky, a grocer or pepperer and a
Member of Parliament for the City of London in 1358. It consisted of hall, solar, pantry and buttery, counting-house, and
store-house.[78]

One can see here that although the house of the carpenter in
the *Miller's Tale,* as well as that of Simkin, appears to have been
relatively small, it was probably similar to the average house which
Chaucer saw every day in his own London.

IV

Medieval English persons who lived in villages or on a lord's
manor occupied cottages of proportions generally very humble.[79]
Several illustrations of such dwellings appear in Chaucer's works.

The Reeve's cottage, of which it is said

> His woning was ful fair upon an heeth
> With grene trees shadwed was his place,[80]

was no doubt one of the better ones. Unfortunately, Chaucer gives
no clue as to its appearance, save that it was upon a heath and
shaded by trees.

The poor widow of the *Nun's Priest's Tale* dwells in a cottage

---

[77] Riley, *Memorials,* 65-66. Incidentally, William Hanigtone agreed to
pay for this house, "the sum of 9 pounds, 5 shillings, 4 pence sterling, half
a hundred of Eastern marten skins, fur for a woman's hood, value 5
shillings, and fur for a robe for him, the said Simon. . ." *Ibid.,* 66.

[78] A. H. Thomas, "Illustrations of the Medieval Municipal History of
London from the Guildhall Records," *Transactions of the Royal Historical
Society,* fourth series, vol. IV (London, 1921), 99-100.

[79] The worst of these houses were little better than mud huts and were
exceptionally dirty and mean. See James E. T. Rogers, *Six Centuries of
Work and Wages* (New York, 1914), 67-68; W. S. Sparrow, *The English
House* (New York, 1909), 166-167.

[80] A *Gen. Prol.,* 606-607.

described by the poet as "narwe."   Like that of the Reeve, this house is surrounded by trees:

> Bisyde a grove, stonding in a dale.[81]

To keep her three large sows, three kine, and her sheep named Malle, to say nothing of the chickens, within bounds,

> A yerd she hadde, enclosed al aboute
> With stikkes, and a dry dich with-oute.[82]

The "stikkes" were probably wattles, such as may be seen in an illustration of the medieval cottage in *Le Bréviaire Grimani;*[83] the ditch may have been the remains of some kind of moat.

The cottage itself has only two rooms, dignified by the names of bower and hall:

> Ful sooty was hir bour and eek hir halle.[84]

On a perch in the hall sat the widow's pet bird—not a falcon such as sat on perches in the halls of noblemen[85]—but a fine cock. There, too, were the seven hens of the barnyard.[86]   Although Chaucer does not say so, it is likely that the pigs and sheep belonging to the widow often wallowed on the rush-strewn earthen floor[87] of the house, or wandered freely in and out of the cottage door.

Still another humble cottage is that in which the marquis, Walter, found Grisilde.   It was in a "throp,"[88] or small village and was

---

[81] B 4012-4013.

[82] *Ibid.,* 4020-4021; 4037-4038.

[83] Cf. "La Tonte et la Moisson," 13.   The widow's cottage may have been very similar to the one shown.   This latter has one main room with a sleeping garret.   It has a louvre or opening in the thatched roof to let out smoke from the house, an enclosed yard, and even a ditch.

[84] B *NPT,* 4022.

[85] *Ibid.,* 4074.   Such a perch was used sometimes for garments and sometimes for birds.   Cf. *infra,* 24, 40, 41.

[86] *NPT,* 4056; 4073.

[87] In later years these floors, into which all the filth of the house was likely to be thrown, were periodically dug up by the "salt-petre man," the nitrous matters in the soil being used for the manufacture of gun-powder. Basil Oliver, *The Cottages of England* (New York, 1929), 5.

[88] E *Cl. T.,* 199.

considered one of the poorest. So wretched was it that apparently
the cattle were housed in one part of it:

> And as she wolde over hir threshfold goon,
> The markis cam and gan hir for to calle;
> And she set doun hir water-pot anoon
> Bisyde the threshfold, in an oxes stalle.[89]

Again, reference is made to Grisilde's having been reared in
poverty:

> As in a cote or in an oxe-stalle.[90]

No other information about the cottage is given, except that it has
at least one room, called by Chaucer a chamber.[91]

The cottage as the poet describes it is, then, small, often filled
with smoke from the fire, and evidently occupied sometimes by
both human beings and domestic animals. Few as are the actual
details which Chaucer enumerates, the realism of the general effect
is great.

Such a dwelling as that of the widow is described by Froissart
in an account of the flight of the Earl of Flanders from a mob in
1382. This house, which Froissart says proved to be "a very unfit
habitation for such a lord," was

> only a small house, dirty and smoky, and as black as jet:
> there was only in this place one poor chamber, over which
> was a sort of garret that was entered by means of a lad-
> der of seven steps, where on a miserable bed, the children
> of this poor woman lay.[92]

Langland, who is more concerned with the living conditions of
the poor than are Chaucer and Froissart, reveals much of the
misery endured by persons living in cottages of the most wretched
kind. These poor can hardly provide sufficient food, he tells us,
for the sobbing children. In the cold of winter they must rise
at midnight to rock the cradle at the bedside, and must work

---

[89] *Ibid.,* 288-291.
[90] *Ibid.,* 398.
[91] *Ibid.,* 324.
[92] *Chronicles of England, France, Spain, and Other Countries,* ed. by
Thomas Johnes, 2 vols. (London, 1844), I, 704.

unstintingly to card and comb wool, to darn clothes, and to put rushes on the floor.[93]

Furnishings in General

The furnishings of the medieval house were generally simple and scanty. The fact that Chaucer mentions in more or less incidental fashion nearly every important article of furniture found in hall and chamber and yet has relatively few allusions all together is indicative of the scarcity. Tables and benches for the hall, shelves for books, chests, perches—all receive but slight attention from the poet. The bed, a hawk's mew, hangings and decorations are more fully described. Nevertheless, a general impression of both hall and chamber are created without much specific attention being paid to the furnishings.

Certain influences, particularly that of the Crusades, had introduced many articles of value and beauty into the home, but only the wealthiest of noblemen could afford them. There was a rapidly increasing love of "the silks of Constantinople, of the cloth of Tars and Alexandrian purple, of golden candle sticks and silver censers, of embroidered satins and superb palls fringed with gold,"[94] but for the most part, people had to indulge that love sparingly. Cushions and coverings for benches and chairs, and hangings for walls, were luxuries and belonged mostly to the halls of the wealthy. Similarly, elaborate hangings for beds, silken coverlets, and fine pillows were rare.

An opportunity of describing in glowing colors the furnishings of the better houses would seem to have been offered Chaucer in his selection of such homes as those of Cambinskan, Theseus, January, and other wealthy persons. Still, the poet is frequently content with referring to the "riche arraye" and with using other similarly vague expressions.

---

[93] *Piers Plowman,* ed., W. W. Skeat, EETS, OS 54 (London, 1873), x, ll., 71-81.

[94] Edmund Dale, *National Life and Character in the Mirrour of Early English Literature* (Cambridge, 1907), 25-26.

The Hall and its Furnishings

In all types of medieval English home—castle, manor, town house, or cottage—the principal room was the great hall,[95] varying according to the rank and wealth of the owner, in size, furnishings, decoration, and uses. In general this room was the place where the lord and his family, together with their guests, gathered for meals, entertainment, and often to sleep. Sometimes, too, they met there to pay their last respects to a departed friend,[96] or even to hear mass.

As is the case with Chaucer's description of the exterior of the castle, his single direct view of the interior of the hall[97] is detailed and greatly elaborated by the imagination.

---

[95] The hall was usually on the first floor of the house, either on the ground level or raised about three or four feet above it, being in the latter case constructed on an under room or cellar. The upper end of the hall was raised above the floor level of the room; this formed a dais upon which the master of the house sat before the high table at feasts. Behind this table was the entrance to other apartments; opposite it was the screen, intended as protection against the wind, hiding the entrances to the kitchen and other houses of office. Sometimes a washing place or lavatory was behind the screen, and a sideboard or recess. The top of the screen did not extend the full height of the hall, being only about ten or twelve feet high. It was connected to the end wall by a floor, which served as a ceiling to the entrance and formed a gallery, called minstrels' gallery, or an upper room.

The floor of the hall itself was either of stone or tiles, or sometimes even of the earth, and was covered with straw or rushes. A fire burned on a hearth in the center of the room, the smoke ascending to an opening or louvre in the roof. Fireplaces have been found in the ruins of old halls, but generally the open fire was used.

The windows of the hall were frequently long and narrow, not unlike church windows in appearance. They were deep-set and within their recesses wooden or stone benches were often constructed. The upper part of the window was sometimes glazed, the lower part having iron or wooden bars and shutters.

Stevenson, *House Arch.* II, 8 ff.; Sidney O. Addy, *The Evolution of the English House,* revised ed. (London, 1933), 68 ff.; Jean J. Jusserand, *English Wayfaring Life in the Middle Ages,* translated by Lucy T. Smith, new edition (New York, 1931), 207, ff.; Gotch, *Growth of the Eng. House,* 22-23; Parker, *Dom. Arch.,* II, 34-40.

[96] A *Kn. T.,* 2870-2881.

[97] *HF,* 1341-1525, *passim.*

The specifications as to the size of the hall are not given, but suggestions are made to its enormous proportions.[98] Of its general appearance the poet says:

> .   .   .   that every wal
> Of hit, and floor, and roof and al
> Was plated half a fote thikke
> Of gold. . .
>
> .   .   .   .   .
> And they wer set as thikke of nouchis[99]
> Fulle of the fynest stones faire,
> That men rede in the Lapidaire,
> As greses growen in a mede.[100]

Across one end of the room is a raised platform or dais, upon which is a throne made all of ruby.[101] The hall is divided into a nave and aisles;[102] looking down the length of it one sees:

> Streight doun to the dores wyde,
> Fro the dees, many a pileer
> Of metal, that shoon not ful cleer.

Upon each pillar is the statue of some character famed in history or literature—such men as Josephus, Dares, Virgil, Ovid, and countless others.[103]

The actual medieval hall is almost lost sight of in the details which Chaucer presents. The golden walls, thickly set with gems, the throne of rubies, and the various kinds of metal pillars holding countless statues—all seem so thoroughly unreal as hardly to deserve consideration as an example of the fourteenth century hall. Yet the outline—the great room with a dais across one end, and even the division into aisles and nave—is true to fact.

---

[98] Note especially the reference to the huge crowds which came into the hall. *Ibid.*, 1526 ff.

[99] Jewelled ornaments.

[100] 1343-1353, *passim*.

[101] *Ibid.*, 1360-1363.

[102] Large halls, like that of Oakham Castle in Rutland, were sometimes so divided by pillars with arches, or there was a row of pillars and arches down the center of the room. Smaller halls were without such divisions. Stevenson, *House Arch.*, II, 10-12.

[103] *HF*, 1420-1516, *passim*.

Chaucer has indeed constructed the hall of Fame on mammoth proportions. Nevertheless, some of the actually existing halls of the time were of so extensive size as to make a modern living room seem dwarfish. Those particularly of noblemen's houses had to be equal to great demands which were often placed upon them at the time of special feasts.[104] A hall built by John of Gaunt at Kenilworth Castle, about 1392, a lofty room with a fine open timber roof, was 90 feet long and 45 feet wide.[105] Westminster Hall, built in the first place by William Rufus and reconstructed by Richard II in the latter years of the fourteenth century, is said to have accommodated ten thousand persons.[106] Many halls ranged from 50 to 60 feet in length and from 30 to 50 in width.[107]

In his account of Queen Isabella's entrance into Paris in 1394, Froissart describes a hall of almost unbelievable dimensions. So many persons were assembled there he says, "that a man could not turn but with much pain;" yet there was brought in for the queen's entertainment a castle, a pavilion, and a ship, all on wheels, the castle being 40 feet long and 20 feet wide, with four towers.[108]

In none of his other works does Chaucer present details such as those describing the hall of Fame. Usually his halls are pictured by implication rather than by any direct enumeration.

Duke Theseus' hall in the *Knight's Tale* the poet describes in a negative manner:

> Ne who sat first ne last up-on the deys,
> What ladies fairest been or best daunsinge,
> Of which of hem can dauncen best and singe,
> Ne who most felingly speketh of love:
> What haukes sitten on the perch above,
> What houndes liggen on the floor adoun;
> Of al this I make no mencioun.[109]

The method is effective, being suggestive of the atmosphere of the room rather than of its physical appearance. Such a descrip-

---

[104] William E. Mead, *The English Medieval Feast* (London, 1931), 13
[105] Abram, *English Life and Manners,* 174.
[106] Mead, *op. cit.,* 129.
[107] Stevenson, *House Arch.,* II, 10 ff.
[108] *Chronicles,* II, 401-402.
[109] A 2200-2206.

tion shows Chaucer's true artistry, even though it fails in conveying to the reader any exact scientific information.

King Cambinskan's hall is somewhat similarly described. There is reference to the "feste so solempne and so ryche,"[110] and to the minstralcye which preceded the King from "his bord, ther that he sat ful hye,"[111] but nothing more definite. A very wide door leading into the hall from the street is suggested by "in at the halle-dore . . . there cam a knight up-on a stede of bras."[112]

The similarity between these two halls is further suggested by reference to the dais:

> This Cambinskan, of which I have yow told,
> In royal vestiment sit on his deys,
> With diademe, ful heighe in his paleys,
> And halt his feste, so solempne and so riche. . .[113]

> Thus been they wedded with solempnitee,
> And at the feste sitteth he and she
> With other worthy folk up-on the deys.[114]

The dais, as has been mentioned before, was the place of highest honor in the hall. Upon it, at least in certain influential men's homes, sometimes stood a stationary table which was assigned to the guests of highest rank and honor. The table was regarded as a sign of ready hospitality,[115] and "to begin the table dormant" signified that one was to take the first place at a feast.[116]

Chaucer alludes specifically to a table dormant as being in the hall of the Franklin:

> His table dormant in his halle alwey
> Stood redy covered al the longe day.[117]

A table such as this, fastened to the floor, was a distinct improve-

---

[110] F *Sq. T.*, 61.

[111] *Ibid.*, 268.

[112] *Ibid.*, 76-85, *passim.* In the romances it was traditional for a rider on horseback to enter the hall. Cf. *Gawayne and the Green Knight;* Sir Thomas Malory, *Le Morte Darthur,* 2 vols. (London, 1900), II, 223.

[113] *Ibid.*, 58-62.

[114] E *Mer. T.*, 1709-1711.

[115] *Our English Home,* 30; Jusserand, *Eng. Wayfaring Life,* 122.

[116] Wright, *Homes of Other Days,* 159.

[117] A *Gen. Prol.*, 353-354.

ment over the ordinary table made of boards laid across trestles which was commonly used in Chaucer's day.

On the whole the poet has but few references to tables. In describing Grisilde's preparations for Walter's wedding feast he mentions the setting of tables;[118] in the *Summoner's Tale* he refers to the lord of the village "eting at his bord;"[119] and he alludes to King Cambinskan rising from his "bord, ther that he sat ful hye."[120] But there are no significant details of description or of arrangement in the hall.

There is likewise no information offered by the poet concerning other furnishings of the hall, except an almost incidental allusion to the hangings, a reference to a cushion, and the bare suggestion of bench coverings.

In the *Book of the Duchess* Chaucer promises to paint the walls and to supply "tapites" (tapestries) of one pattern to anyone who will make him sleep:

> .   .   .   and al his halles
> I wol do peynte with pure golde,
> And tapite hem ful many folde
> Of oo sute. . . .[121]

The reference here to painting the hall with gold is in accordance with the romance tradition. No doubt the wealthy of Chaucer's England frequently decorated the walls by having their arms emblazoned on them[122] or by having certain designs painted; however, the pure gold mentioned by the poet is that which one finds in literature rather than in historical accounts.

Most medieval gentlemen seem to have preferred "tapites"—the favorite ornaments of the period—as hall decorations. Often referred to as "halls" or "hallings," they were hung in doorways to ward off draughts, or across one end of the dais, or on the backs of benches. They were considered of great value and were handed down from one generation to another. Often they were

---

[118] E *Cl. T.,* 975.
[119] D 2167.
[120] F *Sq. T.,* 267.
[121] III, 258-261.
[122] Parker, *Dom. Arch.,* II, 47-48.

richly embroidered with devices of leopards of gold, falcons, swans with ladies' heads, stars, birds, griffins, eagles, and flowers.[123]

Medieval wills furnish numerous examples of "tapites" which may have been similar to those which Chaucer mentions. Edward III bequeathed to the Church at Canterbury "a hall of black tapestry with ostrich feathers and a red border with swans and heads of ladies;"[124] Lady Alice West of Hampshire left to her son "an Halle, with docere, costers and bankers," of the same suit as her bed, which in this case was of blue.[125] Nicholas Sturgeon, a priest, bequeathed to his brother John, "the hallyng of the ix wurthy,"[126] which was evidently a hanging embroidered or painted with the design of the Nine Worthies. Queen Isabella had hangings "figured with lozenges of gold, with the arms of France, England, and Brabant."[127]

The hangings and bench covers of the hall had to be well taken care of; they were probably removed when no guests were present and locked in great chests where they would be safe from the ravages of the fleas or moths which infested medieval houses. Did not that very domestic gentleman, the Goodman of Paris, in teaching his youthful wife how to take proper care of her clothing and the household articles made of cloth suggest that moths and fleas could not get into them if they were placed in a chest or in a bag well tied up, because moths and fleas could not live in darkness and without air?[128]

It was the duty of the marshall of the hall to see that the hallings, coverings and the like, were taken out of the chests, cleaned, and put into place when guests were expected. He was directed to have "all hallynges and costers dressed in þer kynde

---

[123] *Ibid.,* II, 49 ff. Tapestry was often displayed in processions and on state occasions.

[124] *Royal and Noble Wills,* ed. John Nichols (London, 1780), 69.

[125] *The Fifty Earliest Eng. Wills,* 5.

[126] *Ibid.,* 132-133.

[127] Agnes Strickland, *Lives of the Queens of England,* 16 vols. (Philadelphia, 1902), II, 152.

[128] *The Goodman of Paris,* trans. by Eileen Power (London, 1928), 174. This was only one of six different methods the Goodman suggested.

places and shaken or betyn wyth Roddes yef nede be."[129]   One
can imagine Chaucer's host, of whom the poet said,

> A semely man our hoste was with-alle
> For to been a marshal in an halle[130]

directing his assistants to beat the hallyngs with rods, or ordering
them to hang them in certain places.   Grisilde, more capable
than any marshall of a hall, perhaps, directed the servants in
such matters, bidding them

> To hasten hem, and faste swepe and shake.[131]

As has been stated, cushions and coverings for benches and
chairs, as well as hangings for walls, were luxuries and belonged
mostly in the halls of the wealthy.   Criseyde sat upon a cushion
of "gold y-bete,"[132] but there is no indication that there were many
more like it in her house.   However, Criseyde had been leading
a secluded life because of her widowhood and may have acquired
through the industrious use of the needle more than it was customary to have.   Pandarus, in his own house, ran for a cushion[133]
so that Troilus could kneel more comfortably at Criseyde's bedside.   And these two cushions—that of Criseyde and that of
Pandarus—are the only ones mentioned by Chaucer.

To know what furniture a medieval hall of average size and
belonging to a gentleman of moderate wealth might have, and
incidentally to see what little information about it Chaucer actually
gives, one has only to glance by way of contrast at the inventory
of goods in Richard Toky's hall.   Toky, as a grocer, must have

---

[129] *A Fifteenth-Century Courtesy Book,* ed. by R. W. Chambers, EETS,
ES 148 (London, 1914), 11.

[130] A *Gen. Prol.,* 751-752.

[131] E *Cl. T.,* 978.

[132] *TC,* II, 1229. Cushions in the fourteenth century were used on benches,
seats, coffers, and chests in reception rooms.   They were covered with
precious materials, embroidered, woven of bright colors.   Generally they
were square with four buttons or tassels at the corners.   The fifteenth
century gave to the cushion the form appropriate to particular usage.
Viollet-le-Duc, *Dictionnaire raisonné du mobilier français, de l'époque
carlovingienne à la renaissance,* 6 vols. (Paris, 1914), I, 85-86.

[133] *Ibid.,* III, 964.

possessed a town house,[134] in the hall of which were these articles:

> a table with trestles, a sideboard painted in designs to hold cups, another painted cupboard, and two occasional tables of spruce, two chairs for the master and mistress with tapestry dorsers and bankers for back and seat, of "blod" colour, or cardinal red, and also three benches upholstered in the same tapestry for the household. There was an iron candelabrum swinging from the ceiling and an iron candle-stick and two andirons on the hearth. On one or other of the tables stood five basins and three wash-bowls for ablutions before and after meals. On the walls were hangings of light and dark worsted in strips. Of pictures there were none, ornament being supplied by several poleaxes, a cross-bow with tackle, and a lance and a shield. Scattered about were some twenty cushions, all upholstered in the same light and dark red as the wall hangings.[135]

An inventory of the furniture belonging to the Stonors lists equipment for the main room or hall:

> j longa tabula cum j pari trestell. It., alia parva tabula cum j pari de trestell. . . . It., ij formill (benches or forms). It., j plate de ferro pro candell. It., j dosere cum j banker, semble de colore rubeo et nigro.[136]

Two tables, two forms,[137] a candelabrum for furnishings; a dorser[138] and a banker[139] as decorations. Certainly the Stonors possessed little for their hall.

---

[134] Cf. *supra*, 18.

[135] Thomas, "Illustrations," 101.

[136] *Stonor Letters*, no. 50, I, 43.

[137] A form differed slightly from a bench in that it had separate places for each person. An arm divided the places. Viollet-le-Duc, *Dict. Arch.*, II, 101-102.

[138] "The choicest piece of arras in the Gothic hall was that which hung behind the dais, or which was thrown over a rod or screen to form a canopy for the state chair. It was called a dorsar, or dorsel, and the arms and initials of the owner were often embroidered upon it." *Our English Home*, 27-28.

[139] A banker was a piece of cloth or arras thrown over the back of a bench—the raised back being known as a bink or bank. *Ibid.*, 28.

The Solar and its Furnishings

Rapidly supplanting the hall in importance in the medieval house was the principal chamber or solar.[140]   This was a combination sitting-room and bed-chamber, usually belonging to the master himself.[141]   The lady's solar was referred to, especially in the romances, as the bower.   Chaucer does not designate any room by the name of solar, but a brief survey of his references shows that he has this room in mind in his several descriptions of the chamber.

The solar seems to have extended in some cases beyond the outside wall of the house and was so near the ground that people walked or rode under it with difficulty.[142]   A faint suggestion that Criseyde's chamber was of this over-hanging balcony kind is made in the lines:

---

[140] "The evolution of the projecting solar or upper room can be traced by reference to Roman practices.   In Rome the tops or roofs of the colonnades in front of the houses were known as *solaria,* meaning literally 'places for basking in the sun.'   Hence when rooms began to be built over these colonnades such rooms were known as 'solars,' so that the sense of 'basking place' or 'sunning place' originally applied to the tops of the colonnades was afterwards transferred to the rooms built over them."   Addy, *Evolution of the Eng. House,* 118.

[141] The solar had been at first in the lesser mansions but a small apartment raised above the chamber and approached by a flight of stairs outside or sometimes within the house.   In Chaucer's day it had assumed new proportions.   It was still an upper room, usually approached by steps leading up from behind the dais in the hall, and often having also an outer entrance into a garden.   It was built over a cellar, but often both solar and cellar were not so high as the hall, leaving a gable with a window in it free above them.   The solar was placed transversely to the hall and was as long as the hall was wide.   It had a window on each end, and on the other side it sometimes joined on to other buildings or rooms, at least in larger houses.   Parker, *Dom. Arch.,* II, 87; Wright, *Homes of Other Days,* 148-150.

[142] A fourteenth century regulation made in the City of London provided "that the pent-houses and jettees of houses shall be so high that folks on horseback may ride beneath them.   And that they shall be of the height of nine feet at the very least; and that all others shall forthwith be rearranged within forty days, under the penalty of forty shillings."   *Liber Albus,* ed. Henry T. Riley (London, 1861), 89.

> And with that thought, for pur a-shamed, she
> Gan in hir heed to pulle, and that as faste,
> Whyl he and al the peple for-by paste.[143]

Other allusions to Criseyde's chamber—including the paved parlour under the term chamber—are concerned with the interior or with the stairs.[144]   Pandarus, on his first visit to his niece's house,

> . . . fond, two othere ladyes sete and she
> With-inne a paved parlour; and they three
> Herden a mayden reden hem the geste
> Of the Sege of Thebes, whyl hem leste.[145]

The note of charming intimacy in this scene is more significant than many descriptive details of a more formal kind. The intimate touch is emphasized by Criseyde's hospitable reception of her uncle, whom she takes by the hand and sets "doun on a bench."[146]

The freedom with which persons entertained their friends in their chambers is distinctively medieval and is frequently recorded by Chaucer. Both Troilus and Criseyde enjoy some privacy in their rooms,[147] but often, too, they have visitors. Pandarus particularly comes and goes at will, or sometimes at the invitation of Troilus.[148]   At Deiphebus' house, when Troilus is feigning illness and is in the chamber, abed, Pandarus feels it necessary to warn the persons present at dinner that they must not all go into the room. His pretext is that

> .   .   .   the chaumbre is but lyte,
> And fewe folk may lightly make it warm.[149]

---

[143] *TC*, II, 656-658.

[144] External stairs lead from Criseyde's chamber into her garden:
> Adoun the steyre annon-right tho she wente
> In-to the gardin, with hir neces three. (II, 813-814)
> With that they wenten arm in arm y-fere
> In-to the gardin from the chaumbre doun. (*Ibid.*, 1116-1117)
Cf. also a similar allusion to the stairs leading down from Deiphebus' chamber to the garden. (II, 1704-1706).

[145] *Ibid.*, II, 81-84.

[146] *Ibid.*, II, 91.

[147] *Ibid.*, I, 358-359; II, 598-600; II, 1173; IV, 232 ff., etc.

[148] *Ibid.*, I, 549; II, 936 ff.; III, 226 ff.; III, 1555 ff.

[149] *Ibid.*, II, 1646-1647.

Besides, he says, too many visitors may do the "sick man" harm.[150]

Other poems of Chaucer also refer to the use of the chamber for the reception of visitors. The miller in the *Reeve's Tale* provides a bed for his two guests in the chamber where he and his family sleep;[151] old January in the *Merchant's Tale* tells May to go after dinner with all her women to the chamber of his squire Damian and to bring him good cheer;[152] and King Cambinskan, preceded by his minstrels, retires after his festal banquet to his "chambre of parements,"[153] and holds a dance for a select few of the guests.[154]

Pandarus' chamber is of particular interest because of the information it presents regarding the arrangement of several rooms. This chamber is next the hall—"middel chaumbre"[155] as Pandarus calls the latter—and has a second smaller room or "stewe"[156] attached to it. In the chamber Criseyde sleeps, while her women lie in the hall, and Pandarus stays in the "stewe."[157] There is a trap door, probably in the wall, between the chamber and the stewe.[158]

The medieval chamber was less plainly decorated and furnished than the hall. Sometimes, in the houses of the wealthy, there were evidences of much comfort; still, many of the chambers were pitifully cheerless and bare. The gradual evolution of Chaucer's method of description from the conventional to the realistic is plainly observed in his treatment of the chamber. Altogether, though, the poet presents more direct information concerning

---

[150] *Ibid.*, II, 1649-1650.

[151] A 4139 ff.

[152] E 1920-1924.

[153] F *Sq. T.*, 269. Skeat defines parements as rich hangings or ornaments (pert. to a chamber). Manly terms the chambre parements as Presence Chamber, which seems more likely. *Canterbury Tales* by Geoffrey Chaucer (New York, 1928).

[154] F *Sq. T.*, 272 ff.

[155] *TC.*, III, 666.

[156] *Ibid.*, III, 601. Both Robinson and Skeat define the stewe as a closet or small room. Robinson adds "heated room."

[157] I believe he refers to the stewe when he says he will sleep in "that outer hous."

[158] *TC.*, III, 698.

this room and its furnishings than he does any other single aspect of the house. In general, his views of it are his most vivid, most nearly complete, and most realistic.

The chamber in the *Book of the Duchess* seems almost purely imaginary, with its excessively rich, painted walls and its ornate windows:

> .   .   .   my chambre was
> Ful wel depeynted, and with glas
> Were al the windowes wel y-glased,
> Ful clere, and not an hole y-crased,
> That to beholde hit was gret joye.
> For hoolly al the storie of Troye
> Was in the glasing y-wroght thus,
> Of Ector and King Priamus,
> Of Achilles and Lamedon,
> Of Medea and of Jason,
> Of Paris, Eleyne, and Lavyne.
> And alle the walles with colours fyne
> Were peynted, both text and glose,
> Of al the Romaunce of the Rose.
> My windows weren shet echon,
> And through the glas the sunne shon
> Upon my bed with brighte bemes.[159]

The walls of medieval chambers were indeed sometimes beautifully decorated;[160] yet Chaucer's description seems so greatly exagger-

---

[159] III, 321-337.

[160] Painted walls, especially of chambers, were sometimes apparently quite ornamental. Henry III had certain chambers in his royal palaces painted. At Woodstock, for instance, he ordered that "the walls of the queen's chamber. . . be whitewashed and painted with points and flowers to be painted below the points. . . ." The queen's chamber in the Tower of London was to be wainscoted, whitewashed, and painted with roses. The king's own chamber at Keninton was to be painted with stories, "so that the field shall be of green colour stencilled with gold stars." *Calendar of the Liberate Rolls,* Rolls Series (London, 1916), 23 Hen. III, 352, 453, 206.

In romances the walls were often painted brilliantly. Partonope of Blois was on one occasion ushered into a chamber of which "the walles were as bryghte as amber." *Partonope of Blois,* ed. A. Trampe Bödtker, EETS, ES 109 (London, 1912), 31.

ated as to belong to romance[161] rather than to the actual medieval house.

In describing the chamber of Nicholas, the "povre scoler" who dwelt with the carpenter of the *Miller's Tale,* the poet's method is primarily realistic. The room is typically that of a student:

> A chambre hadde he in that hostelrye
> Allone, withouten any companye,
> Ful festisly ydight with herbes swoote;
>
> .   .   .   .   .   .
>
> His Almageste,[162] and bookes grete and smale,
> His astrelabie,[163] longynge for his art,
> His augrym stones[164] layen faire apart,
> On shelves couched at his beddes heed;
> His presse ycovered with a faldyng reed;
> And al above ther lay a gay sautrie,[165]
> On whiche he made a-nightes melodie
> So swetely that al the chambre rong.[166]

Nicholas was particularly fortunate in having a room in the carpenter's house rather than in one of the Halls or Colleges of the University, for here he could be alone, "withouten any companye." In the Colleges, at Peterhouse, King's, Magdalen, for instance, there were at least two students in a chamber; sometimes, in the ground-floor rooms there were three or four, and in the first-

---

[161] The ornate windows seem to have belonged particularly to romance. An interesting comparison with Chaucer's description is that in *The Squyr of Lowe Degre,* ed., Wm. E. Mead (Boston, 1904), ll. 93-96:

> In her oryall ther she was
> Closed well with royall glas;
> Fulfylled it was with ymagery,
> Every wyndowe by and by.

[162] "The name given to Ptolemy's astronomical treatise, and then applied loosely to works on astrology." Robinson, 787.

[163] An astrolabe. See Chaucer's *Treatise on the Astrolabe,* 396-418 (Skeat).

[164] Counters for calculating. See the discussion of these stones in L. C. Karpinski, "Augrim Stones," *Modern Language Notes,* XXVII (Nov., 1912), 206-209.

[165] Psaltery, a kind of harp.

[166] A *Mil. T.,* 3203-3215.

floor rooms three.[167]   Even should a student have certain possessions and comforts which belonged to him alone, it was rare
for him to enjoy the privacy of a chamber.[168]   The regulation had
not as yet been passed which provided that Oxford students
must reside in Halls or Colleges,[169] and fortunately for Nicholas
the carpenter had had a room to let.   It was probably the solar,
too, with steps leading up to it from the main hall;[170] and there
in the best room of the house, Nicholas lived in comparative
comfort.

Being "lyk a mayden meke for to se,"[171] our Oxford scholar was
meticulously neat and attentive to the niceties of life.   The floor of
his room was probably covered with rushes, according to medieval
custom; it was also likely that intermingled with the rushes were
sweet-smelling herbs—mint, sage, lavender and others—picked each
day fresh from the garden near the carpenter's stable.[172]   Would
it not be a source of delight to the carpenter's charming wife
to order the maid, Gille, or the carpenter's knave, Robin, to
gather the herbs for the lodger's room?   And how sweet would
be the odor that arose from the herbs when Nicholas trampled
on them as he walked across the room.   It must have been almost
as refreshing as a walk in the garden itself.   One may hope that
along with the herbs a few alder leaves were scattered on the
floor that fleas might be caught thereon.[173]   "Ful fetisly ydight
with herbes swoote" may imply that sprigs of herbs, tied together in bunches, also hung from the beams of the chamber

---

[167] C. E. Mallet, *A History of the University of Oxford* (London, 1928),
I, 143-144; Coulton, *Social Life in Britain* (Cambridge, 1918), 75.

[168] Mallet, *op. cit.,* 143.

[169] This regulation was made in 1420, primarily because hitherto the
students not residing in Halls nor having Principals, "who are called by
the name of Chamberdekyns, and who sleep all day and at night lurk
about taverns and brothels" committed many misdeeds. See Alfred B.
Emden, *An Oxford Hall in Medieval Times* (Oxford, 1927), 30-31.

[170] See lines 3431-3435, *passim.*

[171] A *Mil. T.,* 3202.

[172] See *supra,* 14.

[173] *The Goodman of Paris,* 173.

ceiling.   Or they may have been like those promised to his
daughter by the King in *The Squyr of Lowe Degre:*

> A cage of gold shall hange alofte,
> With longe peper fayre burning,
> And cloves that be swete smellyng,
> Frankensense and olibanum,
> That whan ye slepe the taste may come.[174]

Perhaps, too, the thoughtful wife of the carpenter sometimes tied
tassels of ferns to the beams of the ceiling to catch bothersome
flies.[175]   She may even have placed on Nicholas' bed some flowering herbs, such as rosemary, that his dreams might be pleasant
and his sleep free from annoyance.[176]

The books, the astrolabe, and the counting stones which Nicholas used were arranged in orderly fashion on the shelves at the
head of his bed.   Study ought not to have been too difficult, with
everything needed so close at hand.   Chaucer, himself, may have
had books at his "beddes head."   Sometimes, he tells us, he read
in bed:

> So whan I saw I mighte not slepe,
> Til now late, this other night,
> Upon my bedde I sat upright,
> And bad oon reche me a book.[177]

Perhaps Nicholas studied in bed.   And when he wearied of mental
pursuits, the young scholar could take from above the shelves his
psaltery, or harp, and play to his heart's content.

Nicholas had extravagant tastes for a rather poor scholar.   This
is indicated by the covering of red falding on his press.   Falding
was a soft woollen cloth[178] which was somewhat rare and consequently expensive.   In fact, red and green cloths generally were
the most expensive ones available; consequently the possession of

---

[174] Ll. 846-850.

[175] *The Goodman of Paris,* 175.

[176] "Fragment on the Virtues of Herbs," *Reliquae Antiquae,* ed. T. Wright
and J. O. Halliwell, 2 vols. (London, 1845), I, 194-196.

[177] *BD.,* 44-47.   See also A *Gen. Prol.,* 293-296.

[178] M. Channing Linthicum, "'Faldyng' and 'Medlee,'" *Journal of English
and Germanic Philology,* XXXIV (Jan., 1935), 39-41.   Cf. also A *Gen Prol.,*
391.

them marked a person as noble or more worldly than others.[179]
The price of one-half yard of scarlet cloth in Oxford in 1379
was fifteen shillings,[180] almost five times as much as a winter
tunic for the warden[181] and nearly as much as the price of a
fat stalled ox had been in 1313.[182] This red cover of Nicholas'
press, together with his psaltery, was probably used by Chaucer
to suggest the character of the scholar.

Unlike the romancers of the period, Chaucer gives no glowing
account of the lady's chamber or bower. His references to Criseyde's room are incidental and lacking in significant details. There
are several casual allusions to the chamber of Emelye. Arcite,
after escaping from the tower, became page to the young lady.
The fact that he could "hewen wode, and water bare,"[183] indicates
that as page of the chamber he had to supply wood for a fireplace
and bring water from a well for Emelye's ablutions, but from such
mere suggestions one gets little information.

No medieval household possession was more highly prized than
the bed of a lord or lady. It was at once the most decorative and
most luxurious article of furniture in the house, being not a
mere frame of wood or iron with mattress and coverlets, but
frame, mattress (often some sort of feather bed), "curtains, hangings, tester,[184] celour,[185] and all necessary appendages."[186]

The bed which Chaucer says he will give to Morpheus or

---

[179] Coulton, *Social Life in Britain,* 72. It is interesting to note that
most of Chaucer's worldly characters affect some red garment.

[180] James E. T. Rogers, *A History of Agriculture and Prices in England*
(Oxford, 1866), II, 541.

[181] *Ibid.,* 541.

[182] John Stow, *Survey of London,* ed. C. L. Kingsford, 2 vols. (Oxford,
1908), II, 162.

[183] A *Kn. T.,* 1422.

[184] The head of the bed—as a panel of wood or more often of embroidered
stuff. Louis F. Salzman, *English Life in the Middle Ages* (London, 1929),
104.

[185] From the top of the tester a canopy or seler (celour) stretched over
the bed, and from each corner of this hung curtains. *Ibid.,* 104.

[186] *Our English Home,* 102.

Juno or to anyone who will make him sleep appears at first sight
to be described in an exaggerated fashion:

> Of downe of pure dowves whyte
> I wil yive him a fether-bed,
> Rayed with golde, and right wel clad
> In fyn blak satin doutremere,
> And many a pilow, and every bere
> Of clothe of Reynes,[187] to slepe softe;
> Him thar not nede to turnen ofte
> And I wol yive him al that falles
> To a chambre;   .   .   .   [188]

Perhaps down of white doves for a feather bed is extravagant,
but neither the stripes of gold nor the fine black satin are extremely elaborate for a medieval bed. "Cloth of Reynes," like the
other materials, may not be the ordinary kind of pillow case
Chaucer used, but one has only to examine some of the wills of
the fourteenth century to see that the bed the poet describes is
not necessarily imaginary.[189]

------

[187] A kind of linen made in Rennes in Brittany. (Robinson)

[188] *BD*, 249-258.

[189] Beds belonging to royal persons were of course particularly fine: Edward II bequeathed to his son, the Black Prince, a bed marked with the
arms of France and England. This was in turn passed on to Richard II, son
of the Black Prince. To his confessor, the Black Prince left a red bed with
his arms embroidered at each corner. Not unlike Chaucer's bed, except that
it is more elaborate, was one which Edmund Mortimer, Earl of March
and Ulster, bequeathed in 1380 to his son Roger. It is described as "a large
bed of black satin, embroidered with white lions and gold roses, with escutcheons of the arms of Mortimer and Ulster." The "Fair Maid of Kent,"
mother of Richard II, left to the King "my new bed of red velvet, embroidered with ostrich feathers of silver, and heads of leopards of gold with
boughs and leaves issuing out of their mouths." *Testamenta Vetusta,* ed.
Nicholas H. Nicolas, 2 vols. (London, 1826), I, 10; 12; 111; 14.

Other medieval persons also had valuable beds to leave their heirs. Lady
Alice West of Hampshire (1395) gave her best bed, "a bed of tapicers werk,
with all the tapites of sute, red of colour, ypouthered with chapes and
schohons, in the corners, of myn Auncestres armes," to her son, Thomas.
With the bed she gave also her best featherbed, "and a blue caneuas, and a
materas, and twey blankettys, and a peyre schetes of Reynes, . . . and sex of
my best pilwes . . . and a bleu couertour of menyuer, and a keuerlet of red
sendel ypouthered with Cheuerons." *Fifty Earliest Eng. Wills,* 4-5.

That the bed of his time was more comfortable than it had been
in earlier centuries Chaucer admits in a poem, "The Former Age."
There were in days past "no paleis-chaumbres, ne non halles,"

> In caves and (in) wodes softe and swete
> Slepten this blissed folk with-oute walles,
> On gras and leves in parfit quiete.
> No doun of fetheres, ne no bleched shete
> Was kid to hem, but in seurtee they slepte.[190]

Illustrations of fourteenth century beds show them as being
narrow and low.[191] The upper part appears to slope slightly upward, so that the person in it is in a semi-reclining position. Such
a bed it may be that Chaucer refers to in *Troilus and Criseyde,*
when he specifies that

> He doun up-on his beddes feet him sette.[192]

If the bed sloped upward, the foot of the bed is the only part upon
which Troilus could have sat comfortably.

Even though the solar often served as a living room, there
seems always to have been at least one bed in it. Thomas, in
the *Summoner's Tale,* of whom Chaucer says,

> Bedrede up-on a couche lowe he lay,[193]

is evidently in the principal room—perhaps even the only one—of

---

Nicholas Sturgeon, a priest, left to one of his cousins a bed of green
silk with a tester and canopy of white and red striped tartarin, and "the
gilde pece wiþ smal stones sett thereon." To another cousin he left a bed
of green worsted, with costers that matched; and to his servant a small
amount of money and "a blew bed with the lyoun Curteynes, coverled,
blankettis, a peyre of shetis and a gowne." *Ibid.,* 132-133.

It is needless to say that in the hands of the romancers the bed became
even more elaborate than it actually was. Cf. for example, *Sir Gawayne and
the Green Knight,* 27-28; *Partonope of Blois,* 31; the "Lay of Gugemar,"
French Medieval Romances from the Lays of Marie de France, trans. by
Eugene Mason, sec. ed. (London, 1924), 11.

[190] *Minor Poems,* 41-45.

[191] See "Le Lit de Mort," *Le Bréviaire Grimani,* 57; "La Naissance de S.
Jean Baptiste," *ibid.,* 70; "The Nativity," *Thirty-Two Miniatures from the
Book of Hours of Joan II, Queen of Navarre,* 2 parts (London, 1899), Plate
XV, fol. 50.

[192] I, 359.

[193] D 1769.

the house. The Friar seats himself upon a bench nearby, re- ℵ
marking, as "fro the bench he droof awey the cat,"[194]

Here have I eten many a mery meel.[195]

Visiting, eating, and sleeping were apparently all done in the
same room.

Often there were several beds in a single room.[196] The miller's
solar, it will be recalled, has three:

And in his owne chambre hem made a bed
With shetes and with chalons faire y-spred,
Noght from his owne bed ten feet or twelve.
His doghter hadde a bed, al by hir-selve,
Right in the same chambre, by and by.[197]

Temporary beds could easily be made, often consisting of only a
few blankets and pillows laid on the floor or on a bench. On one
occasion when Pandarus spends the night with Troilus

. . . on a paillet, al that glade night,
By Troilus he lay, with mery chere.[198]

The fact that later, when Pandarus wishes to talk secretly with
Troilus, he

Up roos, and on his beddes syde him sette,[199]

indicates that the pallet was a temporary bed of some kind.

Aside from the furnishings of Nicholas' chamber, Chaucer has
few references to anything save beds. However, he at least mentions such articles as the perch used either for hawks or for cloth-

---

[194] *Ibid.,* 1775.

[195] *Ibid.,* 1773.

[196] There were six beds in Richard Toky's chamber. Besides, there was
a little press for the master's caps and a bench covered in green . . . four
linen chests, with covers, were doubtless used as seats. Thomas, "Illustrations," 100.

[197] A *Rv. T.,* 4139-4143.

[198] *TC,* III, 229-230.

[199] *Ibid.,* III, 236.

ing,[200] candles,[201] coffers,[202] fireplaces,[203] and benches,[204] so that all together a list of what the chamber generally had by way of furniture is supplied.

An uncommon, but certainly not unfamiliar article of furniture is described by Chaucer in the *Squire's Tale*. This is the mew made by Canacee for the wounded hawk which she finds:

> And by hir beddes heed she made a mewe,
> And covered it with veluettes blewe,
> In signe of trouthe that is in wommen sene.
> And al with-oute, the mewe is peynted grene,
> In whiche were peynted alle thise false foules,
> As beth thise tidifs, tercelets, and oules.[205]

A mew was a coop or cage into which hawks were placed and tenderly cared for while they were moulting. So, too, jays, mag-

---

[200] Cf. B *NPT,* 4074; A *Kn. T.,* 2204, for references to the perch used for birds. In *RR,* Frag. A, 224-226 is an allusion to its use for clothing:

> Upon a perche, weyke and smalle,
> A burnet heng therwithalle.

An interesting account of a perch is also given by Marie de France in the "Lay of Gugemar," *op. cit.,* 16. When the husband of the queen came into her bower and found Gugemar there, he was angry and threatened to kill him. Gugemar, undismayed by the threat, "started to his feet, and gazing round, marked a stout rod of fir, on which it is the use for linen to be hung. This he took in hand, and faced his foes. . . ."

[201] Candles seem to have generally furnished the light in medieval houses. Chaucer refers only casually to them. See *TC,* III, 1141; A *Mil. T.,* 3634.

[202] Coffers were small chests, and like chests were used for clothing, documents, linens, spices, and any other valuables a medieval gentleman might possess. In the chamber of La Beale Isoud's queen-mother was a coffer in which the queen kept "the piece of sword that was pulled out of Sir Marharis' head after he was dead." *Le Morte Darthur,* I, 296. Chaucer, in his allusions to the coffer, does not refer to such unusual contents. See F *Fkl. T.,* 1571-1573; D *WB Prol.,* 308-309.

[203] In several of his references to the fire, Chaucer is so vague that one can not determine whether he alludes to the fire in the center of a room or to a fireplace in the wall. Both types were used, the second being usually in the chamber and the first in the great hall. See A *Rv. T.,* 4116; D *WB Prol.,* 713-714; *TC,* III, 978-980; 1141.

[204] *TC,* II, 91; D *Sum. T.,* 1769.

[205] F 643-648.

pies and other birds were kept in such cages as domestic pets.[206]
Chaucer refers elsewhere to "briddes that men in cages fede,"[207]
and to a bird in a cage of gold. Of the latter he writes:

> Although his cage of gold be never so gay,
> Yet hath this bird, by twenty thousand fold,
> Lever in a forest, that is rude and cold.[208]

Lydgate also writes of a "chorle" who was "so gladde that he his
bridde hadde taken" that "in al haste he cast for to make within
his house a pratie litelle cage and with his songs to rejoice his
corage."[209] As early as 1380 cages were garnished with pearls,
emeralds, and other precious stones.[210]

Canacee's cage may have been made according to specifications
such as those which the Goodman of Paris directed his wife to
employ. If so, it must have been something like this:

> . . . de quatre piés de long et quatre piés de large, et trois
> piés de hault, et soit couverte de bonne toile pour le vent,
> et y ait fenestre pour avoir air. Et en icelle mue ait une
> perche, laquelle sera de demi-pié de hault, et sera l'une
> des moitiés feutrée, et en l'autre moitié de long, aura une
> chanlette courant en laquelle l'en luy donra sa viande sans
> touchier à luy.[211]

Canacee's mew, with its covering of blue velvet, signifying "trouthe
that is in wommen sene," its paint of green in token of the inconstancy of men, and its designs of the false birds painted on
it was highly ornamental and must have brightened the young
lady's chamber greatly. Chaucer's description of it appears
singularly realistic.

---

[206] Percy Macquoid and Ralph Edwards, *The Dictionary of English Furniture,* 3 vols. (New York, 1924) I, 56.

[207] F *Sq. T.,* 611.

[208] H *Mcpl. T.,* 168-170.

[209] "The Churl and the Bird," in *English Verse between Chaucer and Surrey,* ed. Eleanour P. Hammond (Duke University Press, 1927), p. 105,
78-82.

[210] *Dictionary of Furniture,* I, 57.

[211] *Le Ménagier de Paris,* 2 vols. (Paris, 1846), II, 313. The original is
here used, for Miss Power's translation of the book does not include this
material.

Although not describing Canacee's care of the mew she builds, the poet refers elsewhere in the *Squire's Tale* to what was probably the usual manner of caring for a bird's cage. In alluding to the "newefanglenesse" of men, Chaucer compares it to that of birds in cages, saying:

> For though thou night and day take of hem hede,
> And strawe hir cage faire and softe as silk,
> And yeve hem sugre, hony, breed and milk,
> Yet right anon, as that his dore is uppe,
> He with his feet wol spurne adoune his cuppe,
> And to the wode he wol and wormes ete;
> So newefangel been they of hir mete. . .[212]

One may be sure that Canacee, in her tender solicitude for the falcon, would see that the mew was properly tended.[213]

Besides the hall and chamber, Chaucer mentions but few other rooms, and those very casually. In the *Franklin's Tale* is a "studie."[214] In view of the great cost of books at this time,[215]

---

[212] F 612-618.

[213] Dame Juliana Berners, the author of one of the most interesting of early works on sports, gives instructions for the proper care of a mew as follows:

> Dispose your mew so as it be free from weesel or poulcat, or any other vermine, and that it be not annoyed either with winde or cold, or extreame heat, yet let one part of the mew stand so as the Sun may come in for the most part of the day, let also the scituation be so appointed as your hawke may not bee troubled with much noise nor tumult of men, neither let any person come unto her, but onely he that feedeth her: provide to have in your mew a feeding stocke for your hawke, and a long string tied thereunto to make her meate fast withall, for else she will carry it aboute the house, and soile it with dust, and many times hide it till it stinke and be unwholsome; insomuch as it may occasion her death, and therefore when it is bound to the feeding stocke, neither in the feeding, nor in the tiring, neither at her lighting downe, nor at her rising up shall shee doe her selfe any hurte or prejudice, then when as shee hath fedde, take away whatsoever shee shall leave, and at the next time give her fresh and sweete meate, for stale and long kept meate engender- eth manie evill and mortall sickenesses, and looke that you never go to your mew, but when as you doe intend to give her meate. *The Book of St. Alban's,* reprint by Gervase Markham (London, 1595), 9.

[214] F 1213-1214.

[215] Chaucer is said to have had sixty books which were worth as much as a collection of 5,000 volumes of today would be. A book in the fourteenth

it seems hardly probable that this room was wholly devoted to books. It was more than likely a combination chamber and study, semi-private in character. Like Richard Toky's study or counting-house, it may have contained an iron-bound chest for deeds, a money-box, pen box and inkhorn, a quire or two of paper, and a few books.[216]

The kitchen and other houses of office are merely mentioned, although they were of significance in the medieval house. On one occasion the poet writes:

> And al the paleys put was in array,
> Both halle and chambres, ech in his degree;
> Houses of office stuffed with plentee.[217]

and again he alludes to

> Blessinge halles, chambres, kitchenes, boures,[218]

but such references are so incidental as to be of no special importance and to offer no real information. The reason for Chaucer's apparent neglect of these rooms may be that he created no scene around them and found no need to describe them. When one recalls that the poet's intention was not to inform the reader about medieval houses, except incidentally, he is surprised not at the omissions but rather at the many significant details found throughout his works. Chaucer's own excuse for his omissions is generally expressed in some such fashion as this:

> Of which if I shal tellen al th'array,
> Than wolde it occupye a somers day.[219]

As has been seen, the rooms of the medieval house did not have a great amount of furniture. Even persons who could afford two houses had usually only enough for one of their dwellings at a time. Consequently, when the family moved from one house

---

century was a treasure capable of being pawned, often as valuable as a country estate. Wilbur L. Schramm, "The Cost of Books in Chaucer's Time," *MLN*, XLVIII (March, 1933), 139-145.

[216] Thomas, *"Illustrations,"* 101.

[217] E *Cl. T.*, 262-264.

[218] D *WB*, 869.

[219] F *Sq. T.*, 63-64.

to another it was preceded by carts laden with seats, beds, bedding, kitchen utensils, chests of linen and clothing, hangings, and other similar possessions.[220]   Even the king, when moving from one place to another with his brilliant cortege of lords was followed by an army of loud-creaking carts laden with household goods.[221]

In view of the fact that Chaucer's Canterbury pilgrims travel on the public highway on their journey, it would seem only natural to have some allusion to the transportation of household goods. Yet the poet furnishes no information on the subject. His single reference, so incidentally made as to be little more than a suggestion, is in *Troilus and Criseyde:*

> The moeble which that I have in this toun
> Un-to my fader shal I take. . . .[222]

The means of conveying her furnishings may have been square-shaped, massive carts made of planks and placed on two wheels, or lighter wagons fashioned of slats latticed with willow trellis and placed on wheels studded with big-headed nails which were decorative.[223]

Tenants of the Middle Ages frequently removed in their great carts much which did not belong to them when they left houses which they had leased.   Anything which was removable, even the glass of the windows, seems to have been sometimes loaded

---

[220] Jusserand, *Eng. Wayfaring Life,* 91; William H. Helm, *Homes of the Past* (London, 1921), 50-51; *Our English Home,* 105.

[221] Jusserand, *op. cit.,* 91.   In the will of Richard Earl of Arundel and Surrey, in 1392, is mention of bequests of a bed of red silk to his daughter, Charleton, and one of blue stuff to his daughter. Margaret.   The former is referred to as being *usually* at Reigate, and the latter as being *usually* at London.   This must allude to the custom of transporting them from one house to another. *Testamenta Vetusta,* I, 131.

[222] IV, 1380-1381.

[223] See the representations of such carts in Jusserand, *op. cit.,* 90.   The Prior of Durham Abbey had for the transportation of his belongings from one place to another, a long cart, the horses of which were harnessed in red leather.   When all the articles were packed into the cart, they were protected by hides sewed together and secured by cords, in much the same fashion as tarpaulins are used at the present time. *Account Rolls of the Abbey of Durham,* 3 vols.   Surtees Society Publications, nos. 99, 100, 103 (Durham, 1898-1900), III, iv.

on the carts and taken along with the tenant's own possessions.[224]
Criseyde, however, probably had sufficient furniture of her own
without adding to it.

Lodging Houses

Closely related to the medieval house for private families was
the lodging house where "gestes were heeld to bord." These
houses were of two kinds—inns kept by hostelers, and lodging
houses kept by herbergeours. Both were supplemented by cook-
shops, similar to our modern restaurants.[225] The rules of medieval
hospitality further provided for lodgings in private families, where,
like Sir Launcelot, one was "lodged with good will and had good
cheer for him and his horse."[226] When it was time to retire, one
might find himself brought into a fair garret, over the gate, to his
bed,[227] or if there were many guests, he might even be given a bed
on the floor of the great hall.

Chaucer relates in the *Nun's Priest's Tale* the following incident
from an old story concerning two men who had gone on a pilgrimage:

> And happed so, they come into a town,
> Wher-as ther was swich congregacioun
> Of peple, and eek se streit herbergage
> That they ne founde as much as o cotage
> In which they bothe mighte y-logged be.[228]

---

[224] Macquoid and Edwards, *The Dictionary of English Furniture*, I, 23.
Cf. also Koellreuter, *Das Privatleben*, 5. This removal of property by
tenants occasioned an act in the reign of Edward II, providing that tenants
were not to remove certain things:

> Yf they be affixed wt nayles or irne or of tree as pentises glasse
> lockis benchis or ony suche other, or of ellis yf they bee affixed wt
> morter or lyme or of erther or any other morter as forneis leedis
> candorus chemyneis corbels pavemettis or such other, or ellis yf
> plantiz be roetid in the groud as vynes trees graffe stoukz trees of
> frute, etc. Yt shall not be leeful unto such tenauntis in ye ende of
> her terme or any other tyme therin nor any of them to put away
> move or pluk up in any wyse, but yt they shall alwey remayn to the
> owner of yt soyle as percels of ye same soyle or tenement. *Arnold's
> Chronicle* (London, 1811), 138.

[225] Frederick J. Snell, *The Customs of Old England* (London, 1911), 212.
[226] *Le Morte Darthur*, I, 193.
[227] *Ibid.*, 194.
[228] B *NPT*, 4174-4179.

In true medieval indifference to their accommodations, they set out
to find some place where they might stay, with the result

> That oon of hem was logged in a stalle,
> Fer in a yerd, with oxen of the ploughe;
> That other man was logged wel y-nough,
> As was his aventure, or his fortune.[229]

Of a much more fortunate gentleman, a priest who served as
chaplain, Chaucer writes:

> That ther in dwelled hadde many a yeer,
> Which was so plesaunt and so servisable
> Unto the wyf, where-as he was at table,
> That she wolde suffre him no-thing for to paye
> For bord ne clothing, wente he never so gaye.[230]

Not all herbegeours and hostelers were as generous as this wife,
although laws provided that they should be "good folks, proper,
and sufficient, as regards serving their guests well and lawfully;
that so every one who is lodged with them may be sure both
as to body and to chattels."[231] No hosteler, or herbegeour, unless

---

[229] *Ibid.,* 4186-4189.

[230] G *CYT,* 1013-1017.

[231] Riley's *Memorials,* 1256. Probably the regulations made in the time of
Edward III, which were governed by the Old Anglo-Saxon frank-pledge,
were still in effect at this time. In part these regulations provided as
follows:

> No hosteler or herbegeour might entertain a stranger longer than a
> day and a night, unless he undertook to answer for his guest's be-
> haviour, and he was left in no uncertainty as to the course of con-
> duct which he was expected to pursue towards the always unde-
> sirable alien. In many respects his position resembled that of a mas-
> ter of a workhouse rather than a speculative tradesman. Thus, at
> times when it was forbidden to carry arms in the City, it became his
> duty to take possession of his guest's arms and retain them until the
> stranger departed. If the latter did not comply with his demand,
> they were fined and imprisoned. At other times, when the regula-
> tions were not so severe, he had to tell his guests that they were not
> to carry arms after curfew rang, or go wandering about the streets
> of the City. Should it happen that urgent business compelled a
> guest to be absent from the hotel for the night, the keeper was
> obliged to warn him with the best grace he might, that he must take
> care to be back as soon as possible.

he were a common brewer, was to sell ale, except to his stranger guests, and was not to charge for a gallon of the best ale, more than two pence. Likewise he was not to make any bread in his house for sale, but was to buy bread of the common bakers. This bread was to bear the stamp of the baker, "on the pain of having the same punishment as the baker would have had."[232] Such regulations indicate that efforts were made on the part of city officials to protect lodgers from fraudulent dealings and to secure their protection insofar as possible.

References to the treatment of lodgers are numerous in Chaucer's works. Many were the comforts offered by the host of the Tabard, where

> The chambres and the stalles weren wyde,[233]

and the host made good cheer:

> And to the soper sette us anon;
> And served us with vitaille at the beste.
> Strong was the wyn, and wel to drinke us leste.[234]

In addition to these references, Chaucer describes the carpenter of the *Miller's Tale* as

> A rich gnof, that gestes heeld to bord.[235]

That the carpenter was kindly in his treatment of his lodger is suggested in numerous ways. The room which was allotted to Nicholas, the student, has already been mentioned. Further, the carpenter showed interest in his lodger when he was absent, and at Nicholas' request that he bring him drink,

> This carpenter goth doun, and comth ageyn,
> And broghte of mighty ale a large quart.[236]

The miller of the *Reeve's tale,* when called upon to harbour the young men from Soler-halle at "Cantebrigge," agrees to do so.

---

[232] *Ibid.,* 347-348.
[233] A *Gen. Prol.,* 28.
[234] *Ibid.,* 748-750.
[235] A 3188.
[236] *Ibid.,* 3496-3497.

The arrangements made between him and the students seem very realistic:

'Get us som mete and drinke, and make us chere,
And we wil payen trewely atte fulle.
With empty hand men may na haukes tulle;
Lo here our silver, redy for to spende.'[237]

The miller, it will be recalled, then sent his daughter into town to purchase ale and bread for the guests, roasted them a goose, and provided sleeping accommodations in his own room.[238] Unfortunately, from the miller's point of view, the guests eventually departed without having paid their fee for lodging.[239]

*   *   *

A retrospective view of Chaucer's allusions, detailed as well as incidental, shows that a fairly complete and surprisingly realistic account of the English medieval house is given. Even those references for which the poet depends largely upon other literary sources offer significant information when considered apart from the details added by his imagination.

The castle is the most completely described of the four general types of houses. This dwelling is frequently found in the literature of the time and it is perhaps only natural that Chaucer should give it more attention than any other. It is usually of such exaggerated dimensions and such elaborate structure that it appears to be purely of the imagination, or at least primarily of symbolic purport. Yet its features are those of the real medieval castle of Chaucer's own time. There is the strongly fortified wall, with its great gate elaborately carved with various kinds of figures, the surrounding moat, the enormous building with its strongly built tower; there are the architectural ornamentations—the gargoyles, the numerous pinnacles on dwelling and wall, the niches with their sculptured figures in them.

The manor house, called *court* or *halle,* is too casually mentioned to be of much significance. In fact, it is merely named and no more is known of it from Chaucer's works than that it was the house of the lord of a manor or village.

---

[237] A 4132-4135.
[238] *Ibid.,* 4136 ff.
[239] *Ibid.,* 4315.

It is difficult to distinguish between the manor and the town house. Apparently there is little difference except that the latter is within the limits of the city and is the home of that class of society whose wealth did not depend on owning land. Chaucer's allusions to this dwelling are never specific; only by inference, which is perhaps faulty, may one designate any in his works as a town house. The term "paleys," used by the poet to denote a house of spacious proportions, frequently refers to the town house. The nearness of one dwelling to another also appears to imply it.

The exterior of neither of these houses is described. The rooms and their arrangement are in many cases referred to, however, and from implied information nearly the whole interior can be reconstructed fairly well. The carpenter's house has a hall open to the roof, with a bower and the lodger's room at one end, and a stable opposite these at the other. With the exception of the kitchen and other houses of office, which are omitted, this is the typical arrangement of the medieval English house—a great hall with rooms at each end, varied in size and number according to the wealth of the owner. Such rooms as bower, parlour, countour-house, study, and sometimes a domestic chapel—all of which Chaucer alludes to in more or less detailed manner—composed the house of a wealthy person. The village house or cottage was usually very humble, as is seen in Chaucer's poems. In one instance it is depicted in more than usual detail; it is said to be narrow, to be in a dale shaded with trees, and to have a yard surrounded by some sort of crude fence and a dry ditch or moat. Inside, the cottage has two rooms—which Chaucer dignifies by the names of hall and bower—blackened by the smoke from the fire. Another cottage, even more humble than this, perhaps, seems to house both human beings and animals; the ox-stall is evidently attached to it.

In all types of medieval house the hall was the principal room. Chaucer shows its uses as a place for meeting and entertaining guests, as a dining hall for the householder's family and visitors, possibly as a chapel, and as a place where persons met to pay respects to a departed friend. Basically, the hall was a room of large proportions with a dais for the principal table across one end of it. An extraordinarily large hall was sometimes divided into aisles by pillars which extended in two rows down the room. Often the hall door led directly out into the street; it was of unusual width and capable of admitting at least a horse and its rider. The furnishings of the room consisted of tables laid on trestles, with sometimes a stationary table, called a *table dormant* for the master of the household or his privileged guests. The walls were hung with beautiful tapestries (tapites) or painted. People sat on benches which were sometimes made more comfortable by cushions and hangings.

The principal chamber or solar of the medieval house was used as a combination sleeping and reception room. It was more private than the hall, but even in this chamber men and women met and spent many hours in one another's company. Often there were several beds in one's private chamber. Sometimes a smaller room or closet, offering more privacy than the larger one, was attached to it. The walls of the chamber, particularly as shown in romance literature, were elaborately painted. Sometimes the windows were of glass; those in romances, and occasionally those in real life were painted or otherwise brightly ornamented. With the exception of the bed, the chamber furnishings were simple and scanty. A bench or two, a chest for clothing or important documents and other possessions, a perch for hawks or for garments, sometimes a fireplace, a set of shelves for books and small articles, comprised the furnishings. Not many chambers, it may be believed, possessed even all of these articles. In numerous allusions, some of which merely mention one or more pieces of furniture, Chaucer informs the reader of them.

The medieval bed was by far the most important and highly-prized furnishing in the house. In homes of the wealthy it was often elegantly arrayed in coverlets of silk, linen, or fur. The mattress and pillows were made of softest feathers and were covered with fine linen or silk. Chaucer's most complete description of the bed seems to be that of a wealthy person; yet he tells us also that the miller, in making beds for his guests, has bed clothes which are by no means common. Evidently all but the poor provided their households with at least fairly comfortable and attractive beds.

Sometimes ladies kept their falcons in mews or cages in their chambers.   Ornamented, as that of Canacee was, with bright-colored paint and figures, such mews must have been decorative as well as useful.

The sharing of his house with others seems to have been often required of the medieval householder.   The unwritten rules of hospitality demanded that passing guests be treated with kindness and cordiality whether it was possible for them to pay for their lodging or not.   Sometimes lodgings were a source of income; regularly, in this case, certain rooms of a private house were set aside for students or others who were obliged to seek living-quarters for a specified time.   Toward his lodgers the hosteler had definite obligations.   He was not only to offer them a certain amount of protection, but also very courteous treatment.

Chaucer presents much information on this matter.   He treats of the kindly woman who bestows every kindness on a priest-lodger without demanding any pay.   He shows the carpenter as a solicitous host who has rented out to a student what is perhaps the best room in the house.   He further describes the reception of the two students in the home of the miller.   Regardless of the fact that the miller and students have had rather unpleasant business relations, the former accords his guests every privilege of hospitality, making them a bed in his own chamber, setting a good meal before them, and entertaining them until late at night.

In conclusion it is to be noted that in poems which are not essentially domestic in character, Chaucer has given an astonishingly comprehensive view of the English medieval house and its furnishings.   Were one to depend on the poet's information alone, he would derive sufficient knowledge to reconstruct this house with a great degree of accuracy, at least in general outline. Even in poems in which he affects foreign scenes, as for instance in the *Troilus* and in such tales as those of the Knight and the Squire, he supplies domestic life which is essentially English. There are indeed many descriptions based on literary sources, but there are numerous others which are primarily original and apparently based on existing models.   Altogether, the poet's contribution to the history of the development of the English medieval house is considerable.

CHAPTER II

THE GARDEN

This yerd was large, and rayled alle the aleyes,
And shadwed wel with blosmy bowes grene,
And benched newe, and sonded alle the weyes.
In which she walketh arm and arm bitwene.
—*Troilus and Criseyde,* II, 820-823.

The English medieval garden, like the house, bears witness to
the rapidly increasing domestic spirit of the age. Its popularity,[1]
its orderly, well planned arrangement, the interest in flowers for
their own sake, the great variety of plants used, and the recreations enjoyed in the garden—all are manifestations of this spirit.
Chaucer, in more or less significant allusions, presents on the
whole a fairly complete treatment of the subject.

For centuries gardens had been planted and tended in England. The Anglo-Saxons had known and used about 500 plants
for cookery and as medicines;[2] they probably also cultivated small

---

[1] Mrs. Evelyn Cecil, *A History of Gardening in England,* third ed. (London, 1910), 42, says, "By the end of the fourteenth century every small manor
and farm could boast of a garden."

[2] A good account of these plants and their uses is found in *Leechdoms,
Wortcunning and Starcraft of Early England,* ed. by Rev. Oswald Cockayne,
Rolls Series, 2 vols. (London, 1864, 1865). Many curious beliefs and practices attended the use of plants for their healing qualities. Betony, for instance, was scraped, rubbed into dust, and two drachms of it swallowed in
beer to cure a broken head. It was said that "the head healeth very quickly
after the drink," *ibid.,* I, 71. This same plant was seethed in water and
used for sore eyes, blear eyes, nosebleed, toothache, as a preventive of in-
toxication, to cure weariness, to aid digestion, for adder bites, sore throat,
gout, and numerous afflictions. Of nasturtium or cress it was claimed that
"in case a man's hair fell off," the juice of the plant put on the man's nose
would cause the hair to grow again, *ibid.,* I, 117. Bright coloured hydele
was used for "sore of teeth and if they wag," *ibid.,* I, 127. A compound of
mint, sulphur, and vinegar, smeared with a new feather on skin eruptions
relieved soreness, *ibid.,* I, 235. It was believed that diseased minds were
likewise healed by certain plants. Peony was so employed. Clove wort

plots in which flowers were grown for the pleasure they afforded.[3] The Norman invasion, with the attendant disturbances in domestic life, retarded the normal development of the garden; however, nearly every Norman household relied on a small plot of ground,[4] tended generally by the women,[5] for the few vegetables used on the table,[6] and herbs employed in the treatment of illness and wounds. Flowers, too, may have been cultivated, but on the whole the Norman garden was for practical rather than aesthetic purposes.[7]

In the twelfth and thirteenth centuries the art of gardening became more significant than it had ever been before. Crusaders returning from the Orient related tales of the beautiful gardens they had seen, with the result that many attempts were made to reproduce similar ones.[8]

Even more potent, however, was the influence of the Church and its religious Orders on gardening. For centuries the Church had assigned a symbolic meaning to flowers, especially to roses and lilies,[9] and had thus encouraged their cultivation. The garden as a whole had always been regarded as a symbol of a peaceful,

---

wreathed about the lunatic's neck with a red thread, when the moon was on the wane in April, would heal the lunacy by the early part of October, *ibid.,* I, 101.

[3] What these gardens were like is not known. Only an occasional allusion, such as that in which the breath of St. Guthlac is compared to "mellifluous plants, blossoming full joyously throughout the plains, diffuse in places, though firm-set in their stations," suggests them. St. Guthlac, II (B) *Exeter Book,* ed. and trans. Israel Gollancz, EETS, OS 104 (London, 1895), I, 181-182.

[4] These small plots were within castle yards, where at this period there was little room for gardens, because the castles were usually built on hills and did not have large yards. Cecil, *op. cit.,* I, 30-31.

[5] Marie Luise Gothein, *A History of Garden Art,* ed. Walter P. Wright, and trans. from German by Mrs. Archer-Hind, 2 vols. (London, 1928), I, 183.

[6] Most of the food used by the Normans was brought in from the chase, but a few vegetables were used. *Ibid.,* I, 183.

[7] *Ibid.,* I, 176.

[8] Among other things, oriental influence was responsible for the setting of costly baths in the gardens. It was now considered almost a necessity for ladies to bathe their feet there before a meal. *Ibid.,* 190-192.

[9] Charles Joret, *La Rose dans L'Antiquité et au Moyen Age* (Paris, 1892), 392-399.

quiet life, and one may well believe that the men and women of the early monastic establishment viewed it as such. In a sense it may be said that the English garden was preserved and developed by the monks of the Middle Ages.[10] Two of the chief sources of information regarding the medieval garden are the *De Naturis Rerum*[11] of Alexander Neckam, an Augustinian abbot of the latter twelfth and early thirteenth centuries, and the *De Proprietatibus Rerum*[12] of Bartholomaeus Anglicus, a Franciscan encyclopedist of the thirteenth century.

It was in the thirteenth century, with the publication of the French poem, the *Romaunt de la Rose,* that the garden became significant in purely literary works. Previous to this time allusions in literature seem to have been merely incidental, but now the garden as a consciously-used scene, especially for lovers, was definitely introduced.[13] The description of the garden of the *Romaunt* had a tremendous influence on subsequent similar descriptions in medieval literature.

Gardens in General in Chaucer's Work

Chaucer's interest in the garden may have derived primarily from the *Romaunt de la Rose.* As translator of the poem his early works are so strongly influenced by the description given in it that his views of the garden are conventionalized and so marked by the traditional love of enumerating trees, birds, and plants that any realistic touches are scarcely noticeable. There

---

[10] Gothein, *op. cit.,* I, 174.

[11] Ed. Thos. Wright, Rolls Series (London, 1863). In this voluminous work Neckam treats of plants, listing the names of those grown in England, and indicating the general appearance of the garden. He is chiefly concerned with plants having a practical use, but also includes the names of numerous flowers, such as roses, lilies, heliotrope, violets, daffodils, poppies, peonies and others.

[12] A translation of this work is found in *Medieval Lore,* ed. Robert Steele (London, 1893). It appears to include many of the plants named by Neckam and contains many stories and fables concerning the history of plants. Of the use of various plants for medicinal purposes Bartholomaeus also furnishes information. In general, his work augments that of Neckam.

[13] Gothein, *op. cit.,* I, 192-194.

is little or no originality evident in such descriptions, for the poet depends too much upon his source.

In his more mature works, however, Chaucer becomes more realistic in his garden descriptions. There are fewer details than in the earlier ones, but they suggest the poet's acquaintance with actual gardens[14] rather than with those belonging chiefly to previous literary works. Yet even in these more realistic allusions one notes the influence of the conventional garden scene, and it is only in almost inadvertent references that the poet frees himself from the traditional method of describing it. The information which he offers is nevertheless important, for besides including several kinds of gardens, Chaucer shows fairly well their plan, their contents, and the uses to which they were put as recreational centers. From a literary point of view his contribution is, then, worth while, particularly since it is in Chaucer's poetry that the English garden first appears at all realistic.

The Kinds of Gardens in Chaucer's Works

The simplest type of garden in Chaucer's day, and one which the poet himself refers to several times, was the flowery mead. This was a field planted with grass and dotted with low-growing flowers such as violets, daisies, buttercups, and the like. Of it Chaucer writes in his translation of the *Romaunt de la Rose:*

> Ther sprang the violete al newe,
> And fresshe pervinke, riche of hewe,
> And floures yelowe, whyte, and rede;
> Swich plentee grew ther never in mede.
> Ful gay was al the ground, and queynt,
> And poudred, as men had it peynt.
> With many a fresh and sondry flour,
> That casten up ful good savour.[15]

---

[14] Chaucer is said to have drawn inspiration from the beautiful gardens of the Savoy, one of the most magnificent of English medieval residences. The palace was destroyed during the Peasants' Rebellion in 1381. George M. Trevelyan, *England in the Age of Wycliffe,* new edition (London, 1904), 46.

[15] Frag. A, 1431-1438.

Likewise, in the *Legend of Good Women* the poet says,

> Fair was this medew, as thoughte me overal;
> With floures enbrowded was it al.[16]

The mead seems to have been artificially, not naturally, formed. That is, what would correspond to the present-day lawn was planted with flowers in a manner simulating a natural meadow.[17] To keep it in order the plot was returved every three or four years, "the constant care and other attentions of modern times being apparently unknown." [18] Illuminations in old manuscripts abound in illustrations of the mead.[19] They show the ground thickly planted with flowers, like a piece of tapestry or embroidery work. Sometimes there is an enclosing wall or hedge, but often the mead is an open expanse.

More significant in the history of gardening than the mead was the formal garden of Chaucer's time. This type appears in detail, though ideally portrayed, in the *Romaunt de la Rose* and again in the *Parlement of Foules*. It seems to form a standard for other descriptions found more briefly drawn in the poet's later works.

The outside of the garden is first described:

> Enclos it was, and walled wel,
> With hye walles, embatailled,
> Portrayed without, and wel entailled
> With many riche portraitures.[20]

This "walle of masonrye,"[21] with the figures of Hate, Covetousness, Villainy, Felony, Avarice, Envy, Sorrow, and the like, painted "with gold and azure over alle,"[22] was evidently very

---

[16] *Prol.*, 106-107. In describing the dress of the Squire, Chaucer compares it to a mead:

> Embrouded . . . as it were a mede
> Al ful of fresshe floures, whyte and rede. A *Gen. Prol.*, 89-90.

[17] Eleanour Sinclair Rohde, *The Story of the Garden,* third ed. (Boston, 1936), 48.

[18] Sir Frank Crisp, *Medieval Gardens,* 2 vols. (London, 1924), I, 27.

[19] See illustrations in *Le Bréviaire Grimani,* 108, and in Crisp, *op. cit.,* II, Fig. LXXXII.

[20] Frag. A, 138-141.

[21] *Ibid.,* 302.

[22] *Ibid.,* 477-478. The wall surrounding the garden in the *Parlement of Foules* is of green stone. Cf. 11. 121-122.

beautiful. In it was a single entrance, "a wiket smal,"[23] of which Chaucer says:

> Upon this dore I gan to smyte,
> That was (so) fetys and so lyte;
> For other wey coude I not seke.[24]

The first impression of the garden was of its numerous trees, in which countless birds were singing.

> Summe highe and summe eek lowe songe
> Upon the braunches grene y-spronge.[25]

To reach the main part of the yard the poet turned to the right, and in his own words:

> Tho wente I forth on my right hond
> Doun by a litel path I fond
> Of mentes ful, and fenel grene;
> And faste by, withoute wene,
> Sir Mirthe I fond; . . .[26]

That part of the garden to which the path led seems to have had fewer trees than the other, for there was gathered a crowd of fair folk who were enjoying themselves in song and dance.

As he "wente up and doun ful many a way,"[27] that is, as he wandered about over the many paths, he observed this beautifully planned yard:

> The gardin was, by measuring,
> Right even and squar in compassing;
> It was as long as it was large.[28]

The trees, of which there were all varieties, were ranged in rows, so close together and so luxuriant in foliage that the sunlight

---

[23] *Ibid.*, 525-530. Compare this with the gate in *PF*, 123-140.
[24] *Ibid.*, 531-533.
[25] *Ibid.*, 717-718.
[26] *Ibid.*, 729-733.
[27] *Ibid.*, 1345.
[28] *Ibid.*, 1349-1351.

could hardly find its way through them. There, too, were many spices,

> As clow-gelofre, and licoryce,
> Gingere, and greyn de paradys,
> Canelle, and setewale of prys,
> And many a spyce delitable,
> To eten whan men ryse fro table.[29]

This little plot of useful plants may have been separated from the rest of the garden, but the poet does not specify that fact.

Here and there within the enclosure were wells, or fountains, well shadowed by the trees. From them were conduits to carry the water to various parts of the garden,

> Of which the water, in renning,
> Gan make a noyse ful lyking.[30]

The water from the wells and conduits had made the soil especially productive:

> About the brinkes of thise welles,
> And by stremes over-al elles
> Sprang up the gras, as thikke y-set
> And softe as any veluet,
>
> .   .   .   .   .
>
> Through moisture of the welle wete
> Sprang up the sote grene gras,
> As fair, as thikke, as mister was.[31]

---

[29] *Ibid.*, 1352-1372, *passim.*

[30] *Ibid.*, 1408-1416. No doubt these wells were artificial, having been placed in the garden for purposes of irrigation. Thomas Hyll, writing in the sixteenth century, describes methods of irrigation similar to this:

> A garden (and especially for potherbes) must be moist of it selfe, or els easy to be watred for fertilitie sake. . . . It is necessary also to have a well in a garden unles it may be watred with some conduit, or smal river runnynge by, or els be very neare to a river, for water is a great nourisher of herbes. And if there be no wel, then must ther be a pytte dygged, although it wyll be verye laborious to the Gardiners to drawe water therout. . . . But yf you can not well digge a pytte make then a lyttle ponde (or cestern as they name yt) as paladius willeth under the ground, that the rayne fallying all ye wynter may run thereinto (and therby with that water) you may happelye water your garden in the hoote sommer.

A Most Briefe and Pleasaunt Treatyse, Teachynge how to Dress, Sowe, and Set a Garden, first ed. (London, 1536). Not paginated.

[31] *RR*, Frag. A, 1417-1426.

In the lush grass the violets, periwinkle, and other flowers, "yelowe, whyte, and rede," of the flowery mead already referred to[32] grew in profusion.

Further wanderings through the garden led to what was probably the central fountain;[33] at least it seems to have been the most beautiful spot of all:

> And springing in a marble-stoon
> Had nature set, the sothe to telle,
> Under that pyn-tree a welle.
> And on the border al withoute,
> Was written, in the stone aboute,
> Lettres smale, that seyden thus,
> 'Here starf the faire Narcisus.'[34]

This well, or fountain, was delightfully clear, and when one looked into its depths he saw two crystal stones, which took on various hues when the sunlight shifted upon them. The stones acted as a mirror, reflecting everything which stood nearby, "as wel the colour as the figure."[35]

> Among a thousand thinges mo,
> A Roser (rose-bush) charged ful of roses,
> That with an hegge aboute enclos is.[36]

This little enclosed plot, hidden by the hedge from the sight of one passing in the garden, lay revealed in all its beauty in the magic well.

The description of this great garden, in spite of numerous realistic touches, such as the names of the trees and flowers, the references to the conduits and their practical purpose, and the

---

[32] Cf. *supra*, 56.

[33] Traditionally, the fourteenth century garden is said to have had three essentials, namely, enclosure, a well, or fountain, and plants. These elements are expressed pictorially in an illustration copied by Crisp. One picture shows "a wall, a fountain, and three trees," *Medieval Gardens*, II, Plate XCIII; another shows "a wall, a fountain, and two flowering plants." *Ibid.*, XCIV. The arrangements of these parts of a garden were numerous, but on the whole they seem to have assumed a similarity which partly accounts for the conventionality of descriptions of the medieval garden.

[34] Frag. A, 1462-1468.

[35] *Ibid.*, 1554-1587, *passim.*

[36] *Ibid.*, 1650-1652.

apparently exact location of everything in the yard, is primarily idealistic and symbolical. The minutely described wall, the accurate details concerning the arrangement of the trees, the suggestions as to the size and shape of the garden are somewhat deceptive in that they seem to indicate an actual garden, while in reality they are details which belong to one that is largely imaginary, even though probably modelled on what actually existed. This is a formal garden, moreover, planned and cared for by man. It is likewise primarily a pleasure garden rather than a useful one, although fruits, herbs and spices grow therein.

The influence of the foregoing description on Chaucer's other works is most clearly discernible in the garden depicted in the *Parlement of Foules*. Here the poet refers to "a parke, walled with grene stone," to which entrance was gained through a gate. The park was filled with trees of many sorts, and in one section of it was a garden, described as follows:

> A garden saw I, ful of blosmy bowes,
> Upon a river, in a grene mede,
> Ther as that swetnesse evermore y-now is,
> With floures whyte, blewe, yelowe, and rede;
> And colde welle-stremes, no-thing dede,
> That swommen ful of smale fisshes lighte,
> With finnes rede and scales silver-brighte.[37]

Here again were birds of every kind, and various animals; here also grew "every holsom spyce and gras,"[38] and under a tree was a well.

In addition there was an arbour, where the "noble goddesse Nature" sat:

> Of braunches were hir halles and hir boures,
> Y-wroght after hir craft and hir mesure.[39]

An arbour such as this was of great importance in the medieval garden. It was a kind of playing place, either in a wall or in the garden sheltered by a hedge, made of trees intertwined with

---

[37] V, 121 ff.; 183-189.
[38] *Ibid.*, 206.
[39] *Ibid.*, 302-303.

climbing plants—often roses and honeysuckle.[40]   Chaucer claims
to have one in his own garden:

> Hoom to myn hous ful swiftly I me spedde;
> And, in a litel erber that I have
> Y-benched newe with turves fresshe y-grave,
> I bad men shulde me my couche make;
> For deyntee of the newe someres sake,
> I bad hem strowe floures on my bed.[41]

The reference here to the benches freshly turved is significantly
realistic; one feels that the arbour actually existed, although it is
described no more fully than as "a litel erber."   In Deiphebus'
garden the "herber grene,"[42] where Eleyne and Deiphebus went
to read a letter, was probably like this one; again, however, the
poet is provokingly vague as to the description of it.

He is more specific and correspondingly realistic in his description of Criseyde's garden:

> This yerd was large, and rayled alle the aleyes,
> And shadwed wel with blosmy bowes grene,
> And benched newe, and sonded alle the weyes,
> In which she walketh arm in arm bitwene.[43]

Here one notes particularly the general ground plan, which is lacking in the other descriptions.   The walks with rails round them,
the newly made benches, the sanded paths all bespeak order and
formal planning.   However, here Chaucer fails to give any real
information of the types of trees and plants growing in the plot.
"Blosmy bowes grene" is suggestive, but tantalizingly indefinite.
Still, it is in a sense an improvement in method over that
of listing the names of trees—a method which because of its
exaggeration is even less effective than the vague outline of the
later scheme.

The garden which January made for his wife, May, was similar to that of Criseyde.   It was walled with stone, and had in it

---

[40] Cecil, *History of Gardening*, 50; Gothein, *History of Garden Art*, I, 187.
[41] *LGW*, Prol., text A, 96-101.
[42] *TC*, II, 1702-1708.
[43] *Ibid.*, II, 813-823.

a laurel tree, under which was a well.[44]   Again, there were benches of turves "fresh and grene,"[45] where January and May sat to enjoy the beauty of the garden, and many paths.[46]   Only indirect allusions are made to plants and trees; besides the laurel there was a pear tree.[47]   Of flowers the suggestion is indirect and in no way specific:

> Bright was the day, and blew the firmament,
> Phebus of gold his stremes doun hath sent,
> To gladen every flour with his warmness.[48]

The gate or wicket of the garden, for which January had had made a silver key, was not to be opened by anyone except the old man himself.[49]   This suggests that Chaucer meant January's garden to be a kind of *hortus conclusus,* a type which was very popular in the Middle Ages.   Usually such a garden was within a larger one, enclosed by vines and trellises, or perhaps, even, by a wall.   Within it were grown various kinds of flowers, particularly roses and lilies.[50]   It was regarded as a form of devotion to the Blessed Virgin, a symbol of the spouse of the *Canticle of Canticles.*[51]   The medieval gentleman seems to have been partial to this little plot, and must have given it special care.

There is dramatic irony in Chaucer's use of the *hortus conclusus.*   One has only to compare January's address to his wife,

---

[44] E *Mer. T.,* 2029-2037, *passim.*

[45] *Ibid.,* 2235.

[46] *Ibid.,* 2324.

[47] *Ibid.,* 2217.

[48] *Ibid.,* 2219-2221.

[49] *Ibid.,* 2042-2047.

[50] *The Goodman of Paris,* 20.

[51] "My sister, my spouse, is a garden enclosed, a garden enclosed, a fountain sealed up." *Canticle of Canticles,* IV, 12.   The symbolism is expressed pictorially in "Emblèmes Symboliques de Marie," *Le Bréviaire Grimani,* 110.   The picture shows the *hortus conclusus* surrounded by a lattice.   Within it the flower beds are raised, and there grow a lily and a rose bush.   A fountain, too, is in the plot.

when he and she are entering the garden, to the *Canticle of Canticles*[52] to remark the parallelism between the two passages;

[52] Rys up, my wyf, my love, my lady free;
The turtles vois is herd, my douve swete.;
The winter is goon, with alle his reynes wete;
Come forth now, with thyn eyen columbyn!
How fairer been thy breasts than is wyn!
The gardin is enclosed al aboute;
Come forth, my whyte spouse, out of doute,
Thou hast me wounded in myn herte, o wyf!
No spot of thee ne knew I al my lyf.
E. *Mer. T.*, 2138-2146.

. . . Arise, make haste, my love, my dove, my beautiful one, and come.
For winter is now past, the rain is over and gone.
The flowers have appeared in our land, the time of pruning is come: the voice of the turtle is heard in our land:

. . . .

Thou art all fair, O my love, and there is not a spot in thee.

. . . .

How beautiful are thy breasts my sister, my spouse! Thy breasts are more beautiful than wine, and the sweet smell of thy ointments above all aromatical spices.

. . . .

My sister, my spouse, is a garden enclosed, a fountain sealed up.
Canticle of Canticles, II, 10-12; IV, 7, 10, 12.

he has only to observe the character of May to notice the dissimilarity between her and the Spouse of the Canticle.

What is almost a complete summary of Chaucer's various garden descriptions is found in a poem written by Lydgate and probably under the influence of the former poet's work:

> Of length and brede elich square and longe
> Hegged and diched to make it sure and stronge
>
> Alle the aleys were made playne with sonde
> The benches covered with new turvys grene
> Swete herbes with condites at honde
> That welled up ayenst the sonne shene
> Like silver stremes as any cristel clene
> The burbly wawes (in ther) up boylling
> Rounde as birall thair stremes out shewing
> Amyd the garden stode a fresshe laurere.[53]

---

[53] "The Churl and the Bird," *Poetry from Chaucer to Surrey*, 105, 11. 48-57.

Here one observes the main features of the English pleasure garden—the enclosure, the paths all sanded, the benches covered with turf, the sweet-scented herbs, the conduits, the fountains, and trees. Lydgate, like Chaucer, notes the laurel as the centrally located tree. Like him, too, he emphasizes the fact that the benches were freshly turved[54] and that the fountains were clear as crystal.

Attention has already been directed toward the part of the garden of the *Romaunt de la Rose* in which herbs and spices grew.[55] Generally Chaucer is not much concerned with the type of garden known as the herbary. That the widow of the *Nun's Priest's Tale* had at least a bed of herbs in her yard is suggested:

> The same night thurgh-out the hegges brast
> Into the yerd, ther Chauntecleer the faire
> Was wont, and eek his wyves, to repaire;
> And in a bed of wortes stille he lay.[56]

Other allusions to herbs and spices are made, not in the sense of their being in a planted and tended garden, but as growing wild in field or forest.

That the medieval herbary was often as well planned as any other type of garden is seen in the *Tale of Beryn*, a poem formerly believed to have been of Chaucer's authorship. In this poem the Wife of Bath is represented as saying to the Prioress:

> . . . 'Madam! wol ye stalk
> Pryvely, in-to þe garden, to see the herbis growe?'[57]

The Prioress accepted the invitation, and they went out together:

> Passyng forth (ful) sofftly in-to the herbery:
> Ffor many a herbe grewe, for sew and surgery;
> And al the Aleyis feir I-paris, I-rayled, and I-makid;
> The sauge, and the. Isope, I-frethid and I-stakid;
> And other beddis by and by (ful) fresshe I-dight.
> Ffor comers to the hoost, riȝte a sportful sight.[58]

---

[54] These benches were artificial mounds of earth, turved. Cf. Crisp, *op. cit.,* I, 81.

[55] Cf. *supra,* 59.

[56] B. 4408-4411; cf. also the list cited in lines 4153-4156.

[57] *The Tale of Beryn,* 11. 282-283.

[58] *Ibid.,* 287-294.

This appears to have been a garden primarily useful and incidentally for pleasure—almost exactly the reverse of the gardens which Chaucer describes.

Although the vegetable plot must have been of significance in fourteenth century England, there is no allusion to it in Chaucer's works. With the poet's love for realism in at least his later works, it seems surprising that he not so much as mentions that garden which must have supplied the table with onions, garlic, leeks, and the other vegetables which medieval Englishmen liked to eat.

Size and Location of Gardens

As has been seen, Chaucer's general information regarding various types of medieval gardens is, in spite of certain omissions, relatively complete. An examination of his allusions to the size and location of them reveals an interesting fact, namely, that while the size is not given, the location frequently is. This places side by side a study of Chaucer's somewhat tantalizing indefiniteness in certain matters, and his exactness in others, and shows incidentally his appreciation of values in descriptive writing.

Most of the gardens which the poet depicts are circumscribed by some kind of enclosure or wall. Yet the extent of the space enclosed is in no single instance mentioned. The garden in the *Romaunt de la Rose,* for example, is "ful long and brood,"[59] but the only intimation of the enormous size of it is that the numerous trees found therein are set five or six fathoms apart.[60] The imaginary quality of the garden makes appropriate this vagueness; on the other hand, the plausibility of even a dream garden must be emphasized, and this is effected by the apparently rather exact location of it:

> Toward a river I gan me dresse,
> That I herde renne faste by;
> . . . . . .
> And somdel lasse it was than Seine,
> But it was straighter wel away.

---

[59] Frag. A, 137.
[60] *Ibid.,* 1393.

>   .   .   .   .   .   .
> The medewe softe, swote, and grene,
> Beet right on the water-syde.
>   .   .   .   .   .   .
> Tho gan I walke through the mede,
> Dounward ay in my pleying,
> The river-syde costeying.
> And whan I had a whyl goon,
> I saugh a gardin right anoon.[61]

There is not even a vague allusion to the size of the garden in the *Parlement of Foules,* but there again the location is referred to as "upon a river, in a grene mede."[62] Criseyde's garden, described as large,"[63] seems to have been located below the young lady's chamber and entered by means of an outside stairway leading from that room:

> Adoun the steyre anoon-right tho she wente
> In-to the gardin, with hir neces three.[64]

Deiphebus' arbour, itself not described, is in a similar place:

> And rominge outward, ...
> Downward a steyre, in-to an herber grene.[65]

Obviously the normal place for the pleasure gardens which were public or at least used by a large group of persons, as those in the *Romaunt* and the *Parlement of Foules,* was along a riverside. Probably this was on account of more fertile, better-watered soil than elsewhere. The smaller, more domestic pleasure garden appears to have been generally within the owner's yard, and was entered from his chamber.[66] Sometimes, as Chaucer shows in

---

[61] *Ibid.,* 110-136, *passim.*

[62] Minor Poems, V, 184.

[63] *TC,* II, 820. We are told that generally medieval gardens were small, and that as late as 1665 a plot twenty yards square was considered a fair size for a gentleman's flower garden and forty yards square for his orchard. Thirty and eighty yards square respectively were the dimensions of those gardens belonging to a nobleman. Crisp, *Medieval Gardens,* I, 49.

[64] *TC,* II, 813-814. Cf. also II, 1116-1117.

[65] *Ibid.,* II, 1704-1705.

[66] Turner, *Domestic Architecture,* II, 115.

the *Knight's Tale,* such a plot must have been set within the
angle formed by castle walls:

> The grete tour, that was so thikke and strong,
> Which of the castel was the chief dongeoun,
>
> .   .   .   .   .   .
>
> Was evene joynant to the gardin-wal,
> Ther as this Emelye hadde hir pleyinge.[67]

It was directly beneath the iron-barred window of the tower, and
when Palamon, with his jailer's permission, walked in this upper
room, he saw not only the nearby city, but "eek the gardin, ful
of braunches grene,"[68] wherein Emelye roamed.

The garden of the *Miller's Tale,* to which Chaucer makes only
incidental allusion, was apparently at the rear of the house.[69]
Nicholas, in giving the carpenter directions to aid him in escaping
the flood he had predicted, spoke of how they might go "unto
the gardin-ward, over the stable."[70] There is no slight intimation
as to either the type or size of this garden, but it may have been
one in which vegetables, herbs, and even flowers were grown.[71]

Trees, Fruits, Flowers, and Herbs

A study of Chaucer's numerous references to what grew in the
medieval garden, together with his isolated allusions to trees,

---

[67] A 1056-1061. It is interesting to observe that Dryden, in his *Palamon
and Arcite,* describes Emelye's garden thus:

> The tower.   .   .   .   .
>
> .   .   .   .   .   .
>
> Was one partition of the palace wall:
> The garden was inclos'd within the square,
> Where young Emilia took the morning air.

Other examples of similarly located gardens may be found in Crisp,
Medieval Gardens, II, Plate CCCIII; *Le Morte Darthur,* I, 72.

[68] A 1063-1069, *passim.*

[69] This was no doubt the normal place for the general garden of a household. See Rogers, *Work and Wages,* 111.

[70] A 3572.

[71] Often the garden was of this general plan, with flowers, vegetables,
herbs, etc., planted somewhat indiscriminately in the same plot. See *The
Goodman of Paris,* 20-21; Esther Singleton, *The Shakespeare Garden* (New
York, 1931), 4-5; Cecil, *op. cit.,* 50.

fruits, flowers, and herbs[72] contributes not only to our knowledge of the garden, but also to that of manners and customs more or less related to the uses of garden products.

It is somewhat difficult to learn what trees the garden of Chaucer's England had, for the poet in listing them is powerfully influenced by the conventional practice of including exceptionally long lists of trees in descriptions. In his translation of the *Romaunt de la Rose* the poet adheres slavishly to his source, and although most of the names mentioned were probably those of trees grown in England, certain ones were undoubtedly included merely to increase the length of the list, and incidentally to convey the idea of profusion in the garden. Many of the trees bore fruit, but others were evidently for shade. There were some unusual varieties, including pomegranate, almond, fig, date, and the like. Besides, there were many "hoomly" (common?) trees,

> That peches, coynes (quinces), and apples bere,
> Medlers, ploumes, peres, chesteynes,
> Cheryse, of which many on fayn is,
> Notes, aleys (service-berries), and bolas (bullace-plums),
> That for to seen it was solas.[73]

Others, such as cypress, olive, elm, maple, ash, oak, plane, poplar, yew, and linden completed the rows.[74]

In close imitation of the *Romaunt de la Rose,* a list of trees is given in the *Parlement of Foules.*[75] In this poem, however, are omitted the fruit trees, so that the general impression is of a natural park or wood rather than of an orchard. Similarly, in the *Knight's Tale* almost exactly the same list is given.[76] The

---

[72] The Goodman, in discussion of the garden, mentions as its contents: (1) flowers: violet, gillyflower, peony, lily, rose; (2) vegetables: porray and beet, leek, cabbage, parsley, bean, pea, spinach, lettuce, pumpkin, turnip, radish, parsnip; (3) herbs: lavendar, marjoram, sage, mint, dittany, basil, clary, dragonwort, savory, sorrel, borage, orage, and hyssop; (4) fruits: vine, raspberry, currant, cherry, and plum. *The Goodman of Paris,* 20-21.

[73] Frag. A, 1373-1382.

[74] *Ibid.,* 1383-1390, *passim.*

[75] Minor Poems, V, 176-182. The list here given is modelled in part on Joseph of Exeter's *Iliad.* See Robinson, *Chaucer's Complete Works,* 903.

[76] A 2921-2923. This list is not given to describe a garden.

importance of the names of the trees lies particularly in the fact that the poet was apparently not interested in describing actual trees so much as he was in following a particular literary tradition.[77] It is notable that in his more realistic poems Chaucer does not cite lists such as these.

Much more significant in relation to manners and customs of fourteenth century England than the lists of trees the poet presents are occasional, often fragmentary and incidental, allusions to fruits. Such references occur chiefly in the later works and are apparently of Chaucer's own observation rather than dependent on other sources.

Perhaps the longest and most informative of these references is that in which the elderly Reeve is described by being compared to an "open-ers," or the fruit of the medlar.[78] The process by which the medlar is mellowed is particularly mentioned:

> Myn herte is al-so mowled as myn heres,
> But-if I fare as dooth an open-ers;
> That ilke fruit is ever leng the wers,
> Til it be roten in mullok or in stree.[79]

Placed in a heap of refuse or in straw when it was barely ripe, this fruit was kept there until it became soft and tender. As October was generally the month in which it ripened, it was probably late in November before the medlar was palatable. The fruit was eaten much as we eat apples; sometimes, too, it was preserved with sugar or honey.[80]

Apples were also enjoyed by medieval Englishmen, as Chaucer testifies in an indirect allusion. In the *Miller's Tale* is a description of the mouth of the Carpenter's charming wife. It was, the poet writes, as "swete as bragot or the meeth," (ale or mead)

> Or hord of apples leyd in hey or heeth.[81]

---

[77] Robinson, *op. cit.,* 903.

[78] Medlar trees were common in England, growing in orchards or in hedges among briars and brambles. The fruit was generally small and round, but if the tree had been grafted on white thorn, it was as large as small green apples. If eaten too early, medlars were harsh and choking. John Gerarde, *The Herball, or General Historie of Plantes* (London, 1597), 1265-1266.

[79] A *Rv. Prol.,* 3870-3873.

[80] Gerarde, *op. cit.,* 1265-1266.

[81] A 3261-3262.

The practice of storing apples by covering them with hay or grass that they might keep for use in winter was similar to that of mellowing the "open-ers."[82] It is interesting that Chaucer's allusions are to the processes concerned with the fruits rather than with their uses. Perhaps it is not amiss to mention here the domesticity suggested by the care of the medlars and the apples. The medieval Englishman appears as a provident householder, who did not depend for his future supplies on chance, but at least partly on his own good use and care of what he had.

Other than the foregoing references, Chaucer has little to say about fruit. He does, indeed, compare the Carpenter's wife to "a new perjonette tree,"[83] and allude to the pear which January's wife pretends to desire from the tree which grew in their garden,[84] but fruits of other kinds are not mentioned.

In treating of the flowers which grew in the medieval garden, Chaucer is more specific than he is concerning trees and fruits. He may often be influenced by literary tradition, but regardless of this fact, he presents either as translation or as original descriptions much that is significant of medieval flowers and their uses.

Roses, particularly red ones, were the best loved flowers of the Middle Ages,[85] as is shown by countless references to them in art and literature. They were valued primarily, no doubt, for their beauty of form and colour and their sweet scent; besides, they had many practical uses, some of which seem absurd to us, but were important to the people of the earlier age.[86] Chaucer's

---

[82] In certain regions the practice of storing apples in grass or hay, that they may be kept for winter use, is still popular.

[83] This seems to have been an early-ripe pear. It has been suggested by Skeat that it derived its name from the fact that it ripened about St. John's Day. See Robinson, *op. cit.*, 787.

[84] E *Mer. T.*, 2331-2337. Cf. also Robinson, *op. cit.*, 821.

[85] *Goodman of Paris*, 21.

[86] It would be almost impossible to include here all the practical uses made of the rose. A few of the most interesting and perhaps unusual ones will serve to illustrate the somewhat peculiar ideas medieval persons had of it. The Goodman of Paris discusses the practice of sifting rose leaves through a sieve to separate them from any worms which might have been on them and of drying them that they might be spread over a lady's dresses before they were put away for the winter. *Ibid.*, 302-303.

appreciation of this flower is primarily an aesthetic one; the few practical uses of it which he mentions are likewise dependent on the rose's beauty rather than on any special powers it may have been thought to have.

It is in the translation of the *Romaunt de la Rose* that Chaucer best describes the rose.[87] Strongly under the influence of his source, the poet shows the flower in various stages of its development and does so with almost scientific exactness. He begins logically enough by noting the scent of the blossoms:

> The savour of the roses swote
> Me smoot right to the herte rote,
> As I hadde embawmed be.[88]

The knoppes or buds on the rose-bush particularly interest him; he gives a detailed description of them—one which reveals unusual powers of observation:

> Of knoppes clos, some saw I there,
> And some wel beter woxen were;
> And some ther been of other moysoun,
> That drowe nigh to hir sesoun,
> And spedde hem faste for to sprede;
> I love wel swiche roses rede;

Roses, together with the white of an egg and vinegar were used as plasters for stomach afflictions. Hyll, *A Most Briefe and Pleasaunt Treatyse.* As medicine, "the juyce of Roses, especially of Roses that are reddest, or the infusion or decoction of them," was said to strengthen and cleanse the liver, and to be good against hot fevers and the jaundice. Besides, "it is also good to be used against the shaking, beating and trembling of the hart, for it driveth forth and dispatcheth all corrupt and evyl humours in and about the veynes of the hart." Crisp, *op. cit.,* 46-47.

The value of the rose is seen in the custom of tendering one, usually a red one, at midsummer as the nominal rent of land. *Godstow Nunnery Records,* EETS, OS 129, 130 (London, 1905, 1906), 265, 271, 305, 308, 412, etc.

[87] Some commentators are of the opinion that Fragment A of the *Romaunt* was Chaucer's in its original as well as final form. See the discussion of the whole question of its authorship in Robinson, *op. cit.,* 988-990.

[88] Frag. A, 1661-1663.

For brode roses, and open also,
Ben passed in a day or two;
But knoppes wilen fresshe be
Two dayes atte leest, or three.[89]

Here one notes especially the stages in the development of the various buds and the poet's comments on the life of a full-blown flower as compared to that of a bud. The most beautiful of the blossoms is selected and more fully pictured. It was a red rose,

And it had leves wel foure paire,
That kinde had set through his knowing
About the red rose springing.
The stalke was as risshe right,
And thereon stood the knoppe upright,
That it ne bowed upon no syde.[90]

The description is vivified by allusion to "the swote smelle" which seemed to fill the whole place.[91]

Less detailed, but effective, is a further reference to the rose in a simile in the *Parlement of Foules:*

Right as the fresshe, rede rose newe
Ayen the somer-sonne coloured is,
Right so for shame al waxen gan the hewe
Of this formel, whan she herde al this.[92]

The poet's powers of observation and his somewhat personal love of nature is apparent in this picture of the flower as it looked when the sun shone on it. The allusion may indeed be casual, but it is indicative of Chaucer's ability to paint in few words an effect.

---

[89] *Ibid.,* 1675-1684. The Goodman gives a curious method of preserving rosebuds for a whole winter. He thus directs his wife:

Take from the rose tree little buds that be not full blown and leave the stems thereof long, and set them within a little wooden cask like unto a compost cask, without water. Cause the cask to be well closed and so tightly bound up that naught may come in or out thereof, and at the two ends of the aforesaid cask tie two great and heavy stones and set the aforesaid cask in a running stream. *Goodman of Paris,* 203.

[90] Frag. A, 1691-1703.
[91] *Ibid.,* 1704-1705.
[92] Minor Poems, V, 442-445.

Despite his avowed love for the rose, the poet later tells us
that the daisy is his favorite flower:

> That, of alle the floures in the mede,
> Than love I most these floures whyte and rede,
> Swiche as men callen daysies in our toun.
> To hem have I so greet affeccioun,
> As I seyde erst, whan comen is the May,
> That in my bed ther daweth me no day
> That I nam up, and walking in the mede
> To sene these floures agein the sonne sprede,
> The longe day, thus walking in the grene.[93]

"Whyte and rede" daisies, such as Chaucer likes, were common
in England. There were many of other colours also. Daisies
as a whole were of two varieties, classified by Henry Lyte in *A
New Herball* as great and small. Of the latter, there were again
two types, garden and wild. The wild daisies were white with
yellow centers, but the small garden ones were "sometimes white,
and sometimes very red, and sometimes speckled or partie coloured of white and red. . . ."[94] Evidently the flowers which the
poet describes belong to the cultivated or garden kind.

In describing the opening and closing of the daisies Chaucer
gives evidence of having actually witnessed the process. In a
sense, his interest allies him to Wordsworth. The picture he
paints of his observing the little flower as it uncloses includes a
charming view of the flowery mead:

> And doun on knees anon-right I me sette,
> And, as I coude, this fresshe flour I grette;
> Kneling alwey, til hit unclosed was,
> Upon the smale softe swote gras,
> That was with floures enbrouded al,
>
> Of swich swetnesse and swich odour over-al,
> That, for to speke of gomme, or herbe, or tree,
> Comparisoun may noon y-maked be;
> For hit surmounteth pleynle alle odoures,
> And eek of riche beautee alle floures.[95]

---

[93] *LGW,* prol., A version, 41-50.
[94] Henry Lyte, *A New Herball* (London, 1619), 121.
[95] *LGW,* prol., B version, 115-124.

In the poet's eyes, the daisy assumes personality. Earlier in the poem he tells us that the flower closes at night "so hateth she derknesse," and that she spreads cheer in the brightness of the sun, when she opens.[96] This prepares the way for the explanation given of the name of the flower, of which Chaucer says,

> That wel by reson men hit calle may
> The 'dayesye' or elles the 'ye of day.'[97]

Daisies of white with golden centers are described indirectly in the following passage:

> And she was clad in real habit grene.
> A fret of gold she hadde next hir heer,
> And upon that a whyt coroun she beer
> With flourouns smale, and I shal nat lye;
> For al the world, ryght as a daysye
> Y-corouned is with whyte leves lyte,
> So were the florouns of hir coroun whyte.
> But of o perle fyne, oriental,
> Hir whyte coroun was y-maked al;
> For which the whyte coroun, above the grene,
> Made hir lyk a daysie for to sene,
> Considered eek hir fret of gold above.[98]

Chaucer may indeed show in this as in other descriptions of the daisy, his reliance upon the literary traditions of the "marguerite" poets,[99] but nevertheless the impression produced on the reader is that of originality.

To other flowers popular in the Middle Ages, Chaucer has but incidental and sometimes vague allusions. The lily, which was considered the symbol of purity, must have been grown in nearly all gardens of the time, judging from illustrations found in old manuscripts,[100] but the poet's references to it are disappointingly few and of little significance generally. Of King Emetreus, he

---

[96] *Ibid.*, B version, 63-65.

[97] *Ibid.*, B version, 183-185. This name is taken from the Anglo-Saxon, "daegeseage." "The flower was probably so-called because of its resemblance to the sun, to which the term primarily applied." Robinson, *op. cit.*, 956.

[98] *Ibid.*, B version, 214-225.

[99] See Robinson, *op. cit.*, 995-996.

[100] See Crisp, II, *passim*, for examples.

tells us that he bore upon his fist "an egle tame, as eny lilie
whyt."[101]   Similarly, Sir Thopas' armour is said to have been
"as whyt as is a lily-flour."[102] But these are conventional phrases,
showing no original observation on the part of the poet.

No more enlightening is the allusion in the *Second Nun's Tale,*
except that something of the symbolism attached to the flower
is suggested :

> This angel hadde of roses and of lilie
> Corones two, the which he bar in honde ;
> And first to Cecile, as I understonde,
> He yaf that oon, and after han he take
> That other to Valerian, hir make.
> 'With body clene and with unwemmed thoght
> Kepeth ay wel thise corones,' quod he ;
> 'Fro Paradys to you have I hem broght,
> Ne never-mo ne shal they roten be,
> Ne lese her sote savour, trusteth me ;
> Ne never wight shal seen hem with his ye
> But he be chaast and hate vileinye.'[103]

Altogether, the poet's references to the lily are too few and too
slight for one to judge of his knowledge of it or to learn much
concerning the medieval regard for and uses of this plant.[104]

Chaucer is even more vague in offering information regarding
the violet, which also seems to have been a tremendously popular
flower of the times.[105]   Only once does he allude to it, calling it

---

[101] A *Kn. T.,* 2177-2178.

[102] B *Sir Thop.,* 2056-2057.

[103] G 220-231.

[104] The blossom itself seems not to have been often used as medicine, but
the root of the plant was. Among the most curious uses of the lily root
was that of pounding it to mix it with honey and applying it to dislocations
or cut sinews. Further, the root is said to have been mingled with oil or
grease to bring "the heare agayne upon places that have bene either burned
or scalded." Crisp, *op. cit.,* 47.

[105] Violets are said to have held the place of honor in many gardens. Some
of them, called Sweete garden or March violets, were "or a fayre darke
or shining deepe blewe colour, and of a very amiable smell ;" but the
wild ones were "without sauor, and of a faynt, blew, or pale colour." Still
others were double and full of leaves, and as white as snow, while a few
rare ones were "of a dark crimson, or old reddish purple colour, in all
other poynts like to the first." Lyte, *A New Herball,* 105-106.

"the vyolet al newe,"[106] but he probably includes it in referring to "flowers blue and white and red." He missed an excellent oportunity here, of preceding Wordsworth in describing "a violet neath a mossy stone," or at least of leaving a record of some of the peculiar uses to which his fellow countrymen put this little flower.[107] Evidently he did not appreciate the violet as did Froissart, who says in connection with his early affection for little girls,

> In those days I took more account of a chaplet of violets
> to give those little girls, than I take now for several
> marks from the hand of a count. . . .[108]

The carnation, called "clove gilliflower,"[109] was another well loved flower in the medieval garden. Chaucer refers several times to it. He classifies it once as a spice,

> Ther was eek wexing many a spyce,
> As clow-gelofre, and licoryce,[110]

and another time as an herb:

> Ther springen herbes grete and smale,
> The licorys and cetewale,
> And many a clow-gilofre.[111]

---

[106] *RR,* Frag. A, 1431.

[107] Sometimes violets were shredded and combined with onions as a salad. As a syrup or conserve they were used to relieve inflammation of the lungs, pleurisy, coughs, and various kinds of fevers. Crisp, *op. cit.,* 47. They were also said to provoke sleep, and, when "gargelled in the throat," to help cure "that disease called the Squincie." Thomas Hyll, *The Profitable Art of Gardening,* third ed. (London, 1597), 77. Violets pounded "and layed to the head alone, or mingled with oyle, remoueth the extreme heat, swageth head-ach," and were therefore considered good "against dizziness of the head, against melancholy and dulness or heauinesse of spirit." Lyte, *op. cit.,* 106.

[108] *Espinette Amoureuse,* ed. Buchon, III, 477 ff., trans. by Coulton, *Social Life in Britain,* 85.

[109] The flower was of various sorts and colours. It took its name from the fact that the flowers grew at the top of the stalks of the plant, "out of long, round smooth huskes, and dented or toothed aboue like 'the spice called Cloues," and also from their clove-like scent. Lyte, *op. cit.,* 111.

[110] *RR,* Frag. A, 1367-1368.

[111] B *Sir Thop.,* 1950-1952.

This indicates that the plants may have been valued not so much for their aesthetic as for their practical uses.

There were indeed many and varied ways of using clove "gilofres." They were hardy plants, blooming all summer long until late in the season.[112] Sometimes the blossoms were put into wine to add spiciness to its flavor; because of this they were popularly referred to as "sops in wine."[113] They were likewise made into a conserve by the addition of sugar to the flowers and were served as dainties. Such a conserve was said to be "exceeding cordiall," and "wonderfully aboue measure" in comforting the heart.[114] Furthermore, "it prevaileth against hot pestilentiall feuers, expelleth the poison and furie of the disease, and greatly comforteth the sicke. . . ."[115]

From evidence furnished by the Goodman of Paris, it is seen that clove gilofres were sometimes valued as house plants. The method of caring for them and violets so transplanted from the out-of-door garden to pots is thus described by the Goodman:

> *Item.* Both of these, when the frosts draw near, you should plant in pots, at a season when the moon waneth, in order to set them under cover and keep them from the cold in a cellar, and day by day set them in the air or in the sun and water them at such times that the water may be drunken up and the earth dry before you set them under cover, for never should you put them away wet in the evening.[116]

This custom of potting the plants made it possible for the clove-gilliflower to be rendered as quit-rent early in the spring, if need be. That it was so exacted is proved by an account of the rent required of a certain Maude Horsneyl, namely,

> by yere to the chief lordes of the fee servyces dewe thereof, and to her and to her heires or her assignes

[112] Gerarde, *The Herball*, 473.

[113] *Ibid.*, 473. Gerard names a certain variety of clove gilliflower "Sops in Wine."

[114] *Ibid.*, 473.

[115] *Ibid.*, 473.

[116] *Goodman of Paris*, 196-197.

one clowe gelofure at Estir, for all servyce, sute of courte, custome, and exaccion.[117]

Of other flowers grown in the medieval garden, Chaucer refers specifically to very few. He mentions the periwinkle, which he alludes to as "fresshe pervinke, riche of hewe";[118] marigolds, which he calls "yelwe goldes";[119] the primrose, or "prymerole";[120] and the pigsnie, or "piggesnye."[121] He furnishes no description of any of them, but the allusions are significant in that they help one to understand how many and how varied may have been the flowers which grew in gardens such as that of Criseyde, or Emelye, or of January and his wife. In other words, they aid the imagination to interpret Chaucer's tantalizingly indefinite, "yelowe, white, and red." In addition, they show that the poet's descriptions of the garden or of individual flowers and plants are based on those of his own country and times rather than those of legendary lands and ancient times, as they could so well have been for some of his scenes.

As has been previously suggested, Chaucer sometimes classifies certain plants as both spices and herbs, thus making somewhat difficult the consideration of each group. For the sake of simplification, the term *herbs* is here employed to include the plants not grown for the beauty of their flowers but entirely for their practical value, namely, in cookery, as remedies, as deodorizing agents, and for their sweet scent underfoot in garden and in chamber or hall.

Mint, which Chaucer alludes to in his description of the garden in the *Romaunt de la Rose,* was used as it is today, in sauces

---

[117] *Godstow Nunnery Records,* 108.

[118] *RR,* Frag. A, 1432. Periwinkle was called the "joy of the ground," because of its tendency to spread by its jointed branches upon the ground. "The parwenke of prowesse" was an expression used in medieval times to typify excellence in the same way as "the very pink of courtesy," was used in Elizabethan times. Cecil, *op. cit.,* 52.

[119] A *Kn. T.,* 1929.

[120] A *Mil. T.,* 3268.

[121] *Ibid.,* 3268. The pigsnie (lit. 'pig's eye') is a name given to the cuckoo flower in Essex. It is also said to be used in the United States—in Minnesota and other states in the Northwest—for *trillium.* See Manly's *Canterbury Tales,* 560; Robinson, *op. cit.,* 787.

and for flavoring in various dishes.[122]   It was also regarded as good "agaynste the stynkynge of the mouth, and rottines of the gummes and teath," and as an antidote for poison.[123]   It was perhaps often scattered among the rushes on hall or chamber floor to counteract unpleasant odors, too.

Fennel or "fenell," mentioned by the poet along with mint,[124] was an herb of which both leaves and seeds were eaten.   "Poor folk used it to relieve the pangs of hunger or to give relish to unpalatable food on fasting days."[125]

In *Sir Thopas,* Chaucer alludes not only to "licorys and cetewale," but also to nutmeg, each of which had different uses. Licorice, for example, was said "to clense and to open the lunges and the brest and (to) loosen fleume."[126]   Cetewale, a medical herb obtained originally from the East Indies, was fragrant and had a bitter taste; it was used in various medicines.[127]   Nutmeg was "good for them the whiche have colde in theyr hed, and dothe comforte the syght and the brayne, and the mouthe of the stomacke, and is good for the splene."[128]   It also sweetened the breath when chewed, and was held to be "good against freckles."[129] Chaucer adds to these uses of nutmeg:

> And notemuge to put in ale,
> Whether it be moyste or stale,
> Or for to lay in cofre.[130]

The first of these uses is self-explanatory; the latter probably refers to the practice of putting sweet-smelling herbs into coffers

----

[122] Cecil, *op. cit.,* 44.

[123] Hyll, *A Most Briefe and Pleasaunte Treatyse.*

[124] *RR,* Frag. A, 729-731.

[125] Cecil, *op. cit.,* 44.   Langland refers to "a ferthyngworth of fenel seed, for fastyng dayes." *Piers Plowman,* ed. W. W. Skeat, EETS, OS 38 (London, 1869), v, 1. 313.

[126] Andrew Boorde, *Introduction and Dyetary,* EETS, ES 10 (London, 1870), 287.

[127] Skeat, *Student's Chaucer,* glossary.

[128] Gerarde, *op. cit.,* 1354.

[129] *Ibid.,* 1354.

[130] B *Sir Thop.,* 1953-1955.

or chests to impart a sweet scent or to keep out moths and fleas.

Most curious is Chaucer's allusion to the various herbs with which Absolon prepared himself to go to see the Carpenter's wife:

> But first he cheweth greyn (cardamon) and lycorys,
> To smellen swete, er he had kembed his heer.
> Under his tonge a trewe love he beer,
> For ther-by wende he to ben gracious.[131]

Graynes, or cardamon, like licorice, was supposed to be good for the stomach, as well as for the head;[132] but also must have had the virtue of sweetening the breath. The *trewe-love* mentioned here was known as *herbe Paris,* or *herbe truelove.* It was a small plant, having a single stalk two hands high, at the very top of which came forth four leaves directly set one against another, "in maner of a Burgunnion crosse or a true loue knot; for which cause among the aunciencts it hath beene called herbe True-loue: in the middle of the said leaues cometh a starlike flower, of an herbie or grassie colour. . . ."[133] From this blossom, which may have been the part which Absolon held under his tongue, came a blackish brown berry.[134]

To herbs or vegetables which served as food or were used as flavoring, Chaucer makes but few references other than those already mentioned. Yet medieval gardens must often have been planted with many of each. Of the "herbys un-meke," or what we should now call hardy, such as onions, garlic, and leeks,[135] the cooks of that time made great use, but Chaucer mentions only casually of the Sumnour,

> Wel loved he garleek, onyons, and eek lekes.[136]

---

[131] A *Mil. T.,* 3690-3693.

[132] Boorde, *op. cit.,* 286.

[133] Gerarde, *op. cit.,* 328.

[134] *Ibid.,* 328.

[135] Gerarde, *op. cit.,* 328.

[136] A *Gen. Prol.,* 634. It is particularly fitting that the Summoner should like garlic, onions, and leeks.

Without naming any particular plants, he suggests the use of various garden products in cookery, as follows:

> Of spicery, of leef, and bark and rote
> Shal ben his sauce y-maked by delyt,
> To make him yet a newer appetyt.[137]

Another general statement as to the practical value of plants is made in regard to Grisilde. Before this young woman's marriage to Sir Walter, she was always usefully occupied with simple household tasks. Besides,

> . . . whan she hoomward cam, she wolde bringe
> Wortes or other herbes tymes ofte,
> The whiche she shredde and seeth for hir livinge.[138]

Similarly, the poor widow of the *Nun's Priest's Tale* may have shredded and boiled the worts which grew in her yard. Dame Pertolote expatiates at length on their value as remedies, telling Chaunticleer to "pekke hem up right as they growe, and ete hem in."[139]

It is readily seen that although the allusions Chaucer makes to trees, flowers, vegetables and herbs are frequently scattered throughout the poems, and are fragmentary and often vague, when taken together they furnish rather significant information regarding the contents of the medieval garden. Evidently but few of the most popularly grown and enjoyed plants are omitted.

Social Significance of the Garden

In addition to general descriptions of the garden and specific allusions to plants, detailed as well as incidental, Chaucer contributes even more interesting and pertinent information about the rôle which the pleasure garden played in the social life of the people. None of the gardens he describes is primarily of value in the poems because of its arrangement or the plants grown therein. Rather, nearly every one of them is above all else a pleasure-spot— a place to "pleye."

---

[137] C *Pard. T.*, 544-546.
[138] E *Cl. T.*, 225-227.
[139] B 4157.

The garden in the *Romaunt de la Rose* was the scene of particularly gay festivities. A crowd of gentlemen and ladies, in holiday attire, danced and sang; minstrels, jugglers, and various other professional entertainers added to the jollity of the occasion.[140] It is an idealistic picture, full of color and beauty, and charming because it is so.

In the *Parlement of Foules,* St. Valentine's Day is being observed with suitable celebrations. Numerous persons, given type names such as Plesaunce, Aray, Lust, Curtesye, and the like were assembled there; before a temple in one part of the garden danced a group of fair women in a religious rite of some sort.[141] In another portion of the garden, the goddess Nature sat holding a parliament of birds, symbolic of men, who disputed about the subject of love.[142]

Several pictures of the activities enjoyed in the *plesaunce* are painted in the *Troilus.* The most effective of these seems to have been Chaucer's own, in the sense that it is not dependent on the *Filostrato,*[143] and shows Criseyde, her three nieces, and a great number of Criseyde's women as they stroll about at their recreation:

> Adoun the steyre anoon-right tho she wente
> In-to the gardin, with hir neces three,
> And up and doun ther made many a wente,
> Flexippe, she, Tharbe, and Antigone,
> To pleyen, that it joye was to see;
> And othere of hir wommen, a gret route,
> Hir folwede in the gardin al aboute.[144]

For greater entertainment the beautiful Antigone "gan on a Trojan song to singe clere."[145] The song was one concerning love and it evoked from Criseyde a discussion of that subject so near

[140] Frag. A, 743 ff.
[141] Minor Poems V, 218-238, *passim.*
[142] *Ibid.,* 302 ff., *passim.*
[143] Cf. Robinson, *op. cit.,* 930.
[144] *TC,* II, 813-819. Scenes similar to this are found throughout the romances. In *Sir Orpheo,* for example, Queen Erodys walks with two maidens "to pley in hir orchard-syde." Ritson, III, pp. 5-6, 11. 64-70.
[145] *TC,* II, 824 ff.

her heart. Indeed, the ladies remained in the garden talking and walking until the sun set and the stars appeared. Then "she and al hir folk in went y-fere."[146]

Troilus and Pandarus spent some of their time in a garden, too. Their amusements were different from those of Criseyde and her women:

> In-with the paleys-gardyn, by a welle,
> Gan he and I wel half a day to dwelle,
> Right for to speken of an ordenaunce,
> How we the Grekes might disavaunce.[147]

It is to be noted that the avowed purpose of going into the garden was in this case to discuss plans for battle. That the two gentlemen apparently neglected the discussion is not to be wondered at, perhaps. The pastimes enjoyed are thus described:

> Sone after that bigonne we to lepe,
> And casten with our dartes to and fro,
> Til at the laste he seyde, he wolde slepe,
> And on the gras a-doun he leyde him tho.[148]

The pretty custom of gathering flowers and weaving them into garlands[149] to wear on their heads appealed particularly to medieval women. Chaucer merely suggests it in his description of Emelye:

> And in the gardin, as the sonne up-riste,
> She walketh up and doun, and as hir liste
> She gadereth floures, party whyte and rede,
> To make a sotil gerland for hir hede.[150]

Perhaps the flowers mentioned here, "party whyte and rede," were daisies, which, we are told, were among those frequently used for

---

[146] *Ibid.,* II, 876-910, *passim.* Note that Troilus and Pandarus later enjoy similar pastimes. *Ibid.,* III, 1737-1771.

[147] *Ibid.,* II, 508-511.

[148] *Ibid.,* II, 512-515.

[149] The Goodman tells his young wife regarding the making of chaplets, "I am pleased rather than displeased that you tend rose trees and care for violets and make chaplets and dance and sing." *Goodman of Paris,* 22.

[150] A *Kn. T.,* 1051-1055.

such garlands.[151] However, the indefiniteness of the description
compels the reader to use his imagination in regard to the matter.

Sometimes medieval folk went into large gardens, semi-public
perhaps, to indulge in picnicking. Chaucer's single allusion to
this custom is enlightening. Dorigene, urged by her friends, goes
with them to spend the day in such entertainment:

> So on a day, right in the morwe-tyde,
> Un-to a gardin that was ther bisyde,
> In which that they had maad hir ordinaunce
> Of vitaille and of other purveyaunce,
> They goon and pleye hem al the longe day.
>
> .   .   .   .   .
>
> At-after diner gonne they to daunce,
> And singe also.   .   .   .[152]

Strangely like a modern picnic is this—the previous arrangements,
the "vitaille," the entertainment—and it has a convincing touch
that is worthy of far more consistent realists than Chaucer.

Love of nature itself seems often to have lured persons into
the garden, too. The solacing power of the out-of-doors in general, rather than the pure appreciation of flowers for themselves,
appears to have been significant. Chaucer alludes to various persons who seek distraction from their cares and to others who wish
merely to enjoy the quiet, soothing influence of nature.

Dorigene's friends try various means of diverting her attention
from her loneliness caused by Arveragus' absence:

> They leden hir by rivere and by welles,
> And eek in othere places delitables.[153]

Finally, when all else fails, they plan the picnic described above.
Troilus, in love with Criseyde, often leads Pandarus into the
garden, Chaucer tells us,

> And swich a feste and swich a proces make
> Him of Criseyde, and of hir womanhede,

---

[151] The periwinkle, with its trailing leaves, daisies, violets, and roses were
the most commonly used flowers for making chaplets or garlands. Cecil,
op. cit., 54. Chaucer's Summoner wore a garland "as greet as it were an ale-
stake." A *Gen. Prol.,* 666-667.

[152] F *Fkl. T.,* 901-919, *passim.*

[153] *Ibid.,* 898-899.

> And of hir beautee, that, with-outen drede,
> It was an hevene his words for to here.[154]

After this, he entertains his companion by singing of love.[155]
Chaucer describes himself under nature's spell. As soon as
spring comes and he hears the songs of birds and sees the flowers
opening, he says

> Farwel my studie, as lasting that sesoun![156]

Thereafter, he professes to wander in the mead to watch the
flowers unclose in the morning and close in the evening. On one
occasion, after having spent the day in the fields observing these
phenomena, he goes home and in his little arbour lies down on a
couch strewn with flowers where he falls into a slumber disturbed
by dreams of wandering in a flowery mead.[157] The picture drawn
may indeed be idealistic; yet it reveals the attitude of medieval
nature-lovers toward the out-of-doors.

Medieval lovers often kept their tryst in the garden. Daun
John, pretending to read his breviary, walks in the garden chiefly,
perhaps, to meet the merchant's wife:

> This gode wyf cam walking prively
> In-to the gardin, ther he walketh softe,
> And him saleweth, as she hath don ofte.[158]

After the greeting, the two engage in a conversation concerned
especially with a recitation of the wife's marital troubles and Daun
John's sympathetic responses.[159]

January and May spend many hours walking and talking in their
beautiful little garden. To January theirs is an idealistic existence, for no part of the house offers more privacy than this
enclosed plot, the entrance to which is locked. But May is false
to her husband, and agrees with the young squire to circumvent

---

[154] *TC,* III, 1739-1742.
[155] *Ibid.,* 1750-1771.
[156] *LGW,* prol., A version, 32-39.
[157] *Ibid.,* 89 ff.
[158] B *Sh. T.,* 1282-1284.
[159] *Ibid.,* 1288 ff.

January there in the very garden in which the latter had planned to keep May safe for himself from youthful lovers.[160]

These two are unlovely scenes and the ugliness of the deeds perpetrated are quite out of harmony with the beauties of the surroundings. In describing them, Chaucer is essentially realistic. He represents a view of medieval life unfortunately rather common in his day, but as scandalous then as it is at the present time.

On the whole, the social significance of the pleasure garden is fully observed in Chaucer's works. The activities vary from the somewhat idealistic promenade, accompanied by reading or singing or a discussion of love, to the too realistic illicit love affair. Much of the artificiality of a society influenced by the all-absorbing principles of courtly love is clearly evidenced in those garden descriptions which depend most on other sources. But likewise, the normality of other groups of society is depicted in the more realistic, more original works.

*   *   *

It has been seen that the English garden before Chaucer's time was planted and cultivated largely for the practical uses to which its products might be put, namely as medicines, for cookery, and the like. Flowers for their beauty and sweet scents were indeed grown, but they were evidently less significant than herbs and vegetables.

The development of the formally arranged pleasure garden was noticeable in the thirteenth century—a time when men began to have more leisure and greater interest in matters pertaining to domestic life. The French poem, the *Romaunt de la Rose* with its elaborate garden description, appeared in this same century. For the first time, the *plesaunce* was consciously used as a setting. Chaucer's translation of the poem had a tremendous influence on his later nature descriptions; and to it chiefly he owes his most completely depicted gardens. Incidentally, Chaucer is practically the first poet writing in English to deal so fully with this type of garden in a literary fashion. The information he offers is relatively complete.

---

[160] E *Mer. T.*, 2929 ff.

The most popular kinds of English medieval gardens were the flowery mead, the large formal garden, and the *hortus conclusus.* In addition there was the informal garden, public or semi-public in character, where persons might enjoy picnics and similar pastimes. Chaucer mentions in more or less detailed fashion all of these types.

The flowery mead was a grassy plot thickly planted with low-growing flowers, such as violets, periwinkle, and daisies. It may sometimes have been a natural meadow, with the flowers growing wild, but it seems more often to have been an artificial one, in the sense of having been planted by man.

The formal garden was a plot enclosed by a wall, with trees, herbs, and flowering plants arranged in orderly fashion. The trees were sometimes in rows, and the flowers in beds, with sanded paths separating the beds, one from another. Generally a fountain occupied the center of the plot, and from it flowed numerous conduits which supplied water to all parts of the garden.

Sometimes, within the garden in a nook of the wall, or sheltered by a hedge was a little arbour or "pleying place," made of trees intertwined with climbing plants such as roses and honeysuckles. Chaucer describes such an arbour as belonging to his own garden. With its newly-turved benches, it was a delightful place for him to retire into after the day's labors.

Similar to the arbour was the *hortus conclusus,* a small plot within a larger one, hidden by vines and trellises, or a wall. Within it were grown lilies and roses especially. The *hortus conclusus* was regarded as a form of devotion to the Blessed Virgin, a symbol of the Spouse in the *Canticle of Canticles,* but Chaucer makes ironic use of it as a setting for a base love scene.

The herbary, a kind of kitchen garden wherein herbs were grown, was popular in the Middle Ages, but Chaucer makes no specific reference to it. He does mention herbs and spices, but some of his allusions suggest that they grew not only in the garden, but often wild in field and forest. Likewise, the poet does not refer to the vegetable plot, which must have been important as a source of food for the table.

The medieval garden was evidently of modest proportions, generally. Chaucer indicates in one or two cases that certain gardens are "large," but what the term means cannot be ascertained. If, as he suggests, the numerous trees are several fathoms apart, some gardens were rather extensive. These particular gardens, how- ever, in which there are so many trees listed are highly imaginary rather than realistic, and may never have existed even in bare outline.

The location of gardens depended of course on their size and uses. The larger, park-like ones were along the banks of rivers, generally; more intimate ones were attached to the house, being outside the principal chamber or the lady's bower, in an angle formed by castle walls, or sometimes at the rear of the dwelling.

In considering plant-life Chaucer often follows literary con- ventions, at least in making long lists of trees. Many of the trees it is true were native to England, but some of them were not, and the mention of them gives to the garden description more than the usual air of unreality. Among the trees listed are oak, ash, maple, elm, olive, pear, peach, quince, apple, cherry, linden, fig, almond, laurel, yew, and many others.

Fruits were becoming more popular in England than they had hitherto been. Those used somewhat commonly were apples, pears, cherries, peaches, and medlars. Chaucer's allusions are not generally significant, except when he describes, incidentally, of course, the process of covering apples with straw to keep them for winter use and of doing likewise with the medlar that it might be mellowed and thus made more palatable.

Roses, daisies, lilies, violets, marigolds, periwinkle, and clove- gilly flower (carnations), were among the flowers found in the medieval pleasure garden. The rose and the daisy were both widely loved and were traditionally used in literary works. The descriptions of them are fairly complete in Chaucer's poetry, but there is actually not much originality of treatment. All the important flowers grown at that time are mentioned, if only casu- ally as "flowers whyte and blew and red," by the poet. Plants classified both as herbs and spices, were used in medicine or in cookery. Some of the herbs were particularly useful to sweeten the breath, and there were "un-meke" onions, garlic, etc.,—and spices, (leef, bark, and rote) which were valuable in cookery. But little actual and important information is given about them all.

The social significance of the medieval English garden can hardly be over-estimated. People who had been within cold, damp houses all winter especially delighted in getting out into the garden during the summer months. They assembled in large groups, sometimes, and either danced and sang or played games of some sort. Ladies promenaded rather ceremoniously with their waiting women, or one of them read aloud to the others as they sat around on the turved benches or on the ground weaving garlands of flowers.

The garden often offered more privacy than any part of the house did, so gentlemen discussed plans there for attacking the enemy in battle. A lady or a gentleman might walk in the garden and speak confidentially to a friend of love in general or of his or her own affairs of heart. Picnics were popular then as now and there must have been much gaiety on such occasions. Always lovers spent hours together in the garden. Frequently, too, men and women burdened with care, sought solace there, taking pleasure in the songs of countless birds, the fragrance of flowers and herbs, and the ever-desired privacy of the enclosed plot.

There may indeed be much of Chaucer's information on the garden which is borrowed from other literary sources and there may be little which the poet derived from direct observation; still, his is a noteworthy contribution to garden literature in that there is surprisingly complete treatment of the *plesaunce*. Even all that is apparently unreal and highly colored with the imagination is in the main probably based on actual models. One need look no further than Chaucer to understand the significance of the English medieval pleasure garden.

CHAPTER III

MEALS AND TABLE MANNERS

An housholdere, and that a greet, was he;
Seint Julian he was in his contree.
His breed, his ale, was alwey after oon;
A bettre envyned man was no-wher noon.
With-oute bake mete was never his hous,
Of fish and flesh, and that so plentevous;
It snewed in his hous of mete and drinke.
—A *Gen. Prol.*, 339-345.

The story of fourteenth century English meals is one of elaborate feasts, complex recipes, curious table manners and ceremonies, and well-stocked larders. But it is also the story of enforced sobriety, monotonous diet, simple, even crude manners, and sometimes severe want. The details vary according to the different social classes of the time, as one may readily see in the study of the numerous and diverse allusions which Chaucer makes to the subject.

Meals in General in Chaucer's Works

Our author's references to meals occur almost exclusively in his later, more nearly original works and are consequently marked for the most part by accuracy of detail and realism of treatment. There are descriptions, more or less complete, of the feasts held in the homes of the wealthy, and suggestions of the scanty diet of the poor. The names of dishes, incidental allusions to methods of cookery and to servants, and references to table manners further contribute to our knowledge of the customs attendant on meals, their preparation, and serving. Finally, Chaucer allies himself with the medieval preacher and laments that "pryde of the table appereth ful ofte."[1]

---

[1] I *Pars. T.*, 444.

Number of Meals and Time of Eating

Despite the fact that medieval folk are generally believed to have eaten to excess, the regular custom of the English at this time seems to have been to have only two meals a day.[2] Chaucer's evidence for this fact as well as for the hours usually appointed for meals is on the whole valuable, although sometimes insufficient for complete information on the subjects.

In Criseyde's household dinner is served between nine and ten o'clock in the morning. Pandarus, who had intended arriving at his niece's palace at prime, i. e., about nine o'clock,[3] is according to his own words, a little late:

> And faste he swoor, that it was passed prime.[4]

---

[2] In many households, though perhaps not regularly, a third meal or breakfast seems to have been served, too; it was literally a break-fast and often consisted of only bread and wine, or ale. Abram, *English Life and Manners,* 144.

Dame Alice de Bryene, a housewife of the late fourteenth and early fifteenth centuries, records in her household book three meals a day, also. *The Household Book of Dame Alice de Bryene,* trans. by Marian K. Dale and Vincent B. Redstone (Ipswich, 1931), *passim.*

Religious orders, on the other hand, seem to have subsisted on only one meal a day. The Benedictines, for example, were allowed one meal on fasting days, which included the majority of the days in a year; even when two meals were permitted by their Rule the second was hardly more than a collation, taken after Vespers in the evening. Ethelred L. Taunton, *The English Black Monks of St. Benedict,* 2 vols. (London, 1898), I, 79-84; Sir William Dugdale, *Monasticon Anglicanum,* 3 vols. (London, 1718-1723), I, 163; II, 196.

It is hardly to be wondered at that Religious found the practice of one meal a day difficult. Their hours of work and prayer were generally long and arduous, and it is not surprising that some of the monks and brothers yielded to such temptations as absenting themselves from their religious services to take "little breakfasts" of dripping-cakes or "little messes of broth" in the kitchen. *Visitations of Religious Houses in the Diocese of Lincoln,* ed. A. H. Thompson, 3 vols. (London, 1919-1927), III, 232-237. It is also easy to believe that the Gilbertine Canons, who were allowed breakfasts until they were thirty years of age, "and not after, unless sick, or with leave," dreaded to see their thirtieth birthdays come. Dugdale, *op. cit.,* II, 199.

[3] *TC,* II, 992.

[4] *Ibid.,* II, 1095.

After his arrival, there is some delay before Criseyde says, "go we dyne,"[5] but when they do enter the hall for the meal it is apparently ready to be served.   Evidently it is nearly ten o'clock by the time they are seated.

In Deiphebus' household the hour is specified:

> The morwen cam, and neighen gan the tyme
> Of meel-tyd, that the faire quene Eleyne
> Shoop hir to been, an houre after the pryme.[6]

"Meel-tyd" here apparently refers specifically to dinner, for we are told that Deiphebus offers the invitation to his friends

> To holde him on the morwe companye
> At diner . . .[7]

and again the term "diner" is used in allusion to the end of the meal.[8]

Chaucer's Daun John, although a guest in the merchant's house, objects to too long a fast in the morning, and reminds his hostess that it is time, not for breakfast, but for dinner:

> And lat us dyne as sone as that ye may;
> For by my chilindre it is pryme of day.[9]

There is much delay, however, before the meal is served.   The cooks are commanded to prepare the food;[10] then the hostess goes to her husband's counting room to call him;[11] and after that, mass is said.[12]   If, as has been suggested,[13] the mass is said in the hall, another delay in the preparation of the hall for the dinner is occa-

[5] *Ibid.*, II, 1163.
[6] *Ibid.*, II, 1555-1557.
[7] *Ibid.*, II, 1488-1489.
[8] *Ibid.*, II, 1597.
[9] B *Sh.T.*, 1395-1396.
[10] *Ibid.*, 1400-1401.
[11] *Ibid.*, 1402-1439, *passim.*
[12] *Ibid.*, 1441.
[13] Cf. *supra*, 16, 17.

sioned. The meal could hardly have been served before ten or eleven o'clock, even though

> . . . hastily a messe was ther seyd,
> And spedily the tables were y-leyd,
> And to the diner faste they hem spedde.[14]

In old January's household dinner seems to have been even later than the foregoing meal. According to custom, a bride did not appear in the hall for regular meals until "dayes foure or three dayes atte leste"[15] after the marriage feast. Perhaps it is because January and May observe this custom strictly that the dinner is served later than the usual hour; or perhaps it is because "heighe masse,"[16] which probably occupied a longer time than a low mass would have done, was celebrated before the meal. At any rate, Chaucer's allusion suggests that the hour is somewhat later than prime:

> The fourthe day compleet fro noon to noon,
> Whan that the heighe masse was y-doon,
> In halle sit this Januarie, and May.[17]

"Noon" here appears to signify mid-day, as it does at present; apparently the meal begins at about that time of day.[18]

Chaucer refers numerous times to "souper," but he merely indicates in vague terms the time of its serving as "evening." Pandarus, at Troilus' house on one occasion suggests

> But rys and lat us soupe and go to reste,[19]

and then,

> With al the haste goodly that they mighte,
> They spedde hem fro the souper un-to bedde.[20]

---

[14] B *Sh. T.*, 1441-1443.

[15] E *Mer. T.*, 1888-1892.

[16] *Ibid.*, 1894.

[17] *Ibid.*, 1893-1895.

[18] An interesting comparison might here be made with Froissart's account of the peculiar custom observed by the eccentric Gaston Phoebus, Comte de Foix. This gentleman arose at noon and dined then; he supped at midnight. *Chronicles*, II, 95.

[19] *TC*, II, 994.

[20] *Ibid.*, II, 946-947.

Does the poet mean, here, that the meal was eaten late—perhaps after darkness had fallen—or that the gentlemen retired early to bed? One cannot say with certainty, but by comparison with other references made by Chaucer one may perhaps believe the former to be true.

Supper for the Canterbury Pilgrims seems to have been early in the evening, possibly about four or five o'clock. At any rate, after the host has set before his guests "vitaille at the beste," and they have eaten and drunk to their satisfaction, he begins to entertain them with what seems to correspond in general to our modern after-dinner speech, in which he welcomes them to his inn and suggests their participation in a story-telling contest.[21] Then wine is again passed and drunk, and the guests retire.[22]

The evening meal in the miller's household appears to be much later than this one, however. The two young men, Aleyn and John, are unexpected guests and their proper treatment demands that the miller provide extra food. The miller's daughter, it will be recalled, had to go into town for ale and bread. Likewise, a goose was roasted.[23] All of this took time, and it is not surprising that the meal was ended somewhat late:

> They soupen and they speke, hem to solace,
> And drinken ever strong ale atte beste.
> About midnight went they to reste.[24]

King Cambinskan's feast is at least an all-day ceremony, with entertainment between dinner and supper. A service in the temple,[25] corresponding to that described in romances as being held in medieval chapels after big feasts,[26] is attended before the evening meal.

---

[21] A *Gen. Prol.,* 747 ff.

[22] *Ibid.,* 819-820.

[23] A *Rv. T.,* 4136-4137.

[24] *Ibid.,* 4146-4148.

[25] F *Sq. T.,* 296. One notes the pagan element here; the guests repair to a temple rather than to a chapel. This is probably used as a detail to give local color—to suggest the land of Tartary, which is the setting of the story.

[26] *Sir Gawayne and the Green Knight,* ll. 928-932.

Then,

> The service doon, they soupen al by day.[27]

The implication is that supper is served early in the evening and is finished before daylight wanes. However, after the king sees the brass horse which the strange knight has brought him, he returns to his revels. With plenty of wine and spices, probably, the entertainment is enjoyed until "wel ny the day bigan to springe."[28]

Feasts such as this one were for special occasions; hence the hours of beginning or ending them were no doubt variable. Duke Theseus' guests, arriving for the tournament, must have begun their feast late in the morning. They come into the city "aboute pryme,"[29] but all seem to have been taken to their various lodging houses and inns before the feast begins:

> Whan he had broght hem in-to his citee,
> And inned hem, everich in his degree,
> He festeth hem. . . .   [30]

The wedding feast of the Marquis Walter, in the Clerk's Tale, begins at an earlier hour—soon after "undern," or nine o'clock in the morning.[31]

It is to be noted that the allusions which Chaucer makes to the two meals ordinarily served in the English medieval household are to "dinner" and "supper." The time of the former repast is rather definitely referred to as after prime, generally an hour after it; in other words, at ten o'clock in the morning. The poet indicates that the hour sometimes varied, but that this was the usual one. No time is specified as the hour for the evening meal. Suggestions that supper was eaten before daylight had gone, together with somewhat vague inferences drawn from the allusions to the time of retiring, hardly warrant our stating the hour for this meal on

---

Chaucer's evidence alone. Domestic history, however, gives it as four or five o'clock.[32]

Place of Eating

Even ordinary meals were usually served in the great hall[33] in Chaucer's day. Feasts must generally have been there too, although evidence may be cited to show that they were sometimes held, at least in part, out-of-doors, in huge pavilions.[34] The practice of eating daily meals in the chamber was at this time gaining in popularity;[35] so also was that of eating in the kitchen.[36]

Chaucer furnishes no evidence for the practice of eating outside the great hall. All of his characters seem to have preferred the traditional place of taking their meals, and even the jealous January apparently did not conceive the idea of dining elsewhere.[37]

---

[32] *Our English Home,* 33. Quennell, *A History of Everyday Things in England,* 126.

[33] Cf. *supra,* 22.

[34] "Tents of linen or costly stuffs were reared, . . . while above the tables awnings were spread as a protection against sun or rain." Mead, *The English Medieval Feast,* 134.

[35] The romances especially record this custom. Sir Beves, for instance, is ushered into his lady's bower:

> To her chamber she hym lad
> And sett Beues on her bed;
> A bord was sett, a cloth was spred.
> Whan she had on-armed Bevoun,
> At the Bord they set ham down
> And made them well at ease and ffyne
> With riche metes and nobull wyne.
> —*Sir Beues of Hamtoun,* ed. E. Kölbing,

EETS, ES 46 (London, 1885), pp. 51-52, 11. 858-864 (v).

Langland thinks this an abominable practice and rails against it, saying that the hall was made for men to have meat and meals in. *Piers Plowman,* EETS, OS 38, x, 1. 99.

[36] Alfred Franklin, *La Vie privée des premiers Capétiens,* 2 vols. (Paris, 1911), II, 217.

[37] E. *Mer. T.,* 1710 ff; 1889 ff. Undoubtedly May's meals were served in her chamber during the four days after her marriage when she was not appearing in the hall for them; yet the everyday meals were apparently to be served in the hall, where she came on the fourth day to join her husband and the rest of the household.

On an occasion when privacy would seem to have been especially desirable, Criseyde and Pandarus dine in the hall;[38] so, too, the other persons in the poet's works. Chaucer either mentions the hall as the place where meals are served, or by failing to mention it implies it.[39]

Menus for Feasts and Meals

From the number of feasts and ordinary meals referred to in literature as well as in history, it is seen that eating was one of the chief pleasures of medieval life and that much time and energy were devoted to it.[40] The menu often consisted of many courses, varying according to the wealth of the householder and the occasion for which the feast or meal was served. It has been said, without exaggeration, that

> our ancestors ate practically everything that had wings, from a bustard to a sparrow, and everything that swam, from a porpoise to a minnow; but in the matter of fruits and vegetables they came off very badly.[41]

It would seem as if they sometimes planned their menus to include at a single meal as many of their foods as possible. Some menus are veritable dictionaries of medieval eatables.[42]

From Chaucer's allusions alone one learns much about feasts and the daily meals of various classes of society. Some of the information offered is of itself of only slight significance, but when the references are considered all together, the poet's contribution to knowledge of the foods served and the methods of preparing them is surprisingly great.

---

[38] *TC,* II, 1170;

[39] The hall is specifically mentioned as the place for meals in the *NPT,* 4022-4023; E *Cl. T.,* 1119; and F *Sq. T.,* 169; it is implied in the *Kn. T.,* 2200; B. *Sh. T.,* 1440 ff; F *Fkl. T.,* 1215-1216. It is interesting to note that in several cases Chaucer refers to the master as sitting on the dais; this seems to signify the hall.

[40] Mead, *op. cit.,* 48-49.

[41] Charles Cooper, *The English Table in History and Literature* (London, 1929), 3.

[42] Cf. appendix, 255 ff.

Generally, in describing feasts Chaucer follows the literary customs of his time, and although he eschews the lengthy lists sometimes found in the romances, he refers in an exaggerated fashion and in general terms to the sumptuousness of the fare. Often he makes no specific allusions to what is placed on the table before guests, but insinuates that both food and drink are abundant and of excellent quality.

When Troilus and Pandarus visit the home of King Sarpedoun they are feasted each day:

> With al that mighte y-served been on table,
> That deyntee was, al coste it greet richesse,
> He fedde hem day by day, that swich noblesse,
> As seyden bothe the moste and eek the leste.
> Was never er that day wist at any feste.[43]

Similarly, Queen Dido entertains Eneas at a magnificent feast, but Chaucer avoids enumerating the foods served by saying,

> What nedeth yow the feste to descryve?[44]

He relents a little, though, and elaborates in general terms,

> Ful was the feste of deyntees and richesse.[45]

Such references are particularly vague and non-informing.[46]

That the poet could have furnished more valuable information as to what medieval English folk liked and served at feasts is indicated by his allusions to food in the *Squire's Tale*. Again the method is indirect rather than direct, for, he says,

> Of which if I shal tellen al th'array,
> Than wolde it occupye a someres day.[47]

Naïvely, then, and as if in spite of himself, he describes the feast in negative fashion:

> And eek it nedeth nat for to devyse
> At every cours the ordre of hir servyse.

---

[43] *TC,* V, 437-441.

[44] "The Legend of Dido," *LGW,* 1098.

[45] *Ibid.,* 1100.

[46] See also A *Kn. T.,* 2193; B *MLT,* 419; E Cl. T., 265-266; E *Mer. T.,* 1713-1714.

[47] F 63-64.

> I wol nat tellen of hir strange sewes (soups),
> Ne of hir swannes, ne of hir heronsewes (young herons).
> Eek in that lond, as tellen knightes olde,
> Ther is som mete that is ful deyntee holde,
> That in this lond men recche of it but smal;
> Ther nis no man that may reporten al.[48]

Soups, swans, and young herons were indeed only a small part of a medieval feast, but they are suggestive of the kinds of foods often served.

A comparison of Chaucer's allusions with one or two feasts of historical importance shows that his descriptions are somewhat restrained. For instance, when Richard II held his royal Christmas at the Great Hall of Westminster, in 1390, there was so large a concourse of people present and such feasts held "that there was everie day spent twentie eight, or twentie six Oxen, and three hundred sheepe, besides fowle without number."[49] So, also, at the marriage of Lionel, Duke of Clarence, third son of Edward III, with Violente, daughter of the Duke of Milan, "there was a rich feast, in which above thirty courses were served at the table, and the fragments that remained were more than sufficient to have served 1,000 people."[50]

Much of the literature of fourteenth century England contains allusions to feasting which are more detailed than those in Chaucer's works. In fact, the descriptions are much too elaborate to appear real, even though they may have been fundamentally based on facts about actual feasts. The menu found in the *Squyr of Lowe Degre* is an example of this sort of description:

> And sone he set hym on his knee,
> And served the kynge ryght ryally,
> With deynte meetes that were dere,
> With pertryche, pecoke, and plovere,
> With byrdes in bread ybake,
> The tele, the ducke, and the drake,

---

[48] *Ibid.,* 65-72.

[49] Stow, *Survey of London,* II, 116.

[50] James P. Andrews, *The History of Great Britain* (London, 1794), 439. Cf. also Albert S. Cook, "The Last Months of Chaucer's Earliest Patron," *Transactions of the Connecticut Academy of Arts and Sciences,* 21 (December, 1916), 62 ff.

The cocke, the curlewe, and the crane,
With fesauntes fayre, theyr were no wane,
Both storkes and snytes ther were also,
And venyson freshe of bucke and do,
And other deyntes many one,
For to set afore the kynge anone.[51]

One notes especially the kinds of meat mentioned and that they are probably the very rarest of those served at the medieval table. This fact it is which makes the description seem particularly ideal.

As important as were the medieval feasts for special occasions —for birthdays, weddings, tournaments, and the like—they were probably less significant than the ordinary meals of every day. Something of what it meant in his day to have a well-stocked larder and to provide generously for a household and frequent guests, perhaps, is seen in Chaucer's excellent treatment of the Franklin.

This Franklin, who was "the equivalent of the country squire of modern England,"[52] lived in true country-gentleman style. He "wel loved by the morwe a sop in wyn"[53]—a piece of bread toasted or dried on the embers of a fire and dipped into wine—being, according to Chaucer, "Epicurus owne sone."[54] "Pleyn delyt was

---

[51] *Squyr of Lowe Degre*, p. 64, ll. 314-326.

[52] Gordon H. Gerould, "The Social Status of Chaucer's Franklin," PMLA, 41 (June, 1926), 265.

[53] "The virtues of wine sops are extolled in *Regimen Sanitatis Salerni* (1528 version), thus: Here are declared iiij commodities of wyne soppis. The fyrst is / they purge the tethe / by reason they stycke longer in the tethe / than wyne alone or bread alone; therefore the fylthynes of the tethe is the better consumed / and the tethe the better purged. The ij commodite is / that it sharpeth the syghte: for it letteth the yll fumes to ascende to the brayne: which by theyr mynglynge together / darke the syghte. And this is by reason that hit digesteth all ill matters beynge in the stomacke. Thyrdly / hit digesteth perfectly meates nat wel digested: for it closeth the mouthe of the stomacke / and conforteth digestion. Fourthly / hit reduceth superfluous digestion to meane. . . ." Mead, *op. cit.*, 128.

It has been said that a species of apple was known in Cornwall as "Sops in Wine," but it seems not at all probable that the Franklin's sops were such. Cf. Manly, *Canterbury Tales*, 520. Certainly, if as cited above, pieces of toast soaked in wine were valuable in the treatment of digestive disorders, the Franklin would find them particularly beneficial after over-indulgence in foods as rich as those he enjoyed habitually.

[54] A *Gen. Prol.*, 336.

. . . felicitee parfyt,"[55] as far as the Franklin was concerned, and he managed his household in accord with this philosophy:

> An housholdere and that a greet was he;
> Seint Julian[56] he was in his contree.
> His breed, his ale, was alwey after oon;
> A bettre envyned man was no-wher noon.
> With-oute bake mete was never his hous,
> Of fish and flesh, and that so plentevous,
> It snewed in his hous of mete and drinke,
> Of alle deyntees that men coude thinke.
> After the sondry sesons of the yeer,
> So chaunged he his mete and his soper.
> Ful many a fat partrich hadde he in mewe,
> And many a breem and many a luce in stewe.
> Wo was his cook, but-if his sauce were
> Poynaunt and sharp, and redy al his gere.
> His table dormant in his halle alway
> Stood redy covered al the longe day.[57]

Special feasts in the Franklin's house must have been sumptuous, indeed. If the larder was abundantly supplied for daily living, how much the more so it must have been for a great occasion. The menu for a feast such as Chaucer's Franklin may have given is found in "The Boke of Nurture":

> A Franklen may make a feste Improberabille,
>   brawne with mustard is concordable,
>   bakon served with peson,
>   beef or moton stewed servysable,
>   Boyled Chykon or capon agreeable,
>   convenyent for þe seson;
>   Rosted goose and pygge fulle profitable,
>   Capon, Bakemete, or Custade Costable,
>   when eggis and crayme be geson.
>   þerfore stuffe of household is behoveable,
>   Mortrowes or Iusselle ar delectable
>   for þe second course by reson.

---

[55] *Ibid.*, 338. This philosophy is also expressed in E *Mer. T.*, 2021-2027.

[56] St. Julian was the patron of hospitality. Cf. J. G. Graesse, *Jacobi a Voragine Legenda Aurea* (Lipsae, 1850), cap. XXX (4), 142-143; *An Alphabet of Tales,* ed. Mary M. Banks, 2 parts EETS OS 126, 127 (London, 1904, 1905), 285-286. Note also "Seynt Julyan, lo, bon hostel," *HF*, II, 1022.

[57] A *Gen. Prol.*, 339-354.

> Than veel, lambe, kyd, or cony,
> Chykon or pigeon rosted tendurly
> bakemetes or dowcettes with alle
> þen followynge frytours and a leche lovely;
> Suche servyse in sesoun is fulle semely
> To serve with both chambur and halle.
> Then appuls and peris with spices delicately
> Aftur þe terme of þe yere fulle deynteithly,
> with bred and chese to calle.
> Spised cakes and wafurs worthily
> with bragot, and methe, þus men may meryly
> plese, welle bothe gret and smalle.[58]

Even a table dormant would have groaned under such an array of medieval delicacies! One can readily imagine the ruddy-faced Franklin beaming with pleasure as he witnessed the bringing in of the dishes, for "to liven in delyt was ever his wone."[59]

While the Franklin and persons of the higher classes of English society were dining and feasting on foods of finest quality, the poor of the time were having difficulty in supplying their miserable tables with enough to eat.[60]

Chaucer's single reference to the diet of the poor shows that he was acquainted with their manner of living. The widow's table was served with food which was not only very plain, but often scanty:

> Hir bord was served most with whyt and blak,
> Milk and broun breed, in which she fond no lak,
> Seynd bacoun, and somtyme an ey or tweye,
> For she was as it were a maner deye.[61]

---

[58] John Russell, *Babees Book,* ed. F. J. Furnivall, EETS, OS 32 (London, 1868), 170-171.

[59] A *Gen. Prol.,* 335.

[60] Many of the poor, especially in the rural sections of the country, lived chiefly on bread and salted meats, such as salt pork, beef, mutton, and poultry. This extended use of salt provisions is said to have been the cause of scurvy and leprosy, the virulence of which was aggravated by "the inconceivably filthy habits of the people." Rogers, *Work and Wages,* 95-96.

The bread used by the poor was of inferior quality, for it was made of the cheapest kind of flour, sometimes combined with oats, rye, barley, or even peas and beans. Mead, *op. cit.,* 66. It was fortunate that some of the poor had small gardens and farms, from which they eked out their supplies with vegetables, eggs, and milk. Rogers, *op. cit.,* 95.

[61] B *NPT,* 4033-4036.

"A maner deye," that is, the dairywoman of a manor,[62] would certainly seem to have needed more than bread and milk, broiled bacon, and an occasional egg or two, yet on such a diet the widow thrived. Of course, there were advantages to eating so little; at least,

> Repleccioun ne made hir never syk;
> . .   .   .
> The goute lette hir no-thing for to daunce,
> N'apoplexye shente nat hir heed.[63]

There was nothing, however, to lend variety to her board— no "poynaunt sauce,"[64] no wine, either white or red[65]—nothing which most medieval persons especially liked:

> No deyntee morsel passed thurgh hir throte;
> Hir dyete was accordant to hir cote.[66]

The Franklin might indeed have been inclined to live beyond his means; the poor widow, never!

Occasionally there is reference in the literature of the fourteenth century other than Chaucer's works to the fare of the provident as well as to that of the very poor man. A certain plowman, for instance, is described as having a good supply of foods stored for use:

> His hall rofe was full of bakon flytches,
> The chambre charged was with wyches
> Full of egges, butter, and chese,
> Men that were hungry for to ese;
> To make good ale, malte had he plentye;
> And Martylmas befe, to hym was not deynte;
> Onyons and garlyke had he inowe;
> And good creme, and mylk of the cowe.
> Thus by his labour ryche was he in dede.[67]

---

[62] Skeat, *op. cit.*, gloss.

[63] B *NPT,* 4027-4031.

[64] *Ibid.*, 4024.

[65] *Ibid.*, 4032.

[66] *Ibid.*, 4025-4026.

[67] "How the Ploughman Learned his Paternoster," *Reliquae Antiquae,* I, 43.

Although the foods mentioned here do not appear as of great variety, they were real luxuries in the plowman's home.

Another plowman, perhaps more typical of his class than the former, certainly lived on a plain and frugal diet. He had no money to buy pullets, geese, or pigs; nor did he have any salt bacon. Instead, he was very fortunate to have two green cheeses, a few curds of cream, a cake of oatmeal, two loaves of beans and bran, parsley, pot herbs, and plenty of cabbages. These were to last him and his family till the next harvest.[68]

He was unable to satisfy his guest, Hunger, with such food, so his neighbors, though poor like himself, assisted him by bringing in peascods, beans, baked apples, and wild fruits.[69] None of these people seem to have had meat or fish, wheaten or barley bread, wine or beer—the foods which were common among the well-to-do—and they were satisfied with little. When the harvest came, though, and food was more plentiful, they became discontented. Beggars became fastidious about their diet, refusing to eat bread made of beans and asking for the best there was. Likewise, they demanded the best and brownest ale, and would not eat herbs which had lain over night. Bacon no longer satisfied them; they demanded fresh fish, fried or roasted, requesting that it be served to them warm or hot, as their stomachs were cold.[70]

The food of the Middle Ages consisted largely of meat and fish, as may have been observed in the citations given thus far. Meat was the chief dish for ordinary days, and fish for fast days.[71] The Franklin's household fed often on partridge[72] and various

---

[68] *Piers Plowman,* EETS OS 54, vi, ll. 282-291.

[69] *Ibid.,* ll. 294-297.

[70] *Ibid.,* ll. 305-313.

[71] Mead, *op. cit.,* 73.

[72] Roast partridge was considered a great delicacy. It was sometimes prepared in accordance with the following directions:

> . . . tak a fedir and put it in to his hed and let him dye and pulle hym dry and drawe hym and rost hym as yo wold raise the legges and wingys of an henne and mynce hym sauce hym with wyn pouder of guinger and salt and warm it on the fyere and serve it. Mrs. Alexander Napier, *A Noble Boke off Cookry* (London, 1882), 61.

bake metes;[73] but they also had fish of fine quality, among which were bream[74] and luce.[75]   Together with meat and fish, bread seems to have been universally used.[76]   Besides these articles of diet, a reference or two to "deyntees," and an allusion to the Summoner's fondness for "garleek, oynons, and eek lekes,"[77] Chaucer fails to specify any other kinds of foods used, although from contemporary sources one learns that fruits, certain vegetables, nuts, and numerous other kinds were used in varying degrees of frequency.

Chaucer's allusions to the foods most liked by medieval Religious men, ironical though they may be, are particularly interesting, not that they throw much light on the subject of monastic fare in general, but that they are suggestive of certain regulations and abuses.

The friar of the *Summoner's Tale,* whose appetite prompts him to ask for

> . . . of a capon but the livere,
> And of your softe breed nat but a shivere, ⏋
> And after that a rosted pigges heed,[78]

---

[73] According to Mead, "bake meate, which is called flesshe that is beryd, for it is buryd in paast," is the same as pasties or pies. *Op. cit.,* 84.

[74] Bream, a fresh-water fish (Cf. Manly), might be cooked according to a recipe such as this:

> To dight a breme in sauce tak and scale hym and drawe hym at the belly and prik hym at the chyne and broyle hym on a gredyrne till he be enoughe then tak wyne boiled and cast it to pouder of guinger and vergius then lay the breme in a dysshe and poure on the ceripe and serve it. *A Noble Boke off Cookry,* 70. Or a sauce of parsley, sage, and ginger could be used as a variation, *ibid.,* 73.

[75] Luce, or pike, as it was sometimes called, was served with a sauce of water, salt, a little ale and parsley, into which had been cast "ginger, vergeous, mustard," and the like. *Two Fifteenth Century Cookery Books,* ed. Thomas Austin, EETS, OS 91 (London, 1888), II, 101.
    A pike, be it known, "was served whole to a lorde, but cut up in pieces for the commonalty." *A Noble Boke off Cookry,* vii.

[76] Chaucer merely mentions it. Cf. A *Gen. Prol.,* 341; B *NPT,* 4033-4034; D *Sum. T.,* 1840.

[77] A *Gen. Prol.,* 634.

[78] D 1839-1841.

seems by no means to be "a man of little sustenaunce,"[79] as he claims to be. Rather, one suspects that his request for only a capon liver, a small piece of bread, and a roast pig's head is affectedly humble and that if the housewife should take him literally, he would be deeply offended.[80]

The discourse of the friar upon the subject of monastic abstinence is shot through with the most subtle irony. It is delivered while he waits for a repast to be prepared. First, the friar refers to his own disability—the result, he says, of his great mortifications.

> I am a man of litel sustenaunce.
> My spirit hath his fostring in the Bible.
> The body is ay so redy and penible
> To wake, that my stomak is destroyed.[81]

The destroyed stomach permits him to indulge only in light meals —capon liver, bread, and roast pork! But he is not alone in his self-praised abstemiousness; his brethren are all, says he, lovers of poverty and moderation:

> We live in povert and in abstinence,
> And burel folk in richesse and despence

---

[79] *Ibid.*, 1844.

[80] On the subject of over-indulgence as practiced by religious, one of the most popular of medieval tales is that of a Carmelite friar, invited by a certain woman to dine at her house. The woman and her guest are alone and are served by two waiters. They are hardly seated when there is brought to them "la belle poree avec le beau lart, et belles trippes de porc, et une langue de beuf rostie." Before the hostess has disposed of her portion of soup, the friar has eaten the entire course. The hostess then orders a piece of good salt beef and a large choice mutton, which the friar eats at once. Next, the servant brings in a fine ham, which is the only meat left in the house. Of that, the friar leaves only the bone. His appetite is still not satisfied, however:
> Pour abregier, la dam fist mettre à la table ung très bon fourmaige
> gras, et ung plat bien fourny de tartes et pommes et de fourmaige,
> avec la belle piece de beurre fraiz, dont on n'en reporta si petit
> que rien.
When he has finally disposed of all the food in the woman's house, the friar discourses on the parable of the loaves and fishes. There seems to have been no fragments left, however. "Le Carme Glouton," *Les Cent Nouvelles Nouvelles,* ed P. L. Jacob (Paris, 1858), 333 ff.

[81] D *Sum. T.*, 1844-1847.

> Of mete and drinke, and in hir foul delyt.
> We han this worldes lust al in despyt.
> Lazar and Dives liveden diversly,
> And diverse guerdon hadden they ther-by.
> Who-so wol preye, he moot faste and be clene,
> And fatte his soule and make his body lene.
> We fare as seith th'apostle; cloth and fode
> Suffysen us, though they be nat ful gode.
> The clennesse and the fastinge of us freres
> Maketh that Crist accepteth our preyeres.[82]

With Pharisaical glibness of tongue, the friar elaborates upon his theme, giving examples of chosen souls whose poverty and love of abstinence had won them God's favor, concluding with the statement that the prayers of the friar are better than anyone else's because they practise such mortifications.[83] With each sentence he utters his hypocrisy becomes more apparent.

Chaucer's Monk, representative of another group of Religious, is particularly fond of one of the choice meats of the Middle Ages:

> A fat swan loved he best of any roost.[84]

The Monk's taste for the most delicate and most expensive of foods was of course in keeping with "his sleves purfiled at the hond with grys,"[85] his "grehoundes . . . as swifte as fowel in flight,"[86] and "his hors in greet estat."[87]   But was this taste in harmony with the Rule the Monk had professed to follow? The matter has been variously discussed, with no definite conclusion reached.

It is certain that the Monk expresses disregard for the points

---

[82] *Ibid.*, 1873-1884.

[83] *Ibid.*, 1885 ff.

[84] A *Gen. Prol.*, 206. The difference in the value of a swan and other fowls may readily be seen by a glance at the expenses incurred in providing for the feast for the installation of the Prior of St. Augustine's in Canterbury (cf. appendix, 258). Five hundred hens and capons cost only 6 pounds 5 shillings, but 24 swans cost 7 pounds. Similarly, 1,000 geese were purchased for 16 pounds as compared to the 24 swans for 7.

[85] A *Gen. Prol.*, 193-194.

[86] *Ibid.*, 190.

[87] *Ibid.*, 203.

of his Rule which he did not care to follow, for Chaucer says of him:

> The reule of seint Maure or of seint Beneit,
> By-cause that it was old and som-del streit,
> This ilke monk leet olde thinges pace,
> And held after the newe world the space.[88]

In regard to the food which St. Benedict had wished his Monks to have for their daily meals, the Rule specified that there should be two portions, and sometimes a third, of herbs, a pound of bread, and a measure of wine (about three-fourths of a pint), a third of which was to be laid by when the Monks were to sup, as they did on certain days.[89] It was further provided that "all, save the very weak and sick, are to abstain wholly from eating the flesh of quadrupeds."[90]

The question as to whether this latter injunction meant that bipeds might be eaten has been answered in both the affirmative and in the negative. Dugdale sums up the opinions expressed before his time, as follows:

> Many have been of the Opinion, that St. Benedict, having prohibited only the Flesh of four-footed Animals, had tacitly allow'd the eating of Fowls; and among them, Haestenius is of this Opinion, grounding himself on the authority of *St. Hildegard,* and of *Rabanus Maurus;* but *F. Mabillon* says, there is no Likelihood that *St. Benedict,* who had appointed his Monks none but mean Food, and such as could not please the Appetite, would permit those that were in Health to eat Fowls, which was then only serv'd up to the Tables of Kings, as exquisite Dainties, according to the Report of *Gregory of Tours.*[91]

If St. Benedict did mean to exclude fowls from the restriction he had made, it is hardly in accordance with his general attitude to-

---

[88] *Ibid.,* 173-176.

[89] Dugdale, *Monasticon* (1722 ed.), I, 163. Cf. also *The Rule of St. Benedict,* trans. and ed. by Cardinal Gasquet (London, 1925), Ch. XXXIX.

[90] *Idem.*

[91] *Monasticon,* I, 163. See also on this point Dom Cuthbert Butler, *Benedictine Monachism* (London, 1924), 44, n; 308.

ward poverty and abstinence that those of high price should be
on the tables in monasteries, even for "a manly man, to been an
abbot able."[92]   It may be that the saint permitted fowl to be eaten
simply because it was sometimes more easy to obtain than was
other meat; this would be especially true of chickens which could
be raised on monastic farms and of game which could be snared
and taken in the open fields. Just as many persons on farms today have fowl as food, not in any respect as a luxury, so too, in
Chaucer's time it may have been a great saving for the monks
to have it.

Whether or not the Monk was often able to satisfy his liking
for roast swan, we cannot be sure. If he were, it may have been
prepared according to one of the methods explained in part by the
Goodman of Paris to his wife:

> Pluck him like a chicken or a duck and scald or do again
> (in hot water); put him on a spit skewered in four
> places and roast him whole with beak and feet and pluck
> not his head; eat with yellow pepper sauce.
> Item, who will may glaze him.
> Item, in killing split him from head to shoulders.
> Item, they be sometimes skinned and clad again in their
> feathers.[93]

It must be remembered that Chaucer's Monk, like the Friar
and Daun John, was by no means an exemplary Religious. Like
them, he was worldly-minded, vain, and probably a lover of all
fine foods,[94] and although he may have been representative of a
certain group in his monastery who had fallen into laxity as regarded the observance of their Rule, he was not necessarily
typical of his whole Order.

No one can honestly deny that the members of Religious orders
often lived exceptionally well at this period, although their Rules
provided generally that they live frugally, being satisfied with at
most two meals a day and with food of the poorest sort. It is un-

---

[92] A *Gen. Prol.,* 167.

[93] *Goodman of Paris,* 238-239.

[94] Chaucer's allusion to the Monk's love of swans appears to me to be
chiefly used to infer his gluttonous tendencies in general.

necessary to cite here numerous examples of monastic intemperance other than those suggested by Chaucer. Rather, a little information concerning what seems modest supplies of food provided in certain monasteries will indicate what was probably the somewhat typical amount of food used in Religious houses wherein the spirit of poverty and temperance was of at least ordinary strength.

The kitchen charges listed in the accounts of St. Swithun's Priory from Michaelmas, 1334, to Michaelmas, 1335, show not only the kinds and quantities of foods, but also their prices:

Outgoing:			
Wines:—	£	s	d
Red Wine, 40 casks	88	14	4
White wine, 2 pipes	3	0	0
Kitchen Charges:			
536 carcases of sheep	13	17	8
11,300 white herrings	5	13	4
42,000 red herrings	19	18	6
222 salt salmon	8	17	0
salt mullet, conger, lynge, etc.	36	6	7
49 flagons of oil	2	1	6
3 baskets of figs and raisins	0	18	8
garlic and onions	0	12	6
salted provisions	1	0	4
45 qrs. salt	3	1	0
180 qrs. charcoal	2	9	7[95]

Curiously enough, among the charges is one for a "woman cleaning the carcases of pigs, etc." Evidently the pigs were products of the monastic farm, for they are not mentioned elsewhere in the account. The foods, purchased, then, must have been augmented by those raised on the monastic lands. Likewise, dishes were made more palatable to medieval appetites by the use of many spices, sugar, and the like, which are also listed in the account of purchases.[96] Certainly, however, the fare of St. Swithun's was

[95] *The Compotus Rolls of the Obedientiaries of St. Swithun's Priory, Winchester,* ed. George W. Kitchin (London, 1892), 119.

[96] *Ibid.,* 123.

nothing extraordinary, consisting chiefly in wholesome foods—sheep, herrings, salmon—varied sometimes by figs, raisins, garlic, onions, and spices. It may have been better than the average medieval family of moderate means could afford, but it was not sumptuous.[97]

Monastic diet in general has been summed up by Thomas Fosbroke thus:

> . . . bread, beer, soup, beans for soup, all Lent; oats for gruel, Thursday and Saturday in that season; flour for pottage every day in the same season; fried dishes, wastels, or fine bread for dinner and supper on certain feasts; flathos or cakes in Easter; *formictae,* or fine flour cakes, in Advent, Christmas, against Lent, Easter, Pentecost, and certain feasts; fat things (bacon?) were frequent with the Praemonstratensians; black beans and salt with the Clugniacs; general bad fare with the Cistercians.[98]

It would appear from these and similar accounts that for the most part carelessness in matters pertaining to eating was the result of individual disregard of Rules rather than of community negligence.

The evidence from Chaucer's works as presented here shows in regard to what was served at medieval feasts and daily meals (1) the poet's occasional dependence on the conventional methods of describing feasts; (2) an extensive use of realistic material; and (3) a reasonably wide range of information concerning the diet of different classes of society.

---

[97] The amount of food served in a religious establishment such as that at Christ Church, Canterbury, on a fish day, shows no great excess:

> To every two monks, when they had soles, there were four soles in a dish; when they had plaice, two plaice; when they had herring, eight herring; when they had whiting, eight whiting; when they had mackrell, two mackrell; when they had eggs, ten eggs. If they had anything more allowed them beyond this ordinary fare, it was either cheese or fruit or the like. Taunton, *English Black Monks,* I, 80-81.

[98] *British Monachism* (London, 1817), 300-301.

Cookery

To prepare the foods necessary to a medieval meal, and especially for feasts, required a kind of skill unknown in modern cookery. It seems almost as if even the simplest foods had to be disguised in such a manner as to change completely their original taste and appearance.[99] Nearly every dish became a riddle; the most skillful cooks were those who could furnish the best riddle.[100] Something of the problem involved in medieval culinary practices is suggested by Chaucer's Pardoner, who says,

> Thise cokes, how they stampe and streyne, and grinde,
> And turnen substaunce in-to accident,
> To fulfille al thy likerous talent!
> Out of the harde bones knokke they
> The mary, for they caste noght a-wey
> That may go thurgh the golet softe and swote;
> Of spicerye, of leef, and bark, and rote
> Shal been his sauce y-maked by delyt,
> To make him yet a newer appetyt.[101]

The stamping, straining, and grinding here mentioned allude to the common medieval custom of braying foods in a mortar and straining from certain ones the liquid parts, which seem to have been used to help disguise the finally resulting dish. "The ideal," says Mead, "was that nothing should be left in its natural state."[102] Chaucer's Cook was evidently considered capable and had been brought along with the pilgrims on their way to Canterbury to serve in a professional capacity.[103] He knew how

> To boille the chiknes with the marybones,
> And poudre-marchant tart, and galingale.

---

[99] "Practically all ordinary meats and game, fish and poultry, as well as stewed fruit and desserts of every description, were so loaded with cinnamon, ginger, cloves, cubebs, pepper, galingale (cypress root), mace, and nutmeg, one or all, that whatever had been taken as the basis of the dish was made practically unrecognizable." Mead, *op. cit.*, 74.

[100] *Ibid.*, 44.

[101] C *Pard. T.*, 538-546.

[102] Mead, *op. cit.*, 53. Cf. Robinson, *Complete Works of Chaucer*, 835; Manly, *op. cit.*, 619 for a discussion of the Pardoner's lines and their dependence on the *De Contemptu Mundi* of Innocent III.

[103] A *Gen. Prol.*, 379. *For the nones* probably means "for the occasion"; that is, the Canterbury pilgrimage. Robinson, *op. cit.*, 762.

. . . .
Maken mortreux, and wel bake a pye.[104]

Besides, he knew good ale from bad; he could "roste, sethe, and broille, and frye,"[105] and make blankmanger of the best.[106]

Chickens were much used in the Middle Ages, as a glance at any English medieval cookery book will indicate. Boiling them with marrow and spices, such as poudre-marchant and galingale, was probably a common enough way of preparing them.[107] The use of marrow, as Chaucer implies above, was apparently something of a luxury, which betrayed the love of fine foods which medieval persons often indulged in.

Mortreux, sometimes written *mortrewes* or *mortrews,* was thickened soup or pottage;[108] there were numerous recipes used for it, the most common perhaps being something like this:

> Take hennes and pork, and seeth hem togydre. Take
> the lyre (flesh) of hennes, and of the pork, and hewe it

---

[104] A *Gen. Prol.,* 380-384.

[105] *Ibid.,* 382-384.

[106] *Ibid.,* 387.

[107] There are numerous recipes for preparing chickens. A simple one which seems somewhat similar to what is suggested by Chaucer (although it omits the marrow bones) directs that the chickens be scalded; then parsley, sage, and other herbs, and grapes put into the chicken. All are boiled in good broth (perhaps the bones furnish stock for this) which is colored with saffron. Pouderdouce and salt are added just before the chicken is served. See Mrs. Napier, *A Noble Book of Cookery,* 114.

A more elaborate recipe, called Chickens in Bruet (Broth), may at times have been used by the cook. The method of preparing this dish is detailed:

> Take halfe a dosyn Chykonys, & putte hem in-to a potte; þen putte þerto a gode gobet of freysshe Beef, & lat hem boyle wyl; putte þerto Percely, Sawg leuys, Sauerey, noþt to smal hakkyd; putte þerto Saffroun y-now; þen kytte þin Brewes & skalde hem with þe same broþe; Salt it wyl; & but þou haue Beef, take Motoun, but fyrst Stuffe þin chekons in þis wyse: take & seþe hard Eyroun (eggs), & take þe ȝolkys & choppe hem small, & choppe þer-to Clowys, Maces, Hole Pepir, & Stuffe þin chekonys with-al; Also put hole gobettys & mary with ynne; Also þen dresse hem as a pertryche, & fayre coloure hem, & ley uppe-on þis browes, & serue in with Bakoun.

Two Fifteenth Century Cookery Books, 32.

[108] Skeat, *op. cit.,* gloss.

small, and grind it all to doust. Take brede ygrated and do thereto, and temper it with the self broth, and alye it with the yolkes of ayren (eggs), and cast thereon powder-fort (a mixture of the warmer spices—pepper, ginger, etc.); boile it, and do therein powder of gynger, sugar, safroun, and salt, and loke that it be stonding (stiff), and floer (flourish or strew) it with powder gynger.[109]

Blankmanger, which Chaucer's Cook made especially well, consisted of the flesh of poultry, generally capons, boiled with rice and the milk of almonds, and sweetened with sugar. It was garnished with aniseed confectioned red or white, and "with almandes fryed in oile."[110]

To "wel bake a pye" is still an accomplishment of which any cook has the right to be proud, but in Chaucer's day there were so many different kinds of pies that one who could bake them successfully certainly deserved special commendation. The pastry form into which meats, game, fish, or fruits[111] were put must have been similar in composition to modern pastry. It was so shaped before baking as to merit for itself in its finished form the peculiar name of "coffyn."[112]

---

[109] *English Cookery Five Hundred Years Ago,* privately printed (Totham, 1849), ix. See also recipes for mortrewes blank, *idem;* for mortrewes of fysshe, *Two Fifteenth Century Cookery Books,* I, 14; mortrewes of fleysshe, *idem;* also Samuel Pegge, ed., *The Forme of Cury* (London, 1780), 28-29.

[110] *The Forme of Cury,* 24-25. There were many kinds of blankmanger. One was made of fish, boiled with rice, almonds in milk, etc. *A Noble Boke off Cookry,* 111.

[111] The Goodman of Paris seems to have been something of an authority on pies. He tells his wife many useful facts about them. Chickens, for example, are to be set in the pasty on their backs, with slices of bacon on their breasts. Then they are covered—probably with folds of pastry.

Mushrooms, peeled and washed, are combined with oil, cheese and spices and put into pasties. Venison, too, is parboiled, scoured, larded and made into pies. For a beef pasty, the fat is removed from the meat and the lean cooked until it boils. It is taken to the pastry cook to be minced, the fat is mixed with marrow, and all are put into the "coffyn." Or the meat of a beef's cheek is cut into slices and set in a pasty; when it is cooked, the sauce of a young duckling is added to it. *Goodman of Paris,* 269-270.

[112] Abram, *English Life and Manners,* 138.

The Cook was not above practicing deceits in his cook-shop. Of him the Host says,

> For many a pastee hastow laten blood,
> And many a Jakke of Dover hastow sold
> That hath been twyes hoot and twyes cold.[113]

The "pastee" referred to in the first line is probably some sort of meat pie.   What Chaucer means by saying that the Cook had "laten blood" for pasties has not, so far as I know, been satisfactorily explained by scholars.   A possible interpretation is that the Cook cut the throats of capons and hens, thus bleeding them, and then put the fowls into a bucket of very cold water to die. In this way, the flavour of game was given to the capons and hens,[114] and pies made with them as ingredients were perhaps sold as game pies in deceit of the people, just as beef baked in pasties had sometimes been sold for venison.[115]

Whether the term "Jakke of Dover" applies to such pasties is not certain.   Most commentators believe it to mean some sort of meat pie,[116] the exact nature of which is not known.   Manly interprets it as a slang name applied to pies from which the gravy was drawn off, when they were not sold the first day they were

---

[113] A *Cook's Prol.*, 4346-4348.

[114] This process is described in *The Goodman of Paris,* 224.

[115] The "Ordinances of the Pastelers, or Piebakers, as to Pasties," enacted in 1379 in London, included the following:
Because that the Pastelers of the City of London have hitherto baked in pasties rabbits, geese, and garbage (giblets are probably included in this term) not befitting, and sometimes stinking, in deceit of the people; and also, *have baked beef in pasties, and sold the same for venison,* [the italics are mine] in deceit of the people; therefore, by assent of the four Master Pastelers, and at their prayer, it is ordered and assented to . . .
In the first place,—that no one of the said trade shall bake rabbits in pasties for sale, on pain of paying, the first time, if found guilty thereof, 6s. 8d., to the Chamber, and of going bodily to prison, at the will of the Mayor; the second time, 13s. 4d. to the use of the Chamber, and of going, etc.
Also,—that no one of the said trade shall buy of any cook of Bredestret, or at the hostels of the great lords, of the cooks of such lords, any garbage from capons, hens, or geese, to bake in a pasty, and sell, under the same penalty . . . Riley, *Memorials of London and London Life,* 438.

[116] Cf. Robinson, 792.

cooked, that they might keep longer.[117]   At any rate, it seems quite clear that the pies were re-heated and probably sold as fresh ones.

Another phase of medieval cookery suggested by Chaucer is that which in our times is almost the primary consideration, namely, cleanliness.   The Cook is described as being particularly deficient in this matter:

> Of many a pilgrim hastow Cristes curs,
> For of thy persley yet they fare the wors,
> That they han eten with thy stubbel-goos;
> For in thy shoppe is many a flye loos.[118]

The stubble-goose,[119] served as it was with parsley was especially to be eschewed by persons the least bit discriminating; apparently the Cook was not greatly concerned about the fact that his shop was infested with flies.

Considering that probably the Cook served the Pilgrims in his official position, one may conclude that he was surely not among the worst of his class, and that the conditions attendant on medieval cookery were far from ideal.[120]   On the other hand, the notice given of the Cook's failings suggests that it was not an ac-

---

[117] *Canterbury Tales,* 563.

[118] A *Cook's Prol.,* 4348-4352.

[119] Geese fed on stubble were called green.   Frequently geese were put into coops and fattened with a medium quality of flour, mixed with oatmeal and a little water.   The process required only about fifteen days and was therefore often advantageous.   Rogers, *Work and Wages,* 83-84; *Goodman of Paris,* 224.

[120] The sale of putrid foods, especially meats, seems to have been an offense frequently committed; that cooks bought and cooked such foods because they could be cheaply obtained is not difficult to believe.   There are many instances of such practices.   In 1353, for example, one Richard Quelhogge was found guilty of having bought for four pence from one Richard Stevenache, porter, "a pig that had been lying by the water-side of the Thames, putrid and stinking;" from it he "had cut two gammons for sale, and had sold part thereof, in deceit of the people."   In punishment, Quelhogge "was put upon the pillory and the residue of the said gammon was burnt beneath him there."   Riley, *Memorials,* 271.

Similarly, in 1365, John Russelle of Abyndone, a poulterer, was punished for having exposed putrid pigeons for sale, *ibid.,* 328.   See also 448-449 for the sale of putrid pigeons, and 464 for the sale of putrid fish.

cepted custom for persons to eat food cooked under any and all conditions. Tastes may have been less discriminating and less fastidious than they are at present; still, many a pilgrim called down the curse of Christ upon the Cook who dared to disregard the fundamental laws of clean cookery.

This study of medieval culinary practices reveals particularly that recipes popular in Chaucer's day have very little to tempt the modern appetite. The curious combination of meats, spices, sugar, oil, eggs, and the like; the excessive quantities of flesh and fish in the diet; and the too frequent disregard of cleanliness mark medieval cookery as unattractive and certainly different from our own.[121]

The Dining Hall and Service at Table

Even ordinary meals were usually served with great ceremony in the homes of the wealthy,[122] and special feasts were proportionately more elaborate and ceremonious. Chaucer's references to the subject are generally scattered, incidental, and often vague and merely suggestive rather than concrete. As a whole they present broad views of guests being entertained at sumptuous feasts and reveal more of the general atmosphere of merriment and good cheer than of the serving. Individual allusions, however, convey much information regarding such matters as the official titles of servants, the proper seating of guests in order of their rank, the

---

[121] Although one is likely to regard medieval cookery merely as an experimental art, consisting of incongruous mixtures, and excess of spices and sauces, and unattractively served dishes, this is only partly correct. The cooks apparently tried to make the foods they served appear as tempting as possible. They used coloring, such as saffron, sanders, alkenet, mulberries, etc.; likewise they strewed the dishes with flowers, leaves of trees gilded or silvered, and other types of ornaments. *The Forme of Cury*, xiv-xv.

[122] Perhaps no other medieval person observed more unusual customs in having his daily meals served than did the famous Gaston Phoebus. When he went to his chamber at midnight for his supper, this gentleman was preceded by twelve servants, each bearing a lighted torch. The torches were used to light the table. Usually guests were present at the supper and entertainment was provided by minstrels. The Count ordinarily remained at table about two hours. Froissart, *Chronicles*, II, 95.

carving done at table, and the practice of washing before and after meals.

In the *Knight's Tale* there is a general view of a dining scene, which summarizes most of the characteristic features of a medieval feast:

> He festeth hem, and dooth so greet labour
> To esen hem, and doon hem al honour,
> That yet men weneth that no mannes wit
> Of noon estat ne coude amenden it.
> The minstralcye, the service at the feste,
> The grete yiftes to the moste and leste,
> The riche array of Theseus paleys,
> Ne who sat first ne last up-on the deys,
> What ladies fairest been or best daunsinge,
> Or which of hem can dauncen best and singe,
> Ne who most felingly speketh of love:
> What haukes sitten on the perche above,
> What houndes liggen on the floor adoun:
> Of al this make I now no mencioun;
> But al th' effect, that thinketh me the beste.[123]

The mention of the hounds on the floor and the hawks on the perch above the tables lends a realistic touch to this picture, but otherwise the indirect description is not particularly enlightening as to customs observed at table. The whole scene, however, is one suggestive of wealth. The minstrelsy, the rich array, the fair ladies who dance and sing—all bespeak the elegance of the feast.[124]

The minstrelsy was a group of musicians hired for an occasion, or in a great house was maintained as part of the household for the entertainment of guests or sometimes just for that of the lord and his family at table. These musicians usually preceded the guests into the great hall, playing their instruments until all the company had assembled. They also played while the meal was in progress, sometimes being near the high table and at other times in the balcony above the screens.[125]

---

[123] A 2193-2207.

[124] Cf. also *infra*, 120, 121.

[125] Jusserand, *English Wayfaring Life*, 203 ff. See also *supra*, 22, f.n. 95.

Chaucer alludes frequently to the minstrels as evidently an essential part of the feast. At January's wedding celebration,

> Biforn hem stoode swiche instruments of soun,
> That Orpheus, ne of Thebes Amphioun,
> Ne maden never swich a melodye.
> At every cours than cam loud minstralcye,
> That never tromped Joab, for to here,
> Nor he, Theodomas, yet half so clere,
> At Thebes, when the citee was in doute.[126]

Apparently the music here is used to accompany each course of the meal.

King Cambinskan's birthday dinner, which was of great elegance, was also accompanied by minstrels; the players seem to have stood near the King's table:

> . . .   after the thridde cours,
> Whyl that this king sit thus in his nobleye,
> Herkninge his minstralles hir thinges pleye,
> Biforn him at the bord deliciously,
> In at the halle-dore al sodeynly
> Ther cam a knight up-on a stede of bras.[127]

After the meal, King Cambinskan arose from the table, and

> Toforn him gooth the loude minstralcye,
> Til he cam to his chambre of parements,
> Ther as they sownen diverse instruments,
> That it is lyk an heven for to here.[128]

The minstrels must have belonged to the King's household. Probably it was the usual custom of Cambinskan to observe the formality of music at his daily meals and for him to be preceded by minstrels when he entered or left the hall or chamber.

Duke Theseus' minstrels, too, seem to have been attached to the master's household. Besides entertaining his guests, they had duties to perform in Theseus' chamber. The worthy duke, we are told, was "of his sleep awaked with minstralcye."[129]

---

[126] E *Mer. T.*, 1715-1721.
[127] F. *Sq. T.*, 76-81.
[128] *Ibid.*, 268-271.
[129] A *Kn. T.*, 2523-2524.

Besides his several allusions to minstrels, Chaucer includes in nearly all his descriptions of the feast, the important matter of seating honored guests. In the *Merchant's Tale* at the wedding feast, January and May sit

> With other worthy folk up-on the deys.[130]

King Cambinskan, at his own birthday feast,

> In royal vestiment sit on his deys.[131]

But of "who sat first ne last up-on the deys,"[132] in Duke Theseus' house, Chaucer says he will not make mention, for if he told all the details it would occupy a summer's day.

"On the deys" refers, of course, to the place of honor at the feast.[133] The matter of seating guests according to their social ranks was of utmost importance. Whosoever sat on the dais was considered as being at the high table, which in this case was a literally true fact.

When the Marquis Walter was instructing Grisilde about the preparations for his wedding feast, he was particularly solicitous that the guests be received as "royally as it is possible,"

> And eek that every wight in his degree
> Have his estaat in sitting and in servyse
> And heigh plesaunce, as I can best devyse.[134]

Although Grisilde was busy all day long overseeing the decoration of the house, the setting of tables, the making of beds, and all "that to the feste was apertinent,"[135] she met the guests graciously and followed well the instructions she had been given:

> With so glad chere his gestes she receyveth,
> And conningly, everich in his degree,
> That no defaute no man aperceyveth.[136]

---

[130] E 1711.
[131] F *Sq.. T.*, 59-60.
[132] Cf. *supra*, 125.
[133] *Idem.*
[134] E *Cl. T.*, 955-959.
[135] *Ibid.*, 1010.
[136] *Ibid.*, 1016-1018.

Unfortunately, from the point of view of information, the titles of the persons seated on the dais or in their proper order elsewhere throughout the hall, are not given.

Had Chaucer listed the guests, he would perhaps have saved scholars much time and labour in deciding what is meant by a frequently discussed reference to the Knight, namely that

> Ful ofte tyme he hadde the bord bigonne
> Aboven alle the naciouns in Pruce.[137]

Why did the Knight begin the board, since his rank in society was relatively far down from the top? Was it that as a stranger in another country he received special honors? According to English customs this could have been reason enough. At least, etiquette seems to have required that strangers be accorded special privileges:

> More over take hede he must to aliene comers straungeres,
> and to straungers of þis land, resident dwelleres,
> and exalte þem to honoure if þe be of honest maneres.
> þen alle oþer aftur þeire degre like as case requires.[138]

There was at this time, as had been established by the Teutonic Order of Knights, what was known as the *Table of Honor,* used to attract distinguished knights from foreign lands to the service of the other country.[139] According to Professor A. S. Cook, it

---

[137] A *Gen. Prol.,* 52-53. In the rules of precedence, property was not considered as worthy as royal blood and the latter prevailed over the former at table, for it was possible that "royal blood may become King." In part the order observed was as follows:

1. Pope, King, Prince, Archbishop, and Duke.

2. Bishop, Marquis, Viscount, Earl.

3. Mayor of London, Baron, Mitred Abbot, three Chief Justices, and Speaker.

4. The other ranks (three or four to a mess) equal to a Knight, namely, Unmitred Abbot, Master of the Rolls, Under Judges, Doctor of Divinity, Protonotary, Mayor of Calais, etc.
Paraphrased from John Russell, "Boke of Nurture," *Babees Book,* 188.

[138] *Ibid.,* 75.

[139] Albert S. Cook, "Beginning the Board in Prussia," *JEGP,* 14 (July, 1915), 376. See also Cook, "The Historical Background of Chaucer's Knight," *Transactions of the Connecticut Academy of Arts and Sciences,* 20 (February, 1916), 161-240.

was this particular board to which Chaucer had reference.[140] This would perhaps account for the various military expeditions of the Knight, but it seems to be unnecessary to so interpret the lines.

Professor Manly is of the opinion that "Chaucer does not appear to have been referring to these Tables of Honor, for he says the knight began the board 'ful ofte tyme,' whereas Cook says we know of only five Tables of Honor from 1377-1400." Manly believes that Chaucer thought the honor of beginning the board was assigned at every formal feast.[141] One hardly need look further than the poet's own references to the seating of guests, directly or incidentally made, to agree with this opinion. Other literature of the period likewise helps to point to the fact that persons of special merit or of high renown were sometimes given the highest place, regardless of the regular order which should have been normally followed. In *Sir Beves of Hamtoun,* for example, Josian says to the Palmer,

> Palmer, thou semest best to me,
> Therfore men shal worshyp the:
> Begyn the borde, I the pray,
> Thou semest best, withouten nay![142]

Here one notes the element of personal approval as the standard of selection. The "withouten nay" suggests, however, that the Palmer was also unanimously approved to begin the board. Would Chaucer's Knight, whose fine qualities commanded great respect from all, have been less enthusiastically offered the highest place at table when in a foreign country? Probably not.

The serving of a meal, especially for an important occasion, required a corps of servants trained to work efficiently. Medieval ceremonies were elaborate—sometimes ridiculously so—and each servant was obliged to perform his duties skilfully. Chaucer fails to give a detailed description of the process of serving, but he presents in scattered and almost incidental allusions at least the more important officials of the dining hall and implies something of their duties.

---

[140] "Beginning the Board," 376.
[141] *Canterbury Tales,* 501; Robinson, *op. cit.,* 754.
[142] Page 104 (v), 11. 1955-1958.

Besides the squire Damian, who "carf biforn the knight ful many a day,"[143] old January's list of servants included "a squyer, that was marchal of the halle,"[144] and various other squires who assisted with the serving, but whose official positions are not mentioned.[145] In King Cambinskan's establishment there must have been numerous servants, but only the steward, the ushers, and squires in general are named:

> The styward bit the spyces for to hye,
> And eek the wyn, in al this melodye.
> The usshers and the squyers ben y-goon,
> The spyces and the wyn is come anoon.[146]

The Knight's son, the gay young Squire, counted among his many accomplishments that of being an efficient serving-man:

> Curteys he was, lowly, and servisable,
> And carf biforn his fader at the table.[147]

The Host, too, Chaucer says, would be a worthy official among the servants; he is "a semely man . . . to han been a marshal in an halle."[148]

A summary of the foregoing references reveals that Chaucer mentions specifically only the marshal, the steward, the ushers, and the Squire who carved the meat; to all other servants who assisted in the setting of tables and serving the guests, he alludes only in a general manner, or, as in a few cases, implies their existence by referring to the tasks performed.

It is only by studying other sources than Chaucer that one may interpret somewhat fully the significance of these titles and may understand in part what it meant to be a marshal, a steward, and the like. Certainly these were positions considered of much more importance than similar ones today would be. The ability to carve and to serve table properly seems actually to have been regarded as accomplishments of equal rank with those of hunting,

---

[143] E *Mer. T.*, 1773.
[144] *Ibid.*, 1930.
[145] *Ibid.*, 1902. "His squyres stoden ther bisyde."
[146] F *Sq. T.*, 291-294.
[147] A *Gen. Prol.*, 99-100.
[148] *Ibid.*, 751-752.

harping, writing poetry, singing, and so on. It has been aptly said that "manly exercises, manners and courtesy, music and singing, knowledge of the order of precedency of ranks, and ability to carve were . . . more important than Latin and Philosophy."[149] They were taught to the sons of gentlemen at an early age by the servants of another household where the youth spent a period of training.[150]

First in rank among the servants was the steward. He it was who directed all the others, instructing them in their various duties. He also aided the cook in buying food, helped keep accounts of expenditures, and in general managed the dining hall.[151] His office was of such significance that, according to Langland, bishops and bachelors, and tonsured clerics sometimes "serve as servants to lords and ladies, and sit in the seats of steward and butler."[152]

The marshall was likewise an official of importance at the feast. His duties, some of which have been listed above,[153] were of such a nature as to command the respect of his fellow workers. About a half hour before the lord of the house was to dine, the marshall was to take the Rod, a staff signifying his office, and with it in hand was to command the panter and ewer to "make redy for þe lorde and for þe houshold."[154] When everything in the ewery and pantry was prepared, the marshall, together with the server, went to inform the lord, "so þat he may knowe þer by when his mete is redy."[155] Then, with server and esquires, the marshall took his place behind the screen,[156] where with special ceremonies the hands of the lord and his guests were washed.

Meanwhile, the panter and ewer, officers of the pantry and of the ewery or napery, with the assistance of several esquires and

---

[149] *Babees Book,* iv.

[150] *Ibid.,* iv. ff.

[151] *Ibid.,* 196-197 (John Russell "Book of Nurture").

[152] *A Fifteenth Century Courtesy Book,* 11.

[153] Cf. *supra,* 27, 28.

[154] *A Fifteenth Century Courtesy Book,* 11.

[155] *Idem.*

[156] *Ibid.,* 12. In many households the guests washed their hands in the hall itself, rather than in the screens. Mead, *op. cit.,* 150.

grooms covered the tables with cloths laid according to very specific directions, and placed the bread, trenchers,[157] salt, spoons,
knives, and other dishes on the tables. Ridiculous ceremonies attended these duties. Obeisances were made in the middle of the
hall and before the dais, although the lord and his guests were
not yet present. A single example of part of the ceremony will
suffice to illustrate it:

> then the Marshall and the Panter must stande styll, and
> the Caruer must go to the Table, and there kneele on his
> knee, and then aryse with a good countenance, and prop-
> erly take of the Couerpane of the Salt, and geue it to the
> Panter, which must stande styll.[158]

By the time the tables were laid, the lord and his guests were no
doubt ready to enter the hall. As has been seen, they entered preceded by minstrels, or a trumpeter, and were quickly seated according to their social rank.

The duties of the ushers were probably those of minor officials,
namely, to assist the marshall in keeping the hall in order, to
direct guests to their places, to keep the aisles between tables clear
for the servers, and other similar tasks.[159]

Chaucer's only references to this preparation of the hall for
a meal are singularly vague, consisting merely in such expressions
as the following:

> . . . spedily the tables were y-leyd,[160]

and

> . . . with that word she gan the hous to dighte,
> And tables for to sette. . . . .[161]

Doubtless, however, some of the squires he mentions would have
been occupied in tasks such as those described above.

The first requisite of a skillful server at table was the ability to
carve. As has been mentioned, the Squire was capable of carving

---

[157] Trenchers were squares of bread used for plates.
[158] *A Fifteenth Century Courtesy Book,* 18.
[159] *Ibid.,* 11.
[160] B *Sh. T.,* 1442.
[161] E *Cl. T.,* 974-975.

at his father's table.[162]   The Squire Damian, too, in the household of January, was efficient, having carved before his master
"ful many a day."[163]   As soon as this young man was absent from
the feast January missed him and in a speech lamenting his illness
praised his capabilities in words which reveal to the reader the
qualities which a worthy serving-man of the times was expected
to have :

> He is a gentil squyer, by my trouthe!
> If that he deyde, it were harm and routhe ;
> He is as wys, discreet, and as secree
> As any man I woot of his degree ;
> And ther-to manly and eek servisable,
> And for to been a thrifty man right able.[164]

Ironically enough, at the time his master was praising him, Damian
was suffering the pangs of courtly love occasioned by his attraction
to the old man's wife.

Just what did it mean for a young man to be a skillful carver?
To understand something about the procedure he had to observe,
one has only to look at a few of the directions given him.   First
of all, there were certain basic rules to be followed, no matter
what kind of meat was to be carved.   These included having a
sharp knife and knowing the proper way to hold it :

> Son, thy knyfe must be bryght, fayre, and clene,
> and þyne handes faire wassche, it wol þe welle be sene.
> holde alwey thy knyfe sure, þy self not to tene,
> And passe not ij fyngures and a thombe on thy knyfe so kene ;
> In mydde wey of thyne hande set the ende of þe haft sure,
> Unlasynge and mynsynge ij. fyngures with þe thombe that ye
> may endure.[165]

In carving flesh, the squire was directed to cut the brawn on the

---

[162] Cf. *supra*, 124.

[163] E *Mer. T.*, 1773.

[164] *Ibid.*, 1907-1912.

[165] "Boke of Nurture," *op. cit.*, 137.   Wynken de Worde gives an interesting list of terms used in carving.   Some of them are as follows : Breke
that dere, rere that goose, lyft that swanne, sauce that capon, spoyle that
henne, unbrace that mallarde, disfygure that pecocke, etc.   "Boke of
Keruynge," *Babees Book*, 265-286.   The squires must have had difficulties
sometimes in learning such a vocabulary as their lessons in carving included.

dish and lift off the slices with his knife. He was warned, too,
to "pare þe fatt þerfrom" and "to beware of hide and heere."[166]
Large roasted birds, such as geese, teel, mallards, swan, and the
like were disjointed, and the wings and legs placed on a platter
around their bodies.[167] All this and much more the carver had to
learn if he would perform his duties to the satisfaction of his lord.

Medieval romances are full of allusions to serving at table;
many of them are, indeed, more detailed than Chaucer's, and
equally as realistic. It is unnecessary to enumerate examples of
such references; a single one will serve to indicate the extent of
some of the descriptions. The Squire of Low Degree, as marshall of the hall, is pictured as wearing a costume comprised of a
scarlet gown, with a belt trimmed in broad bars. On his head was
a chaplet, and when he entered the hall he carried a white staff or
wand, symbol of his office.[168] To serve his master he "set hym
on his knee" and presented to him the various dishes of the feast,
mentioned above.[169]

In this poem, one finds summarized the names of most of the
important servants in a medieval household:

> The squyer came fro the chambre tho.
> Downe he went into the hall,
> The officers sone gan he call,
> Both ussher, panter, and butler,
> And other that in office were.[170]

The position of the marshall is seen here again to be one of power
over the other officers. He directed his subordinates "to take up
the borde everychone,"[171] and he himself, "lowe he set hym on his
kne," before the king

> And voyded his borde gentely.[172]

---

[166] "Boke of Nurture," *op. cit.*, 141.

[167] *Ibid.*, 24-26.

[168] *The Squyr of Lowe Degre*, 11. 301-313.

[169] Cf. *supra*, 100, 101.

[170] *Squyr of Lowe Degre*, 11. 457-461.

[171] *Ibid.*, 463. *Taking up the borde* refers not only to the removal of the
dishes, cloths, etc., from the tables, but also to the actual taking up of
the boards which lay on trestles and served as tables.

[172] *Ibid.*, 467. To *voyde* or *empty* the board consisted partially in removing
the old trenchers, now soaked with gravy and other liquids, and collecting

It is obvious that there is nothing particularly original in Chaucer's allusions to the serving of a meal. The details are realistic and are inserted just frequently and incidentally enough to seem very natural. There are a few other references than those cited herein which imply certain customs of serving, but they deal principally with washing before meals,[173] and the retiring of the guests to another room where wine and spices were served.[174]

Table Manners and Miscellaneous Matters

Along with the sensuous delight which medieval persons often took in eating there was developing a whole system of table manners not unlike those observed in any age of culture and refinement. Such manners seem almost out of place at tables where guests waited with something like animal eagerness to seize upon great quantities of food. Yet, as one writer has put it, "in theory, at all events, the feast was not merely an occasion for vulgar feeding but a school of manners."[175]

In describing the table manners of his Prioress, Madame Eglentyne, Chaucer sums up the chief points of etiquette which a medieval lady must always have attempted to acquire:

> At mete wel y-taught was she with-alle;
> She leet no morsel from hir lippes falle,
> Ne wette hir fingres in hir sauce depe.
> Wel coude she carie a morsel, and wel kepe,
> That no drope ne fille up-on hir brest.
> In curteisye was set ful much hir lest.

---

them in special containers; the taking away of the dishes, and the stripping the tables of the cloth. All was done with ceremonies similar to those of laying the tables. Cf. *A Fifteenth Century Courtesy Book*, 13-15.

[173] Cf. *TC*, II, 1184.

[174] This refection of wines and spices (a term which included all sorts of sweets of the confectionery kind) was termed the "voydé." (Cf. *TC*, III, 674). It has been suggested that the meaning of the word is a transfer of the term from the utensil to the ceremony, a voyder being a kind of tray, still in use, for the purpose of moving glasses from one room to another. See Chaucer's references to this custom of serving wines and spices: B *Sir Thop.*, 2041-2046; F *Sq. T.*, 291-294, etc.

[175] Mead, *op. cit.*, 156.

> Hir over lippe wyped she so clene,
> That in hir coppe was no ferthing sene
> Of grece, whan she dronken hadde hir draughte.
> Ful semely after hir mete she raughte.[176]

Just what it signified to see someone carry her food to her mouth without letting it fall,[177] dip her fingers into her sauce without getting them wet, and take her meat from the spit[178] or platter without grabbing for it may be understood by comparison with the manners described by St. Bernard in discussing uncleanness at table. The saint's language is forceful; the picture he paints is anything but attractive:

> Some men at table, in their haste to empty the dishes, wrap the table-cloth, or even cast upon it, four-square fragments of crust still moist and dripping with the fat of gravy; until at length, having eaten out of the bowels of the pasty, they cast back the remnants into their former place. Others, as they drink plunge their fingers half-way into the cup. Others, wiping their greasy hands on their frocks, turn again to handle the food. Others fish for their potherbs with bare fingers in lieu of spoon, striving (as it would seem) to wash their hands and refresh their bellies in one and the same broth. Others dip again into the dishes their half-gnawed crusts and bitten morsels; thus, in their haste to make a sop for themselves, plunging that which their teeth have spared into the dish.[179]

That St. Bernard did not overdraw this picture is seen from a study of the rules given in etiquette books of the time and later. Many of the exhortations there included indicate an almost utter

---

[176] A *Gen. Prol.*, 127-136.

[177] Food was generally conveyed to the mouth with one's fingers. Forks had not as yet come into general use, although there is record of several of them in the possession of certain persons. Piers Gaveston, favorite of Edward II, is said to have had among his treasures some silver forks "for eating pears." Quennell, *Everyday Life in Eng.*, 125-126.

[178] The spit was frequently brought in from the kitchen with the roast on it and was passed to the guests, who helped themselves to the meat from it. Wright, *Homes of Other Days*, 168-169.

[179] Quoted by G. G. Coulton, *Medieval Garner* (London, 1910), 98-99, from Hugh of St. Victor, "Rules for Novices," XII-XXI, Migne, *Pat. Lat.*, v. 176, col. 941.

disregard for manners which are now observed by even the rudest of civilized folk. A few of these rules are as follows:

> lik not with þy tonge in a disch, a mote to haue owt.
>
> .   .   .   .   .
>
> Good son, þy tethe be not pikynge, grisynge (grinding), ne gnastynge (gnashing);
>
> .   .   .   .   .
>
> enbrewe (soil) not youre table for þan ye do not ryght
> ne þer-vppon ye wipe youre knyffes, but on youre napkyn plight.[180]
> Let neuer þy cheke be Made to grete
> With morselle of brede þat þou shall ete;
>
> .   .   .   .   .
>
> Ne suppe not with grete sowndynge
> Noþer potage ne oþer þynge.[181]

Further, one was not to let dirt fall on the table, or pick his teeth at meals, or stroke the cat or dog.[182]

Moralists and preachers of Chaucer's time could not but object to the excesses to which their contemporaries had gone in the matter of feasting. Although the subject is too great a one to be considered in detail here, it is interesting and profitable to review briefly the share Chaucer has in reproducing some of the medieval opinions on it. The Pardoner attacks the subject first from the standpoint of gluttony, illustrating his discussion with examples, and crying out in true medieval style:

> O glotonye, ful of cursednesse,
> O cause first of our confusioun,
> O original of our dampnacioun,
> Til Crist had boght us with his blood agayn!
>
> .   .   .   .   .
>
> O, wiste a man how many maladyes
> Folwen of excesse and of glotonyes,
> He wolde been the more mesurable
> Of his diete, sittinge at his table.[183]

Here are no concrete examples such as the Goodman told his

---

[180] "Boke of Nurture," *op. cit.,* 135-138, *passim.*
[181] "The Boke of Curtasye" (Sloane MS., 1986), *Babees Book,* 301-302.
[182] *Ibid.,* 301.
[183] C *Pard. T.,* 498-516, *passim.*

wife. or are found in other sources;[184] rather, they are rhetorical outbursts, strictly conventional.

The Parson's objections are apparently more sincere and based on more varied and more realistic details. In fact, the Parson epitomizes the medieval feast with a great deal of truthfulness and vigorous language:

> Pryde of the table appereth eek ful ofte; for certes, riche men been cleped to festes, and povre folk been put awey and rebuked. Also in excesse of diverse metes and drinkes; and namely, swiche manere bake metes and dish-metes, brenninge of wilde fyr,[185] and peynted and castelled with papir, and semblable wast; so that it is abusion for to thinke. And eek in to greet preciousnesse of vessel and curiositee of minstralcye, by whiche a man is stired the more to delyces of luxurie, if so be that he sette his hert the lasse up-on oure Lord Jesu Crist, certein it is a sinne; and certeinly the delyces mighte been so grete in this caas, that man mighte lightly falle by hem in-to deedly sinne.[186]

Much more forcible than the Pardoner's outburst, this one would probably make even medieval gluttons wince.

It is perhaps unfortunate that Chaucer's allusions to meals are principally to feasts. With the exception of suggestions concerning the daily fare of the Franklin, who after all lived more extravagantly than most persons probably did, and a rather detailed account of the poor widow's diet, the poet really has no other concrete description of the ordinary meals served in medieval homes. In giving his attention mainly to the feast, Chaucer is following the literary tradition of his times and although there is certainly an amount of realism observable in the details presented, yet there is much which could have been of greater descriptive value.

---

[184] These stories are in the nature of tales, but exemplify the excesses of the period in an interesting, if not always edifying manner. Most of them are purely fictional. Cf. *The Goodman of Paris,* 83-84; Coulton, *A Medieval Garner,* 200; 231-232, etc.

[185] For spectacular effects, wine was sometimes poured on food, especially meats, and then lighted.

[186] I *Pars. T.,* 444-446.

The general impression of medieval over-eating is created by too much insistence on the feast, which after all was only occasional—to celebrate a wedding, a tournament, a birthday, for instance—and not characteristic of everyday life. That the people of his England were conscious of rules of temperance and that they often tried to observe them is clearly seen in one or two allusions of the poet. Personal health was by no means flagrantly disregarded. Daun John's advice to the merchant, that he govern his "diete atemprely, and namely in this hete,"[187] shows that temperance in warm weather was especially necessary.

The Physician, with his knowledge of medical science, realized, too, the need of restraint of the appetite and of a well-regulated diet:

> Of his diete mesurable was he,
> For it was of no superfluitee,
> But of greet norissing and digestible.[188]

Here, indeed, is one who not only knew that "many maladyes folwen of excesse and of glotonyes,"[189] but also practiced a praiseworthy moderation.

To enter here into a discussion of the various kinds of wines which are alluded to in Chaucer's works seems of relatively little moment in the consideration of meals and manners. However, it is interesting to observe the names of the most widely used drinks and to study any customs connected with their serving which might differ from those of modern times.

The wines of Chaucer's time are said to have been usually harsh, strong, and sweet, crushed from Tuscan grapes, with which the stalks were often fermented, or brought from Cyprus, Sicily, and other countries.[190] There is much information given in Chaucer's works about the names of some of these wines. Daun John, for instance, brings to his so-called cousin and his wife,

> . . . a jubbe of Malvesye,[191]

---

[187] B *Sh. T.*, 1451-1452.
[188] A *Gen. Prol.*, 435-437.
[189] C *Pard. T.*, 513-516.
[190] Dorothy M. Stuart, *Men and Women of Plantagenet England* (London, 1932), 148.
[191] *Malvesye*, or Malmsey, was a wine of Malvasia (now Napoli di Malvasia), on the eastern coast of the Peleponnesus. Robinson, *op. cit.*, 838.

> And eek another, ful of fyn Vernage,[192]
> And volatyl, as ay was his usage.[193]

Of the Shipman the poet says

> Ful many a draughte of wyn had he y-drawe
> From Burdeux-ward . . .[194]

and of Absolon we are told that as a treat for Alison, besides wafers, "pyping hote out of the glede,"

> He sent hir piment, meeth, and spiced ale.[195]

Other beverages mentioned include ale, Ypocras,[196] white wine of Lepe,[197] and claree.[198]   Frequent references are made to wine without its being specifically named.   So also, to ale, which was widely used.

Wines were generally served with spices.   Often they seem to have been taken to the guests after the meal either in the hall or in another room to which all had gone after the feast.   Diomede, when visiting Criseyde in her father's tent, enjoys wine and spices as he chats with Criseyde:

> The spyces and wyn men forth hem fette.[199]

In January's household wine is served after the feast, while the dancing is in progress:

> And after that, men daunce and drinken faste,
> And spyces al aboute the hous they caste.[200]

---

[192] *Vernage* (Ital. *vernaccia,* the name of a grape) was red wine from Italy, *ibid.,* 838. Cf. also *Mer. T.,* 1807.

[193] B *Sh. T.,* 1260-1262.

[194] A *Gen. Prol.,* 396-397.

[195] These wines are of the sweet kind.   Spiced ale seems to have been a special delicacy.

[196] C *Words of the Host,* 306; E *Mer. T.,* 1807. *Ypocras,* or *ipocras* was a kind of "beverage composed of red wine, spices, and sugar," said to have been so named because a strainer was known as "Hippocrates' sleeve." Robinson, *op. cit.,* 833.

[197] C *Pard. T.,* 563. Lepe: near Cadiz. Cf. Manly, *op. cit.,* 619.

[198] E *Mer. T.,* 1807. "*Claree,* a mixed drink of wine, honey, and spices." *Ibid.,* 776.

[199] *TC,* V, 852.

[200] E *Mer. T.,* 1769-1770. Cf. also A *Gen. Prol.,* 819.

Then after the guests have departed, January again takes wine—ipocras, claree, and vernage—before he retires.[201]

In King Cambinskan's household the wine and spices are apparently taken to the guests in the *chamber of parements* whence they have retired after the banquet to dance and otherwise entertain themselves:

> The styward bit the spyces for to hye,
> And eek the wyn, in al this melodye.[202]

In homes of less wealth ale was served after the meals in the same manner, that is, while persons entertained themselves.[203]

One sees from this brief and perhaps very inadequate review of Chaucer's references to wines that the poet was well acquainted with the names of various kinds[204] and that in general wines were often served with spices after the main courses of the meal.

*   *   *   *

From Chaucer's evidence one learns much exact information concerning medieval meals and manners. The poet's allusions may at times be vague, even almost accidental, but they are generally accurate in detail and but little influenced by conventional descriptions in other works.

Medieval Englishmen had but two regular meals a day, called according to Chaucer, dinner and supper. The first seems to have been served generally at some time after prime, frequently, no doubt, at ten o'clock or later. Supper was served in the evening, and although Chaucer fails to mention any exact hour for it, the inferences to be drawn from his allusions suggest a time before dark, which would vary some according to the season, but must have been about five o'clock ordinarily.

Meals were usually served in the great hall, although the kitchen, chamber, and in some cases pavilions out-of-doors were becoming popular for those of the family and a few guests. Chaucer either

---

[201] *Ibid.,* 1807.

[202] F *Sq. T.,* 291-292.

[203] A *Rv. T.,* 4146-4147.

[204] Chaucer's father was an importer of wine and had a house in Thames Street near Fish Street, a part of the city called the Vintry, because of the wine-merchants. Cf. Manly, *op. cit.,* 619.

mentions the hall directly or suggests it as the place of dining. It seems a little strange that he should not allude to the other rooms in their rather new use.

To the menus served at meals and special feasts there are many references. Some of these are general, being little more than broad statements as to the richness and daintiness of the foods. There are also lists of the names of foods, but unlike his contemporaries, Chaucer limits these lists, usually mentioning only three or four foods which are typical of those served. Of the provident householder whose generous treatment of guests merited for him the title of St. Julian, the poet's information is particularly significant insofar as it lists foods, shows a medieval Epicurean, and suggests the practice of keeping one's larder well stocked.

The poor lived on a meagre diet which is described with remarkable completeness. Incidentally, Chaucer's attitude toward this diet is that usually taken by the well-to-do toward the fare of the poor, namely, that a slender diet had its compensation—it prevented gout and illness. The poet stresses the monotony of the poor widow's meals which were without any sauces or wine to lend variety.

In general the medieval menu was composed largely of fish and flesh, bread, and occasionally dainties, probably sweets or desserts of some sort. Religious, who were bound by virtue of their vocation to lives of abstinence and mortification, are described as being very solicitous about their food. They liked fine meats especially well and did not hesitate to eat them, even though they were departing from the spirit of their profession by so-doing. Much more is suggested than told directly about religious and their fondness for good food.

Of the methods used in preparing foods for consumption there is a general summary, referring to the pounding and mincing of foods, the use of marrow, spices, and the like, and the invention of many sauces to stimulate the appetite. A recipe for cooking chicken with marrow bones and spices is given in vague terms; the particular names of several dishes, such as mortreux, blankmanger, and Jack of Dover are cited. Then a suggestion of deceitful practices in cooking for the public is made.

The serving of a meal in medieval times was accompanied by many ceremonies and required a corps of capable servants. The officers of the dining hall and kitchen were of different ranks and titles, according to their tasks. The cook was of course of great importance; so also were the marshall of the hall, and the steward; various minor serving-men or squires assisted in the work. Chaucer's allusions to servants and their duties are somewhat incidental and scattered throughout the works; yet they serve the purpose of acquainting the reader with some of the titles and a few of the tasks of these men.

Of the custom of having music and dances at meals, particularly at feasts; of the bringing of hawks and hounds into the hall; of the order of precedence observed in seating guests at table; of the code of etiquette followed; of the wines drunk after meals; and of the attitude taken by preachers and moralists regarding eating Chaucer treats in more or less realistic and accurate fashion.

However, to say that the poet gives a complete picture of medieval manners and customs in relation to meals and feasts one would have to overlook his neglect of several important aspects of the subject. It is strange, indeed, that there is no great medieval kitchen with its huge fireplaces wherein whole oxen could be roasted,[205] its ever useful mortars and pestles,[206] and curious pots and pans[207] somewhere in the poet's works. Of course there is no scene in which a kitchen is actually needed, but it is perhaps regrettable that there is not more than a single, vague allusion[208] to this office. Medieval literature was the literature of hall, chamber, and

---

[205] Medieval kitchens sometimes had three or four such ovens. Several of them are known to have been as much as fourteen feet deep. Monastic establishments, especially, along with royal ones, had need of such large ovens. Henry J. Feasey, *Monasticism* (London, 1898), 193.

[206] The mortar and pestle are frequently found listed as bequests in medieval wills. The great love of chopped foods made them popular.

[207] Quoting from Alexander Neckham's *Liber de Utensilibus,* Thomas Wright, "Medieval Manners," *The Art Journal,* XII (Jan. 1, 1860), 45, lists among other kitchen utensils used in the thirteenth century, ". . . pots, trivets or tripods, an axe, a mortar and pestle, a mover, or pot-stick for stirring, a crook, or pothook, a caldron, a frying-pan, a gridiron, a posnet or saucepan, . . . a mier, or instrument for reducing bread to crumbs, etc."

[208] D *WBT,* 869. "Blessinge halles, chambres, kitchenes, boures."

bower rather than of houses of office; it dealt with persons of high rank, usually, and with their amusements rather than with the lower classes and their occupations. Chaucer in this instance, then, clings somewhat closely to contemporary patterns, only occasionally inserting original details or using borrowed ones in an original manner.

Besides neglecting the kitchen, the poet has very little to say about the "greet preciousnesse of vessel"[209] which ornamented the medieval table. The Wife of Bath, alluding to St. Paul's words, remarks that

> . . . a lord in his houshold,
> (He) hath nat every vessel al of gold;
> Some been of tree, and doon hir lord servyse.[210]

Sir Thopas drinks his mead from a "maselyn,"[211] that is, a bowl made of maple wood, but further than these two references, the poet does not present any views of the interesting though scanty tableware of his time.

Other phases of meals and their serving are likewise neglected or treated lightly. There is really no complete menu, no single meal in progress from beginning to end, and no exact description of table serving. Monastic practices are merely suggested and cookery is given only in general outline; many dishes are mentioned, but many are left out. Yet the sum total of the effect produced by a survey of Chaucer's allusions to the subject is that medieval meals and manners are treated with a considerable amount of realistic detail.

---

[209] I *Pars. T.*, 445.
[210] D *WB Prol.*, 99-101.
[211] B *Sir Thop.*, 2041-2042.

CHAPTER IV

DRESS AND PERSONAL ADORNMENT

Allas! may men nat seen, as in oure dayes, the sinful
costlewe array of clothinge, and namely in to muche
superfluitee, or elles in to desordinat scantnesse?
—I *Pars. T.,* 414-415.

In accord with their general attitude toward most things domestic, English men and women of the later Middle Ages showed a
love for fine wearing apparel.[1] Chaucer depicts the attire of various social groups—knights, clerics, professional men, country men,
wives, and nuns to cite but a few—in such a manner as to reveal
the fashions, materials, and accessories which made the dress of
his time distinctive and of significance in the history of English
costume. Further, he indicates the extravagances[2] of the period

---

[1] Among the influences felt on dress of the fourteenth century, that of
the Norman Invasion was perhaps the most powerful. It had been the
cause of numerous changes, chief among which were: (1) a more general
use of furs and silks, (2) the importation of Flemish weavers and the
consequent weaving of better materials, (3) the formation of guilds and
the regulation of cloth-making, (4) some innovations in styles and more
elaborate decorations, and (5) the extension of the toes of shoes. Joseph
Strutt, *A Complete View of the Dress and Habits of the People of England,*
2 vols. (London, 1842), I, 83-111, *passim.*

[2] The influence of a single man's ideas on dress was a great force in the
history of costume in the fourteenth century. It was under the leader-
ship of Piers Gaveston, foppish favorite of Edward II, that the early
years of the century were marked by unusual extravagance in dress. It
has been said that "the germs of all remarkable changes originated in the
court of the unfortunate King Edward II." H. A. Dillon, *Fairholt's Costume in England,* 2 vols. (London, 1896), I, 104.

In the time of Edward III, love of the tournament, increasing interest in
heraldry, and closer communication with foreign countries advanced the
cause of extravagance. The king was no lover of particularly fine dress
and extravagant styles, but his reign was marked by numerous innovations.
Mary M. Wilton, *The Book of Costume* (London, 1834), 120.

Renewed influences of foreign countries—notably Italy, Bohemia, Poland,
Spain, and France—in the reign of Richard II augmented existing peculiari-

and prepares the reader for the tirade of the Parson against them.

Dress in General in Chaucer's Works

There is probably no other phase of medieval manners and customs which Chaucer treats in a more detailed, accurate fashion than he does dress and all that is related to it. Even though he occasionally treats the subject rather broadly or mentions single articles of clothing without describing the complete costume, his usual method is that of the realist. In his translation of the *Romaunt de la Rose* and in other early poems, he shows his dependence on literary models, describing wearing apparel as elaborate and richly ornamented. In his later works, however, particularly in the *Prologue* of the *Canterbury Tales,* he is generally dependent only on his own powers of observation and depicts the attire of his characters more simply and with great exactness of detail. His portraits appear as clearly as those of the illuminations in old manuscripts, having the finish which only a master artist can obtain.

Masculine Dress and Accessories: Civil, Military, Clerical

By far the greater number of Chaucer's characters are men, and thus the knowledge of costume derived from his works is principally of masculine fashions. The allusions include the styles of head dress, of arranging the hair and of trimming the beard, the body clothing worn, footwear, and ornaments of various sorts affected by men to make themselves more attractive. The poet is primarily concerned with persons of the middle classes of society, yet he also more or less completely portrays the dress of several persons of the upper and lower groups.

I

The costumes of royal and noble personages were in Chaucer's lifetime often of remarkable elegance, being extreme of style and

---

ties of fashion by numerous novelties and excesses hitherto unknown in the realm. This was the period of the long-toed shoes, the wide-flowing sleeves which trailed in the dust, and the immodestly short cote-hardies. In the words of Fairholt, "the freaks of everchanging fashion were as varied as the whims of the king—himself the greatest fop." *Costume,* I, 122.

expensive of materials.[3]   The poet's familiarity with court life would seem to have offered him an unusual opportunity to present excellent portraits of gentlemen of high rank; however, his treatment of such persons generally lacks realism, being marked by conventional, sometimes meaningless expressions.   There are possibly one or two exceptions to this, as will be seen by a survey of the author's allusions to royal personages and their costumes.

Although some idea of the elaborately ornamented garments of Nero is obtained from the description Chaucer gives, still there is nothing individualistic about it:

> Of rubies, saphires, and of perles whyte
> Were alle his clothes brouded up and doun;
> For in gemmes greetly gan he delyte.[4]

Certainly this description could be applied to almost any royal robe in any period or country; nothing of the way in which it was fashioned, of its color, or of the material composing it is given.

The attire of Duke Theseus is even more vaguely referred to. He is said to be "arrayed right as he were a god in trone."[5]   So, too, the Marquis Walter is "richely arrayed."[6]   King Cambinskan

> In royal vestiment sit on his deys,
> With diademe, ful heighe in his paleys.[7]

---

[3] An inventory of royal valuables which King Richard II deposited in 1377 with the City of London as security for a loan of 5,000 pounds gives an idea of this monarch's wardrobe.   Besides numerous jewels and plate the garments included were as follows:

 . . . two hoods, one scarlet, embroidered with rubies, balasses (a variety of ruby), diamonds, sapphires, and large pearls; and the other murrey, embroidered with large pearls, without any stones. Also,—one hat, made of blue satin, embroidered with stones and pearls.   Also,—two hats of beaver, embroidered with pearls.   Also, —two coronets for the king's bacinet, with a nouche of five pipes (five vertical flutings) to set in the middle of one of the said coronets.   Also,—one coat of cloth of gold, with a green ground, buttoned with bells of gold, and embroidered with large pearls around the collar and sleeves.   Also,—one doublet of tawney satin, with sleeves embroidered with stones and pearls. . . . Riley, *Memorials of London and London Life,* 411.

[4] B *Mk. T.,* 3658-3660.

[5] A *Kn. T.,* 2529.

[6] E *Cl. T.,* 267.

[7] F *Sq. T.,* 58-60.

The impossibility of forming any kind of satisfactory picture of any of these royal characters is obvious.

Different from the allusions summarized above, the descriptions of the visiting kings at Theseus' tournament are vivid if not entirely characteristic of English manners of dress. Ligurge, the king of Thrace, is in unusual attire:

> In-stede of cote-armure[8] over his harneys,
> With nayles yelwe and brighte as any gold,[9]
> He had a beres skin, col-blak, for-old.[10]

His long, black hair was "kembd bihinde his bak" and on his head he wore a huge wreath of gold, set full "of fyne rubies and of dyamaunts."[11] This description is not entirely original,[12] but it is more impressive than the others so far considered.

Emetreus, the king of Inde, was more elegantly clothed than was Ligurge:

> His cote-armure was of cloth of Tars,[13]
> Couched with perles whyte and rounde and grete.
>
> . . . . .
>
> A mantelet (short mantle) upon his shuldre hanginge
> Bret-ful of rubies rede, as fyr sparklinge.[14]

---

[8] Coat showing the arms, coat-of-arms. Cf. A *Kn. T.*, 1016 ff., ". . . by hir cote-armures. . . .

> The heraudes knewe hem best in special,
> As they that weren of the blood royal
> Of Thebes, and of sustren two y-born.

Cf. also *HF*, 1323 ff., "a vesture which . . . men clepe cote-armure, en-browded wonderliche riche."

[9] "This refers to the ancient practice of gilding an animal's claws when its hide was worn as a cloak." Robinson, *Chaucer's Complete Works*, 780.

[10] A *Kn. T.*, 2140-2142.

[11] *Ibid.*, 2143-2146, *passim*.

[12] It "combines features from Boccaccio's description of Agamennone and Evandro." Cf. Manly, *Canterbury Tales*, 555.

[13] *Cloth of Tars* was "a fine silk imported from Tartary," *idem*. Cf. also Robinson, *op. cit.*, 781.

[14] A *Kn. T.*, 2160 ff.

His yellow hair,[15] hanging in ringlets,[16] was adorned by a garland of green laurel.[17] He rode on a horse trapped in steel covered with cloth of gold[18] and bearing a saddle of "brend gold newe y-bete."[19] Evidently Chaucer here considers the costume worn by an ancient king as like that of his own times. It has been said that the description of Emetreus is somewhat suggestive of Richard II.[20]

The knowledge here gained of royal robes is so slight as to be hardly worthy of notice. The wearing of a garment displaying one's coat-of-arms[21] and richly decorated with jewels of different kinds, the use of the mantle as an outer cloak, the fashion of having the hair uncut and curled, and the adorning the head with garlands of gold or of leaves and flowers are the only exact details given. These, together with the references to the trappings of the horse, suggest certainly the love of fine garments and the extravagant use of jewels and gold.

More definitely characteristic of noblemen's fashions are the allusions found in the *Romaunt de la Rose.* Depending largely upon the French poem, as they do, the descriptions here given are, nevertheless, probably as typical of English as of French costumes.[22]

Cupid and Sir Mirth, in spite of their symbolic significance, may be regarded as representatives of medieval noblemen. Their apparel is strikingly elaborate. Cupid, for example, is clad not in silk, but in a garment so richly embroidered that it seems to be

---

[15] Yellow hair was extremely popular; dyes were probably sometimes used to color hair which was not originally of this shade. Cf. A *Gen. Prol.,* 675; also B *Sir Thop.,* 1920.

[16] The hair was at this time usually worn long. "By the dandy it was elaborately pressed and curled at the ends." Dion C. Calthrop, *English Costume,* 4 vols. (London, 1906), II, 48.

[17] A *Kn. T.,* 2165 ff.

[18] *Ibid.,* 2157-2158.

[19] *Ibid.,* 2162. *Y-bete* may refer to thin sheets of beaten gold, often used for decorative purposes, or to embroidery work. Cf. Manly, *op. cit.,* 542.

[20] Cf. Manly, *op. cit.,* 542.

[21] Cf. Strutt, *Dress and Habits,* II, 29.

[22] At this time French influence on English fashions was notably great, *ibid.,* II, 83-111, *passim.*

"of floures and flourettes." It is painted with *amorettes,* probably love-knots,[23]

> And with losenges[24] and scochouns,[25]
> With briddes, libardes, and lyouns,
> And other beestes wrought ful wel.
> His garnement was everydel
> Y-portreyed and y-wrought with floures,
> By dyvers medling of coloures.
>
> .   .   .   .   .
>
> And many a rose-leef ful long
> Was entermedled ther-among:
> And also on his heed was set
> Of roses reed a chapelet.[26]

Again one notes the heavily embroidered robe and the chaplet of flowers.

The garb of Sir Mirthe is similar in respect to the rich embroidery and the garland of roses, but otherwise his costume is more minutely described as to details of material and style:

> And in samyt, with briddes wrought
> And with gold beten fetisly,
> His body was clad ful richely.
> Wrought was his robe in straunge gyse,
> And al to-slitered for queyntyse[27]
> In many a place, lowe and hye.[28]

Doubtless this robe, made of a rich, glossy silk[29] similar to our satin, embroidered with birds and overlaid with beaten gold, was a long, loose-flowing garment, its edges slashed in imitation of leaves.[30]   It probably had also the voluminous sleeves so popular

---

[23] Cf. Robinson, *op. cit.,* 991.

[24] *Lozenges*—small diamond-shaped shields.   Skeat, *Student's Chaucer,* gloss.

[25] *Escutcheons*—painted shields, *idem.*

[26] Frag. A, 890-908 *passim.*

[27] *Queyntyse,* ornament.   Skeat, *op. cit.,* gloss.

[28] Frag. A, 836-841.

[29] Skeat, *op. cit.,* gloss.   Cf. also *TC,* 109—"In widowes habit large of samit broun."

[30] Cf. Herbert Macklin, *The Brasses of England* (London, 1907), 58-60; *Fairholt's Costume,* I, 126-127; II, 134; Joseph R. Planché, *History of British Costume,* third ed. (London, 1874), 168.

in the later Middle Ages. The costume was completed by shoes fashionably cut and laced,[31] and the almost inevitable garland of roses which his sweetheart had made[32] for him. Such attire is found illustrated in nearly all the popular works dealing with later medieval costume.

Actually, Chaucer's own treatment of the dress of the upper classes differs in several respects from the usual treatment accorded it. Chiefly to be noted is the lack of detail in his method, which can best be observed by a comparison with several contemporary works. Sir Launfal, for example, is dressed in a purple garment elaborately trimmed in white ermine.[33] Sir Gawayne, although wearing garments which are all green, is described with much more attention to his clothing than Chaucer gives to that of most of his royal and noble characters:

> And al graþed in grene þis gome and his wedes:
> A strayt cote in ful streʒt, þat stek on his sides,
> A mere mantile abof, mensked withinne
> With pelure pured apert, þe pane ful clene
> With blyþe blaunner ful bryʒt, and his hode boþe,
> þat wat laʒt fro his lokke and layde on his schulderes;
> Heme wel-haled hose of þat same grene,
> þat spenet on his sparlyr, and clene spures vnder
> Of bryʒt golde, vpon silk bordes barred ful ryche,
> And scholes vnder schankes ere þe schalk rides.[34]

The knight, dressed all in green as he was, does not exemplify the use of many colors which the people of his country often liked. The straight, close-fitting coat, which "stek on his sides," was

---

[31] Frag. A, 842-843. The shoes in Chaucer's time were of extreme length, the toes having increased in length to about six inches. They were made of nearly any kind of material, "sewn with pearls on cloth or velvet, stamped with gold on leather, or the leather raised." The points of the shoes were stuffed or wired into the desired shape, or were allowed to hang limp. Calthrop, *op. cit.,* II, 128-129; Mary Evans, *Costume Throughout the Ages* (Chicago, 1930), 125.

[32] Frag. A, 845-846.

[33] "Sir Launfal," Ritson, p. 359, 11. 416-418. An illustration of just such a costume is that of the King pictured with St. Etheldreda (the Queen). In this latter the King wears a gown of red, trimmed with bands of ermine. See George Clinch, *English Costume* (London, 1909), facing 49.

[34] *Sir Gawayne and the Green Knight,* 5-6, 11, 151-160.

evidently the cote-hardie,[35] and the gay mantle adorned with fur lining, the lining trimmed down so as to show only one colour ("with pelure pured apert"),[36] were distinctly realistic. So, too, the hood which was laid back on the knight's shoulders, the close-fitting hose of green, and the *scholes,* or shoes having the long, pointed toes. His was indeed a noble costume.

It is unnecessary to cite further examples of the realistic treatment accorded dress by the writers of romances. The subject has been discussed recently by Mr. Harvey Eagleson who agrees that in general the romances describe the styles of their own times.[37] Since they are concerned with persons of royal or noble birth, they generally present the habiliments of these classes and it is from the romances, then, that much of our most valuable information on this subject is obtained. In many instances Chaucer improves their methods; but in describing the costume of the upper classes he does not.

In considering the allusions which Chaucer makes to the dress of persons of lower classes of society, it is well to bear in mind that the characters of these groups are found chiefly in the *Prologue* of the *Canterbury Tales.* This is significant, because it imposes upon the poet the obligation of moderate treatment. He may, and does show the pilgrims as dressing in fashion but not in the extreme manner adopted by many persons of the time. Factors contributing to his limitations are: (1) the pilgrims, be-

---

[35] There seem to have been several types of dress worn by the men of Chaucer's day, the types varying according to the wealth and caprice of the wearer, but in outline being as follows:

(1) close tunics, or cote-hardies, buttoned down the front and reaching to the middle of the thighs. These were worn with tight hose or breeches and long-toed shoes. Often an ornamental girdle about the hips supported a small dagger or anelace;

(2) a plain gown and hood with no buttons. Low, pointed slippers;

(3) a long tunic, sometimes voluminous and again rather close-fitting, and a wide mantle buttoned on the right shoulder and thrown over the left arm.

Macklin, *op. cit.,* 58-60; Fairholt, *op. cit.,* I, 126-127; II, 134.

[36] *Gawayne and the Green Knight,* gloss.

[37] "Costume in the Medieval Metrical Romances," *PMLA,* 47 (June, 1932), 339-345.

ing on a journey which is at least ostensibly motivated by religious zeal, would not be likely to appear in their most elaborate garments; (2) they are riding horse-back over dusty or perhaps muddy roads and could ill afford to wear their finest clothing; and (3) they are not of the classes, i. e., royal and noble ones, who most indulged in the excesses of the time.

It is natural that the Squire should appear more attractively dressed than most of the Canterbury pilgrims. He was a young man, and "a lovyere" who probably did more than bear himself well in battle "in hope to stonden in his lady grace."[38] Indeed he has rightly been considered a fourteenth century Beau Brummell, with his locks curled "as they were leyd in presse,"[39] and his fashionable gown with its long, wide sleeves,

> Enbrouded . . . as it were a mede
> Al ful of fresshe floures, whyte and rede.[40]

Chaucer neglects to tell us the colors of the gown, but the Ellesmere Manuscript shows it as green, lined with red, and embroidered or "poudred" with tiny white figures.[41] Such a combination is truly suggestive of a field of flowers. If the gown was actually meant by Chaucer to be of this color, the symbolic significance is not to be disregarded.[42]

The poet does not completely describe the youthful Squire's garments, as is here seen. In the Ellesmere Manuscript, however, it is shown as including a tall-crowned blue hat[43] with an embroidered

---

[38] A *Gen. Prol.*, 88.

[39] *Ibid.*, 81.

[40] *Ibid.*, 89-93, *passim.*

[41] Robinson's suggestion (*op. cit.,* 754) that these lines refer to the Squire's complexion seems to me an unnecessary, if not far-fetched interpretation.

[42] Green seems to have been the symbol of amorous passion. Johan Huizinga, *The Waning of the Middle Ages* (London, 1924), 249. It is interesting to note that in the *Squire's Tale* green is used as a sign of inconstancy; blue of fidelity. Cf. 644-647.

[43] Cf. *supra,* 141, f.n. 3. The blue hat belonging to Richard II may have been similar to this one of the Squire. Medieval gentlemen wore various styles of hoods and hats, including fur or felt caps which were round with rolled-up brims, and a peak; tall-crowned round hats with close, thick brims; and long peaked hats with a single feather as decoration. The most popular hood was the chaperon, which had developed from a hood and cape worn

design, possibly of pearls, thereon, white pantaloons, a girdle decorated with small ornaments, and sharp-pointed shoes.

Of the professional men of medieval England, Chaucer's Man
of Law and Physician are outstanding examples. These gentlemen
held positions of importance and could afford to wear fine garments. However, there is little indication that either of them in
this instance was garbed in clothes of extraordinary quality or
style.

The Man of Law, we are told,

> . . . rood but hoomly in a medlee cote
> Girt with a ceint of silk, with barres smale."

Medlee, or *medley,*[45] was a cloth of mixed weave, sometimes parti-
colored.[46] The Ellesmere Manuscript shows the Man of Law in
a robe of red and blue trimmed with fur. He wears a white hood
and coif, indicative of his profession; his hose are red and his
shoes pointed. This illustration is perhaps fairly accurate, at least
in accord with the usual costume adapted by the medieval sergeant
of law; the ordinary dress of the lawyer at this period was "a long
priest-like robe with a cape around the shoulders furred with
lambskin, a hood with two labels such as doctors of the law wear
in the universities, and a white coif of silk."[47]

The silken *ceint* or girdle, with its "bars," which the Man of
Law wore, furnishes an example of one of the most colorful of
medieval accessories of dress. Until the fourteenth century, gowns

---

separately, but later joined so that they might be put on at once. The peak
of the hood had been lengthened until it reached the feet of the wearer.
Then it was twisted about the head, with the end of the cape protruding like
a cockscomb. This chaperon was worn by men of practically all classes.
Calthrop, *op. cit.,* II, 106-130, *passim.*

[44] A *Gen. Prol.,* 328-329.

[45] One finds many references to medley in the old records. In the will of
one Blase de Bury, skinner, for example, is mention of a cloak of Red-
melle (red medley). *Calendar of Wills,* ed. R. R. Sharpe, 2 vols. (London, 1889), II, 257; in the will of Wm. de Madeford, "one curtpy of black
medlet," *ibid.,* II. 13.

[46] Cf. Linthicum, " 'Faldyng' and 'Medlee,' " *JEGP,* 34 (Jan., 1935), 39-41.

[47] J. M. Manly, *Some New Light on Chaucer* (New York, 1926), 143.

had generally been allowed to flow in loose folds from the shoulders; with the increasing love of finery, however, there arose the use of highly ornamented belts or girdles. Inventories and wills bear witness to the unusual value of many of these articles; nearly every gentleman had at least one to bequeath to his heirs. William Brangewayn, a vintner, left to his wife "his silver girdle de Wreches (riches);"[48] Thomas de Frowyke, to his son, "all his girdles harnessed with silver."[49] Still other wills showed bequests of "a girdle of blue silk with griffons of gold,"[50] "a silk girdle with imitation roses in silver,"[51] and "a silk girdle powdered with pearls."[52] Besides being ornamental[53] to a costume, girdles were used to suspend knives or daggers, as was the fashion, especially when short gowns were worn. The Franklin, it will be recalled, wore an *anlas,* or knife, and a *gypser,* or purse hanging

> . . . at his girdel, whyt as morne milk.[54]

The Physician was, like the Man of Law, richly gowned.

> In sangwin and in pers he clad was al,
> Lyned with taffeta and with sendal.[55]

Sangwin (blood-red) and *pers* (light blue) seem to have been a usual combination for garments in the Middle Ages; illuminations frequently show them parti-coloured in these two shades. Chaucer's Physician wears, according to the Ellesmere Ms., a plainly fashioned gown or tunic of this bright red colour, with trimmings of blue. The sleeves of the gown are of medium fulness, the hood is trimmed with white fur, and the shoes are of the fashionable

---

[48] *Cal. Wills,* II, 41.

[49] *Ibid.,* 170.

[50] *Ibid.,* 190.

[51] *Ibid.,* 214.

[52] *Ibid.,* 97.

[53] The girdle of Rychesse in the *Romaunt de la Rose,* A, 1103-1105, was very ornamental. It had a buckle of stone "ful precious," and

> The barres were of gold ful fyne,
> Upon a tissu of satyne,
> Ful hevy, greet, and no-thing light.

[54] A *Gen. Prol.,* 357-358.

[55] *Ibid.,* 439-440.

pointed-toe variety. That the dress was rich in spite of its apparent simplicity of cut is indicated by the reference to the silken linings. *Taffata* and *sendal* were frequently used not only for linings as in this case, but also for the garments themselves. The former, a heavy quality of silk, probably somewhat similar to present-day taffeta, seems to have been popular with persons of the wealthy classes; Queen Isabella, for example, is said to have had many gowns "of shot taffety," i. e., of changeable coloured taffeta.[56] Sendal, a softer and thinner silk, was perhaps more commonly used.[57]

The descriptions Chaucer gives of the garments of other pilgrims belonging to the business and working classes are if anything more distinctive in general than those of the foregoing characters. The Merchant, belonging as he did to a group which was rapidly becoming wealthy and consequently influential, is pictured in a fashionable and somewhat expensive costume. His forked beard was in itself a sign of the Merchant's attention to the latest styles, and his attire was further evidence of it:

> A Marchant was ther with a forked berd,
> In mottelee, and hye on horse he sat,
> Up-on his heed a Flaundrish bever hat;
> His botes clasped faire and fetisly.[58]

Motley here refers to "cloth woven with a figured design, often parti-coloured," which was in "regular use for members of various gilds and companies," and was the distinctive dress of the Merchants of the Staple to which he probably belonged.[59] His hat,

---

[56] Strickland, *Lives of the Queens of England,* II, 152.

[57] It is said that fine linen may also have been called sendal. In 1350, in regulations as to wages and prices in the City of London, it was provided "that the tailors shall take for making a gown garnished with say (serge) and with sendal, 18 d." Riley, *Memorials,* 254.

In a schoolboy's inventory of about 1380 are included "to sendall gownys." The inventory may have been of Edmund de Stonor's son. *Supplementary Stonor Letters and Papers,* No. 338, 2.

[58] A *Gen. Prol.,* 270-273.

[59] Robinson, *op. cit.,* 759.

manufactured in Flanders,[60] and his stylish boots with their "faire" clasps[61] further marked the Merchant as a man of wealth.[62]

It is interesting here by way of comparison to glance at the inventory of Richard Toky's[63] wardrobe. Toky, as a grocer, probably belonged to the same class as Chaucer's Merchant; his wardrobe may perhaps be taken as representative of that possessed by the average merchant of the fourteenth century. In part, the inventory includes:

> . . . one long shirt, one night-gown and one night-cap; one vernicle;[64] two fossers, one pair of gloves; . . . one gown slashed with russet, furred with lambswool; one short gown; two pieces of woollen cloth of shot colours; one slashed gown of the Grocers' livery; one gown of russet with caps; one gown of black fresed; one fur of otir; . . . six caps; five pairs of hose; . . . *one beaver hat;* one gown of blood-colour furred with crestigray; one gown of blood colour furred with crestigray (of less value than the other); one russet gown furred with bys. . . .[65]

This was indeed no mean wardrobe for a gentleman of Chaucer's day.

The Miller's costume is less fully described than that of the Merchant. Again the beard is referred to; this time, however, the cut of it is less fashionable:

> His berd as any sowe or fox was reed,
> And ther-to brood, as though it were a spade.[66]

---

[60] According to Manly, such hats were worn by the upper classes. They were of various shapes and prices. They could be bought in London, although the Merchant may have purchased his abroad. *Canterbury Tales,* 514.

[61] These boots were probably half-boots with clasps up the front. See *Fairholt's Costume,* II, 67-68. Cf. also F *Sq. T.,* 555, "Ne were worthy unbokele his galoche."

[62] "The dress and appearance of the Merchant were designed to impress the public with a sense, not of his sedateness, but of his wealth." Manly, *op. cit.,* 513.

[63] Cf. *supra,* 18, 28.

[64] Cf. *infra,* 169.

[65] *Calendar of Select Pleas and Memoranda of the City of London,* ed. Arthur H. Thomas (London, 1926), III, 210 ff.

[66] A *Gen. Prol.,* 552-553.

In remarkably few yet vivid words the Miller's clothing is depicted:

> A whyte cote and a blew hood wered he.[67]

The coat was probably a long robe with wide sleeves; the hood a type of the chaperon.[68]

Another miller, namely, Simkin of the *Reeve's Tale,* is pictured as being particularly fond of accessories:

> And by his belt he baar a long panade (knife),
> And of a swerd ful trenchant was the blade.
> A joly popper baar he in his pouche:[69]
> Ther was no man for peril dorste him touche.
> A Sheffeld thwitel[70] baar he in his hose.[71]

Besides his knives and dagger, Simkin wore two distinctive articles of dress; one was a hood with the fashionable tippet, the other a pair of red hose the same shade as his wife's gown. The picture of this miller and his wife on their way to church on holy days is a striking one, though brief in its details:

> On haly-dayes biforn hir wolde he go
> With his tipet bounden about his heed,
> And she cam after in a gyte of reed;
> And Simkin hadde hosen of the same.[72]

Other examples of civil costume worn by fourteenth century men are found in Chaucer's description of the Reeve, the Shipman, the Plowman, and Sir Thopas. The Reeve, who describes himself as an elderly man,[73] wore his beard shaved as close as

---

[67] *Ibid.,* 564.

[68] Cf. *supra,* 147, f.n. 43.

[69] A popper was a dagger. *Pouche* here probably means pocket. Skeat, *op. cit.,* gloss.

[70] A *Sheffeld thwitel* was a knife manufactured in Sheffield, a place "famous then as now for its cutlery." Robinson, *op. cit.,* 790.

[71] A 3929-3933. The knife was probably carried in some kind of garter round the miller's leg.

[72] *Ibid.,* 3952-3955.

[73] A *Rv. Prol.,* 3869. "This whyte top wryteth myne olde yeres," etc.

possible. His hair was close-cropped, as was the custom for persons in servile positions,[74] and of his dress Chaucer says that

> A long surcote of pers up-on he hade,
> And by his syde he bar a rusty blade.[75]

This long outer gown of light blue he had fastened up about his waist, probably with a girdle; "tukked he was, as is a frere,"[76] the poet says.

The Shipman was garbed

> In a gowne of falding[77] to the knee.[78]

More than this we do not know about his costume, except that he had a "laas" or string about his neck, and from it hung a dagger.[79]

The Plowman, lowliest of the Canterbury pilgrims, was the most simply dressed. He wore a tabard,[80] or a kind of sleeveless jacket of which Chaucer mentions neither the kind of material nor the color. We may believe it was a nondescript garment such as only the poorer classes of the time would be obliged to wear.[81] It is interesting to compare this costume with that worn by the shepherd in "A Tale of King Edward and the Shepherd," written in the early fifteenth century. The shepherd is described as wearing a russet kirtle and a courtpy. On his head he had a black furred hood which was especially well-fitting, and of which the author says, "that wel fast to his cheke stode, the typet myght not wrye"[82] (become awry). It is clear that this was a much better costume than that worn by the Plowman.

Further allusions to civil costume as worn by men of the middle and lower classes add but little to our information on the subject.

---

[74] Robinson, *op. cit.*, 768.

[75] A *Gen. Prol.*, 617-618.

[76] *Ibid.*, 621; cf. Robinson, *op. cit.*, 768.

[77] Cf. *supra*, 36, f.n. 178.

[78] A *Gen. Prol.*, 391.

[79] *Ibid.*, 392-393.

[80] *Ibid.*, 541;

[81] Cf. Manly, *op. cit.*, 530. Note the description of the ploughman's dress in *Piers the Ploughman's Crede*, ed. W. W. Skeat, EETS, OS 30 (London, 1867), ll. 421-429.

[82] C. Hartshorne, ed. *Ancient Metrical Tales* (London, 1829), 60.

The Haberdasher, Carpenter, Weaver, Dyer, and Tapestry-worker
are

> . . . clothed in o liveree,
> Of a solempne and greet fraternitee.[83]

However, Chaucer furnishes no description of this livery other
than it was fresh and newly trimmed.[84]   Their knives, he says,
were *y-chaped,* that is, had metal ends on their sheaths[85] made not
of brass but of silver, and their girdles and pouches were wrought
with silver, "ful clene and weel."[86]

What appears to have been the typical costume of the medieval
huntsman was worn by the Knight's Yeoman and by the Yeoman
in the *Friar's Tale.*   The former "was clad in a cote and hood of
grene";[87] the latter "hadde up-on a courtepy[88] of grene," and "an
hat up-on his heed with frenges (strings) blake."[89]   Both carried
"arwes brighte and kene."   The Knight's Yeoman wore on his
breast a *Cristofre*—a small image of St. Christopher, the patron
saint of foresters—made of silver and worn as a talisman.[90]

It is difficult to say how seriously one should regard Sir Thopas'
garb.   His hair and beard, yellow "lyk saffroun" seem absurd,
particularly since the beard "to his girdel raughte adoun,"[91] in the
fashion of an earlier time, but neither the shoes of "Cordewane"—
a fine leather, "Cordovan," manufactured originally in Spain[92]—
nor his brown hose of cloth made in Bruges[93] appear to be so.
The material of his robe was "ciclatoun,"[94] an expensive cloth
"supposed to have been brought from Persia,"[95] but Chaucer gives

---

[83] A *Gen. Prol.,* 363-364.
[84] *Ibid.,* 365.
[85] Skeat, *op. cit.,* gloss.
[86] A *Gen. Prol.,* 366 ff.
[87] *Ibid.,* 103.
[88] A courtpy was a short, jacket-like garment.   Skeat, *op. cit.,* gloss.
[89] D 1382-1383.
[90] A *Gen. Prol.,* 115; cf. also Robinson, *op. cit.,* 754.
[91] B *Sir Thop.,* 1920-1921.
[92] *Fairholt's Costume,* II, 131.
[93] B *Sir Thop.,* 1922-1923.
[94] *Ibid.,* 1924.
[95] Fairholt, *op. cit.,* II, 120.

no further description of it than that it "coste many a jane."[98] Certainly these garments do not befit the knight so popular in English medieval social life. Rather, the description of them suggests the merchant or, as Manly puts it, the tradesman, and is probably designed to satirize the bourgeois knight of Flanders.[97]

The foregoing consideration of civil costume as seen in Chaucer's works shows that with some degree of accuracy the poet has presented practically all of the significant distinctions in the dress of various groups of medieval men. It may be true that he is not particularly interested in the attire of royal or noble personages; nevertheless his descriptions of it indicate the extravagant use of fine materials and elaborate ornamentation, together with some of the characteristic garments—the *cote armure* and the mantle—affected by them.

Further, the poet shows something of the combinations of colors, the kinds of cloth, the trimmings and linings, and the fashions which such persons as the Man of Law, the Physician, the Miller, the Plowman and others used. He describes accessories, emphasizing the carrying of knives and daggers, the wearing of different types of hats, colorful hose and pointed shoes, and the use of garlands of flowers as head dress. He indicates also the growing tendency to adopt garments made in foreign countries, in one case satirizing it as an affectation of certain types of persons. With a few exceptions in the descriptions of the upper classes, the poet's treatment of costume is startlingly realistic and effective.

II

Although Chaucer has but a few references to armour, which was in his time the accepted military costume, his treatment of it is surprisingly complete. He approaches the subject in two distinct ways—seriously and satirically—and it is in some cases difficult to distinguish between the real and the absurd. However, a careful consideration of all the references helps one to reach certain conclusions which, if not entirely trustworthy, may throw some light on armour in general.

---

[96] B *Sir Thop.*, 1925.
[97] *Op. cit.*, 630.

The institution of Chivalry had already begun to decline in the fourteenth century, with the result that the knight's accoutrement[98] was now beginning to be determined more and more by individual caprice. Chaucer, himself, suggests this fact in succinct fashion, when after describing the armour of Palamon's knights, he says,

> Armed were they, as I have you told,
> Everich after his opinion.[99]

What an array of various parts of knightly accoutrement this manner of arming themselves produced is indicated in at least a partial list of what these knights wore:

> Som wol ben armed in an habergeoun,
> In a brest-plat and in a light gipoun;
> And somme woln have a peyr plates large;
> And somme woln have a Pruce sheld, or a targe;
> Somme wol ben armed on hir legges weel,
> And have an ax, and somme a mace of steel.
> Ther nis no newe gyse, that it nas old.[100]

Certainly some of the principal features of fourteenth century armour are included in this list. The habergeoun, for instance, seems to have comprised the main part of the armour covering the upper half of the body, and to have been the most important piece. Originally it had been a sleeveless jacket of mail or scale,

---

[98] In general, it may be said that the latter half of the fourteenth century, if it had a distinctive type of armour, had turned from the use of chain mail to that of plate. There were some remains of the chain, such as the camail—a kind of collar or cape of mail, attached to the helmet—the gussets of chain at the joints, and some remnants of the chain apron; but the main part of the armour seems to have been of plate. The head was protected by the bascinet, or helmet, which was equipped now with a visor, or moveable face-guard, and the feet by sollerets having overlapping plates which were riveted together. Over the body of the armour was worn a *gipoun,* or *jupon,* which had replaced the surcoat of earlier days. Other pieces of armour were sometimes added to these, but in general this comprised the knight's accoutrement. Cf. Planché, *op. cit.,* 134-137; Macklin, *op. cit.,* 50 ff.; Charles H. Ashdown, *Armour and Weapons in the Middle Ages* (London, 1925), 101 ff., etc.

[99] A *Kn. T.,* 2126-2127.

[100] *Ibid.,* 2119-2125.

smaller and lighter than a hauberk, but sometimes apparently the same as that.[101] In the *Buke of the Order of Knyghthood* the author compares the habergeoun to a castle made of stones; composed of pieces of mail, it protects the knight from his foes.[102] Whether this breast plate, as it may perhaps be called, was worn over or under the gipoun is difficult to tell, and is not an important enough matter to have received all the attention given it by various authors.[103]

The discussion of the habergeoun and gipoun has arisen from Chaucer's allusions to them in regard to the Knight's costume:

> Of fustian he wered a gipoun
> Al bismotered with his habergeoun.[104]

The gipoun is generally described as "a close-fitting tunic without sleeves,"[105] which reached to mid-thigh. It was laced up the back, or at one side, in which latter case it was generally at the left. The hem was either scalloped or dagged, and in most cases elaborately embroidered.[106] The one worn by the Knight, however, seems to have been very plain. It was made of fustian, generally described as "a kind of coarse cloth made of cotton and flax,"[107] although Fairholt says that woollen fustians were made as early as 1336.[108] The Knight's gipoun was by no means a garment of rich workmanship; certainly it was not emblazoned with jewels

---

[101] Planché, *op. cit.*, 161. There are many references to the habergeoun in wills and medieval literature. Cf. *Cal. of Wills*, II, 149; *Fifty Earliest English Wills*, 19; "Amis and Amiloun," in *Early English Romances of Friendship*, ed. Edith Rickert (London, 1908), 48; *Piers Plowman's Vision and Creed*, ed. T. Wright, 2 vols. (London, 1887), II, xviii, 11. 12116-12118.

[102] Trans. from the French by Sir Gilbert Hay, Knight, ed. by Beriah Botfield (Edinburgh, 1847), 39. This fifteenth century work is significant in the study of the chivalric system, particularly in regard to the symbolism of the various parts of armour, the colors used in heraldry, etc.

[103] Macklin, *op. cit.*, 50; Hinckley, *Notes on Chaucer*, 7; Ashdown, *op. cit.*, 100 hold that the habergeoun was worn under the gipoun. Planché, *op. cit.*, 176 holds that it was worn over it.

[104] A *Gen. Prol.*, 75-76.

[105] Macklin, *op. cit.*, 50.

[106] Ashdown, *op. cit.*, 101.

[107] NED; cf. also Strutt, *Dress and Habits*, II, 13-14.

[108] *Costume*, 175.

or ornately embroidered as such a garment sometimes was. In the Ellesmere Manuscript it is pictured as a plain, fully-fashioned gipoun of a grayish color, with rust stains on it, but no embellishments of any kind. It appears in this case, at least, that it had been worn under the habergeoun, which had probably been removed before the Knight set out on his journey.[109] Having but lately come from his "viage," the Knight was evidently more concerned about his pilgrimage to Canterbury than he was about any gay external trappings. Besides, he had been in haste to join his companions and it mattered little to him that his gipoun was "al bismotered with his habergeoun."

The arming of Sir Thopas, the pseudo-knight of Chaucer's own tale on the Canterbury journey, has long been of interest to students, having been variously regarded either as an exact account of what the well-armoured knight of the period wore,[110] or as an absurd description meant to satirize the armour of the times.[111] What the poet's intention in portraying Sir Thopas was, can of course not be determined; the details of the arming of the knight must speak for themselves and each reader interpret as he will. It is certain that Chaucer's description gives the effect of verisimilitude:

> He dide next his whyte lere (skin)
> Of clooth of lake fyn and clere
>   A breech and eek a sherte;
> And next his sherte an aketoun,[112]
> And over that an habergeoun
>   For percinge of his herte;

---

[109] Planché, *op. cit.*, 176.

[110] Among those who consider the description in this light are Samuel R. Meyrick, *A Critical Inquiry into Antient Armour* (London, 1842), II, 76; Oswald Barron, "Arms and Armour," *Encyclopedia Britannica*, eleventh ed. (1910), II, 587; Planché, *op. cit.*, 176-178; Irving Linn, "The Arming of Sir Thopas," *MLN*, 51 (May, 1936), 300-311. Cf. also Robinson, *op. cit.*, 845.

[111] James M. Manly, "Sir Thopas: A Satire," *Essays and Studies* (Oxford, 1928), XIII, 70 ff.

[112] The *aketoun* (haqueton, haketon) was "a tunic of leather, buckram, etc., stuffed with wool or tow . . . and was worn beneath the hauberk (habergeoun?) so as to diminish the weight of the chain mail." Clinch, *op. cit.*, 71.

> And over that a fyn hauberk,
> Was al y-wroght of Jewes werk[113]
>   Ful strong it was of plate;
> And over that his cote-armour
> As whyte as is the lily-flour,
>   In which he wol debate.[114]

The discussion as to the realism of Sir Thopas' armour need not be reviewed here, since it has recently been treated in a capable manner by Mr. Irving Linn;[115] however, there may be added to Mr. Linn's observations on the subject several others which may be of only slight importance, but which seem to aid in the interpretation of Chaucer's description.

Even though Mr. Manly had been right in his assertion that "the knight armed for battle or tournament did not wear next his skin breeches and shirt of silk, linen, or any other thin cloth,"[116] is it not fitting that Sir Thopas—a knight of unusually fine sensibilities—should have done so? Whatever the heavily-padded garment usually worn under the armour—be it aketoun, or "jerkin" (as Manly suggests)—would it not perhaps have been of leather, buckram, or some similar material which would have scratched or prickled the knight's skin unless something were worn between it and the body? In short, the silken shirt and breeches are at least realistic in their use by Sir Thopas as Chaucer has betrayed him. Mr. Linn, aided by Strutt's work, further shows that the hero of romance frequently wore such garments.

Strictly speaking, the aketoun appears to have gone out of use

---

An interesting regulation affecting the aketoun was made in about 1322 by the armourers of London. It provided:

> That a haketon and a gambeson (stuffed and quilted vest) covered with sendale, or with cloth of silk, shall be stuffed with new cotton cloth, and with cadaz (flocks of silk, tow, cotton, or wool), and with sendales, and in no other manner. And that white haketons shall be stuffed with old woven cloth, and with cotton, and made of new cloth within and without.

Riley, *Memorials,* 145.

[113] Jews seem to have been famous as armourers and workers in metal from early times. Cf. Robinson, *op. cit.,* 845.

[114] B *Sir Thop.,* 2047-2059.

[115] *Loc. cit.,* 300-311.

[116] "Sir Thopas: A Satire," 71.

some time before 1348;[117] still that would not prevent individual knights from retaining it as a part of their armour. Sir Thopas, being pictured as one not bound by the fashions of his time (cf. the long beard) and likewise only blusteringly brave, would probably have preferred the added protection of the well-padded aketoun to being in style. Similarly, the absurdity of the double protection of the habergeoun—which may have been of the chain mail variety—and the hauberk, which was of plate may lie rather in this over-solicitation of Sir Thopas for personal safety than in their being worn, one on top of the other.

Granted that the white cote-armour refers to the absence of armorial bearings,[118] there seems further significance in the fact that it is described as "white." White, as one of the colours used symbolically in their application to armour, is said to have signified cleanness, purity, and innocence.[119] Satirical though Chaucer may have been in his allusion to Sir Thopas as "chast and no lechour,"[120] and to "the lily-flour," a symbol of purity, which he wore in his crest,[121] still the white cote-armour is again in harmony with the characteristics assigned to the knight.

It is to be noted that although Chaucer described very briefly the armour of the pilgrim Knight, he does contrariwise with that of Sir Thopas. Even to the jambeux (the leg protectors) of quirboilly,[122] his sword sheath of ivory, his metal helmet, and his cypress spear, Sir Thopas is completely protected. His gold shield, ornamented with a "bores heed" and a stone as precious as the "charbocle," give added brilliance to his array. All these details have elements of realism. Jambeux were worn, even though they were usually of metal rather than of quirboilly in the

---

[117] Macklin, *Brasses*, 50. The last figure which shows the aketoun is that of Sir John Giffard, 1348.

[118] Manly, *op. cit.*, 71.

[119] *Buke of Knyghthood*, 83.

[120] B *Sir Thop.*, 1935.

[121] *Ibid.*, 2097.

[122] This was a boiled leather. Prepared in oil and softened, it could be moulded into the desired form. As it dried it toughened. It was much used at this period, not only for armour, but also for other work such as for effigies and the like. Cf. Planché, *British Costume*, 177.

latter part of the century. Just so, the material of the sword sheath, of the helmet, and of the spear bespoke the artificial character of Sir Thopas as a knight. That the sword and spurs were not mentioned gives evidence of unmistakable satire,[123] for no true knight was ever without sword and spur, unless he were in disgrace.

From all the allusions made by Chaucer to the proper arming of a knight, even though some of them are vague and incomplete and others are strongly marked with satire, one discerns that the poet is primarily concerned with the actual accoutrement of his own times. His vocabulary is similar to that used in records and other literary works and even though much remains unmentioned by him which might have made the picture of the knight's armour more distinct and less subject to discussion, the cumulative effect is that of realism.

III

More fully and clearly described than any other costumes in Chaucer's works are those of religious men. The poet seems to show here to the fullest extent his powers of accurate observation, his ability to express much in few words, and his remarkable use of concrete detail. He presents various types of religious habit in a manner to reveal not only the conditions existing in certain monastic establishments but also the characters of the wearers of the garments.

Chaucer's Monk was one of the most extravagantly dressed of the pilgrims, especially considering the ideals of simplicity and poverty professed by his religious order. So noticeable to the other pilgrims was his fine habit that the Host remarks:

> Alas! why werestow so wyd a cope?[124]

---

[123] Linn, *op. cit.,* 310.

[124] B *Monk's Prol.,* 3139. The cope, properly speaking, was an ecclesiastical garment used in the Church services much as it is today. It was semicircular in form, without sleeves, and fastened across the breast by a morse or clasp. It was generally embroidered or otherwise decorated in beautiful designs. The cope mentioned here as in other medieval literature, such as that of Wyclif and Langland, was probably not an ecclesiastical garment, but a modification of it—a kind of mantle of circular form sewed together in front over the neck and chest, and used as a part of the religious' full dress.

Chaucer, in the rôle of one of the pilgrims, observes much else which is not in keeping with the Monk's profession:

> I seigh his sleves purfiled at the hond
> With grys, and that the fyneste of a lond;
> And, for to festne his hood under his chin,
> He hadde of gold y-wroght a curious pin:
> A love-knotte in the gretter ende ther was.
>
> .   .   .   .   .
>
> His botes souple, his hors in greet estat.
> Now certeinly he was a fair prelat.[125]

It is true that the Benedictine Rule, which the Monk professed to follow,[126] provided that monks going on a journey might wear garments "somewhat better than those in ordinary use,"[127] but apparently he had interpreted this with a considerable amount of latitude, or indeed had scorned obedience to the Rule which he regarded as "old and somdel streit."[128]   He could hardly have claimed exemption from the Rule on the basis of his being a "keeper of the celle,"[129] that is, superior of a subordinate monastery, for it had been enjoined by the Pope that "Monks who reside in the outer Priories be conformed to their Abbies, in performing Divine Service, in Decency of Habit,"[130] and the like.

It was not necessarily black, but may generally have been so. . . . Cf. *Fairholt's Costume,* II, 130-131; Anastasia Dolby, *Church Vestments* (London, 1868), 101; *Catholic Encyclopedia* (article by Herbert Thurston).   The width of the monk's cope bespeaks his extravagance.

[125] A *Gen. Prol.,* 193-197; 203-204.

[126] *Ibid.,* 173.

[127] This portion of the Rule seems somewhat vaguely worded, a fact which suggests that St. Benedict trusted his monks to interpret it properly.   It states that

> Those who are sent on a journey shall get hosen from the wardrobe, which, on their return, when washed, they shall return.   Let their cowls and tunics on such occasions be somewhat better than those in ordinary use.   *Rule of St. Benedict* (Gasquet's trans.), LV, 96.

"Somewhat better than those in ordinary use" are words which certainly allow for individual interpretation.

[128] A *Gen. Prol.,* 174.

[129] *Ibid.,* 172.

[130] Dugdale, *Monasticon,* II, 189.

Whatever may have been the spirit of the Monk or the motive which prompted his foppish love of fine clothing and display,[131] it is certain that his grys-trimmed sleeves,[132] his wide cope, and his supple boots,[133] not to mention the curious pin of gold with the love-knot in the greater end, with which he fastened his hood under his chin,[134] were not the ordinary habit and accessories of the Benedictine monk. Nor was it fitting that his bridle was hung with tinkling ornaments or little bells.[135]

St. Benedict had indeed been very exact in his specifications of the costume to be worn. Each monk, at least in ordinary places, was to have a cowl[136] and tunic, "in winter the cowl being of thicker stuff, and in summer of finer or old cloth."[137] He was likewise to be furnished with a scapular[138] for working purposes, and shoes and stockings. Further, provision was made for a second habit to be worn at night and for the convenience of washing. "Anything beyond this is superfluous," says the Rule, "and must be cut off."[139]

---

[131] This love is seen not only in the dress and accessories, but also in the possession of "ful many a deyntee hors" in his stables, the fine grey hounds which accompanied him on his journey, and the beautiful brown horse which he rode. See A *Gen. Prol.,* 168-207, *passim.*

[132] The use of grys, one of the richest furs of the Middle Ages (believed to have been the fur from the back of a squirrel during the winter months) was obviously an extravagance, especially for a monk. See *Cal. of Wills,* II, 214, note 4; and 215, note 1.

[133] To keep leather boots from becoming hard it was necessary to keep them well greased. But the Monk's boots were either so new that they had not yet become hard, or they had been especially well cared for—which latter was difficult, generally, on account of the high price of grease.

[134] The love-knot was an intertwined device; certainly it would be an expensive ornament for a monk.

[135] A *Gen. Prol.,* 170.

[136] Clinch, *op. cit.,* 244, describes the cowl as "a large loosely hanging garment with a hood attached to it and hanging sleeves." I believe the term is in modern times used to refer to the hood alone.

[137] *Rule of St. Benedict,* LV, 95.

[138] The scapular was similar to a tabard, but longer. In some cases there was a hood attached to it; and "the Carthusians wore it with the front and back connected by broad bands." Cf. *Fairholt's Costume,* II, 359.

[139] *Rule of St. Benedict,* 96.

Evidence that other monks than the one Chaucer describes frequently failed in the strict observance of the regulations regarding attire is seen in various exhortations such as those expressed in the statutes made by Pope Gregory IX and revived by Pope Innocent IV, concerning the Reformation of the Black Monks. One might almost think these statutes had been made exclusively for Chaucer's Monk, so well do they touch on the extravagances which he allowed himself:

> The Monks shall behave themselves decently, wearing their common and religious Garments, as well going abroad as in the Cloister; nor are they to go out without a Coul, and regular Habit. Nor are they to have a coloured Cloak. Nor is any Man to presume to ride with a costly or irregular Saddle, or superfluously adorn'd with Nails. They that ride shall not wear gilt or silver'd Spurs, nor have any Iron Ornament on their Bridles; nor finger'd Gloves, nor sharp-toed Boots, but Shoes ty'd with Thongs, round, and not sharp.[140]

The reference here to colored cloaks suggests that monks had sometimes worn such garments. St. Benedict had not, it is true, regulated the color of the habits for his monks. From pictures it appears that "the Garment the first Benedictines wore was white, and the scapular black."[141] Probably the cloak was meant to be black, or at least of some dark color which would not soil easily.

The Monk of the pilgrimage may indeed have been representative of a large group of lax religious; still, he was not necessarily typical of the majority. One may be sure there were many who rode on pilgrimages or other journeys wearing garments which bore witness to most exact observances of their vows of poverty. Such a monk as this is presented in Lydgate's "Prologue to the Sege of Thebes." He is in direct contrast to Chaucer's Monk:

> In a Cope of blak and not of grene
> On a palfrey slender, long and lene
> With rusty brydel mad not for the sale,
> My man to forn with a voide male.[142]

---

[140] Dugdale, *op. cit.,* II, 188.
[141] *Ibid.,* II, 164.
[142] Hammond, *English Verse from Chaucer to Surrey,* 121, 11. 73-76.

Further, Lydgate describes this monk's bridle as having "neither boss nor bell," and alludes to his threadbare hood.

The Friar, probably a Franciscan,[143] is described by Chaucer as another religious who took his Rule lightly. Of his wearing apparel the poet writes:

> For there he was nat lyk a cloisterer,
> With a thredbar cope, as is a povre scoler,
> But he was lyk a maister or a pope.
> Of double worsted was his semi-cope,
> That rounded as a belle out of the presse.[144]

His was a shapely garment, a short cope,[145] richly made and probably lined so that it retained its circular form well. This was no mantle of "vyle and course clothe,"[146] such as St. Francis had commanded his friars to wear, but was of double worsted.[147] It could perhaps be said of this Friar, as it was of those religious in *Piers the Ploughman's Crede,*

> þat in cotynge of his cope is more cloþ y-folden
> þan was in Fraunces froc whan he hem first made.[148]

Superfluous cloth was required, however, if one would have a cope which "rounded as a belle out of the presse."

The regulations which St. Francis had made for his friars were if anything more exacting than those of St. Benedict. In part they were as follows:

> And they whiche arre professid and have promysed obedience shall have oone cote and a hode (*a libertee*) and a nother withoute a hoode that wille have yt, and suche as they have nede or as ar constreyned by necessyte may were shoone. (Equivalent to a commandment). And alle the bretherne must be clothid with symple and vyle clothinge. (*A libertee*). And they may pece them

---

[143] Robinson, *op. cit.,* 758.

[144] A *Gen. Prol.,* 259-263.

[145] Robinson, *op. cit.,* gloss.

[146] Cf. *infra,* 166.

[147] Apparently the cope is made of fine quality woollen cloth. Double seems to indicate a lining, which certainly would help keep the cope in shape.

[148] P. 11, 11.292-293.

and amende them with pecis of sak clothe, or with other
pecis, with the blessyng of God. (An exhortation) . . .[149]

Further, the exact measurements of the habit were given. The
breadth of the hood, for instance, was not to pass "the sholder-
boone," and the length of the habit "shall nat pas the lenkithe of
hym that werethe yt, and the breddith thereof have nat past xvi.
spannys at the most, nor less than xiiij., that is, unless "the
gretnes of the brodre require more after the mynd of the warden."[150]   Of the mantle to be worn it was required that it be "of
vyle and course clothe, nat curiously made or pynched aboute the
necke, nat towching the ground by a whole spanne."[151]

The Friar's cope was probably not the only extravagance which
that gentleman allowed himself. The allusion made to his tipet,
namely that it was "ay farsed ful of knyves and pinnes for . . .
faire wyves,"[152] may indicate that this long pendant hanging from
his great hood was of unusual length and in that sense superfluous. Whatever departure the Friar had made from his Rule
he could probably have excused himself in much the same manner as Friar Daw Topias did when rebuked by Jack Upland, as
recorded in a popular medieval poem. In part, Friar Daw says:

> But if my cloth be over presciouse,
> Jakke, blame the werer;
> ffor myn ordre hath ordeyned
> al in good mesure.
> Thou axist me, Jacke, of my grete hood,
> What that it meneth,
> my scapelarie and my wide cope,
> and the knottide girdil.
> What meenith thi tipet, Jakke,
> as long as a stremer,
> that hangith longe bihinde
> and kepith thee not hoot?
> An hool cloath of scarlet
> may not make a gowne;

---

[149] *Monumenta Franciscana,* ed. Richard Hawlett, 3 vols. (London, 1882),
II, 67.

[150] *Idem.*

[151] *Idem.*

[152] A *Gen. Prol.,* 233-234.

. . . . . .
Why is thi gowne, Jakke,
widder than thi cote,
and thi cloke al above
as round as a belle.
. . . . . .
My grete coope that is so wiid,
signifieth charite. . . .[153]

In addition, the friar says that his great hood is a sign that he will receive reproof for God's sake, and that his scapular signifies obedience to superiors.[154] Undoubtedly he gives the real symbolic meanings attached to the various parts of his habit; but he likewise apparently seeks excuses for garments of extra proportions.

The Canon who overtook the pilgrims at "Boghten under Blee" was anything but foppish in his dress. Rather, he went to the opposite extreme and appeared in exceptionally untidy garments. He wore the usual habit of the Augustinian Rule, black gown and white surplice,[155] but his cloak or "oversloppe" was not "worth a myte," and was dirty and torn.[156] His hood was attached to the

---

[153] "The reply of Friar Daw Topias, with Jack Upland's Rejoinder," *Political Poems and Songs,* ed. Thomas Wright, Rolls series (London, 1859), II, 69.

[154] *Ibid.,* II, 70-71.

[155] The Canons Regular of St. Augustine in Chaucer's time had changed the color of their habits, according to a command of Pope Benedict XII made in 1339, which provided that "the Regular Canons should not in their Garments use any other Colours but White, Brown, Black, or almost Black." Earlier, there had been no specified color, with the result that some of the canons had adopted garments of black, red, or purple, as their tastes prompted them. Dugdale, *Monasticon,* III, 66.

The habit itself consisted of a cassock, generally lined with fur, a white surplice with long-flowing sleeves, and a loose-flowing mantle or cloak with hood attached. The habit of the Canons Secular seems to have been practically the same as this. Clinch, *op. cit.,* 244; Dugdale, *op. cit.,* II, 126. See the illustration of a Canon Regular in Cardinal Gasquet, *English Monastic Life* (London, 1904), facing p. 224.

The surplice at this period had been shortened from its length to the ground so that it now came only to the middle of the shin. Dolby, *op. cit.,* 122-123.

[156] G *CY Prol.,* 557-571, *passim.*

cloak, and a hat hung sloppily down his back by a string.[157]   His apparel was so disreputable looking that the Host inquired of the Canon's Yeoman,

> "Why is thy lord so sluttish, I yowe preye?"[158]

The Host could not understand how a man who was supposed to be able to turn the road to Canterbury "up-so-doun, and pave it al of silver and of gold,"[159] should not have "power better cloth to buy."[160]   Chaucer volunteers no information as to why the Canon was so "sluttish," but the inference is that he was so deeply absorbed in his alchemy that he neglected even the ordinary care of his personal appearance.   Evidently he had little respect for his religious habit, else he would have kept it at least neat and clean.

Like the Canon, the Clerk of Oxenford was poorly clad:

> Ful thredbar was his overest courtepy,
> For he had geten him yet no benefyce,
> Ne was so worldly for to have offyce.[161]

There is no evidence that his courtepy was untidy and dirty.   The Clerk had but little money and preferred to spend whatsoever he might receive as gifts for other things than clothes.[162]

This Clerk in his love of study and the consequent neglect of buying garments for himself is strikingly similar to St. Richard of Chichester, of whom it is said that he had such love for learning "that he cared little or nothing for food or raiment," and that he and two companions who lodged together had only one gown and their tunics between them.   "When one, therefore, went out

---

[157] *Ibid.*, 571-574.

[158] *Ibid.*, 636.

[159] *Ibid.*, 624-626.

[160] *Ibid.*, 637.

[161] A *Gen. Prol.*, 290-292.

[162] The Clerk especially liked to buy books:
> For him was lever have at his beddes heed
> Twenty bokes, clad in blak or reed,
> Of Aristotle and his philosophye,
> Than robes riche, or fithele, or gay sautrye.
> —*Ibid.*, 293-296.

with the gown to hear a lecture, the others sat in their room, and so they went forth alternately. . . ."[163] Apparently St. Richard and his friends, like the Clerk, preferred "twenty bokes clad in blak or reed" to clothing.

The Parish Clerk of the *Miller's Tale* seems not to have suffered thus the effects of poverty. This Absolon, of whose vanity more will be said later, affected the curled hair of the medieval dandy:

> Crul was his heer, and as the gold it shoon,
> And strouted as a fanne large and brode;
> Ful streight and even lay his joly shode.[164]

He was appropriately clad in a kirtle[165] of light blue, over which he wore a gay surplice "as whyte as is the blosme up-on the rys."[166] Still more striking to the eye than the blue and white costume, however, were the fine shoes the clerk wore,

> With Powles window corven in his shoes,
> In hoses rede he wente fetisly.[167]

The shoes, similar probably to ones pictured in *Fairholt's Costume*,[168] were of a cutwork design resembling the rose-window of St. Paul's Church. They were displayed to full advantage by the fashionable red hose worn beneath them.

Chaucer's other characters connected more or less closely with the Church are not particularly significant in the study of costume. The Pardoner had "trussed up in his wallet" his ordinary hood and was wearing a cap, upon which he had sewed a vernicle;[169] the

---

[163] Coulton, *Social Life in Britain*, 61; cf. also the *Catholic Encyc.*, XIII, 43.

[164] A 3314-3316. *Shode* is the parting of the hair. Skeat, *op. cit.*, gloss.

[165] The kirtle was a kind of tunic or surcoat. Often it was worn next the shirt and was covered by the outer cloak or cope. Strutt, *Dress and Habits*, 349. I believe the kirtle here mentioned to have been like the modern cassock.

[166] A *Mil. T.*, 1320-1324.

[167] *Ibid.*, 3318-3319.

[168] II, 65, fig. 11.

[169] A *Gen. Prol.*, 681-685. A vernicle was "a small copy of the handkerchief of St. Veronica preserved at Rome." According to tradition St. Veronica gave her handkerchief, or a towel, to Christ when she met Him on the way to Calvary carrying His cross, and when He returned it to

Nun's Priest and the Parson are not considered in regard to their dress. From the fact that the former rode on a "horse bothe foule and lene,"[170] and that the latter was "a povre Persoun of a toun,"[171] it may be assumed that both wore garments which accorded with their poverty.[172] The omission of details of costume here is not significant; even without such information Chaucer's view of clerical dress is sufficiently comprehensive for one to have a fairly complete idea of it.

Without exception, it seems, the poet's treatment of clerical costume is realistic. The wearing of elaborate copes, sometimes trimmed extravagantly in fine fur, the affectation of the best shoes and hose available, the use of expensive materials, and the wearing of worldly accessories were characteristic of certain lax religious whose love of finery and personal comfort outweighed their regard for the Rules of their orders. So, too, a careless disregard of cleanliness, an unbecoming lack of neatness, and undue inattention to dress bespoke the religious whose interests were elsewhere than in his ordinary religious life. There is practically every large group of religious represented in the poet's works; hence, knowledge of their customs of dress and personal adornment is remarkably inclusive.

Along with a description of men's dress, Chaucer gives many suggestions of that failing which often accompanies extravagance and a love of fine garments, namely marks of vanity. The Squire Damian, for example, when he knows that May loves him, rises from his sick bed—where he had lain a victim of the pangs of love—and dresses himself with great care:

> He kembeth him, he proyneth him and pyketh.[173]

In other words, he combs his hair and makes himself neat and tidy. Similarly, the lover Absolon, who rose at the "first cock-

---

her it bore the imprint of His features. "Copies of this portrait, called *veronicae,* or *veroniculae*—in English *vernicles*—were often brought home by pilgrims to Rome." Cf. Manly, *op. cit.,* 537; cf. also *Piers Plowman,* EETS, OS 54, VIII, 1. 168; and *supra,* 151, f.n. 64.

[170] B *NP Prol.,* 4002-4003.
[171] A *Gen. Prol.,* 478.
[172] Cf. Ellesemere Ms. for a picture of the Parson.
[173] E *Mer. T.,* 2011.

crow" to visit Alisoun, took particular care of his personal appearance :

> And him arrayeth gay, at point-devys (with great neatness),
> But first he cheweth greyn and lycorys
> To smellen swete, er he had kembd his heer.
> Under his tonge a trewe love he beer,
> For ther-by wende he to ben gracious.[174]

The chewing of herbs or spices to sweeten the breath, again the combing of the hair, and the placing of a "trewe love"[175] under the tongue were all efforts to make himself attractive. The chewing of the herbs may be considered also as a practical necessity; if Absolon, like many other medieval persons, had a special liking for onions and garlic, he was wise to make some attempt at sweetening his breath before going into company.

Certainly Chaucer affords the reader a generous view of men's costumes. In spite of any obligations he is under to other literature, and in spite of his omissions, particularly regarding the dress of the upper classes, there are so many different types of costumes, so many fashions, and such excellent use of colors and other concrete details that one can hardly help gaining much useful knowledge about the subject.

Feminine Dress and Accessories: Civil and Religious

Contrary to what one might expect, women's dress in the time of Chaucer was hardly more elaborate or indicative of vanity than men's. In some respects, indeed, there is marked similarity between their costumes, and were it not for men's beards it would in some cases be difficult to distinguish in the illustrations of the period masculine from feminine attire.

Except for the numerous descriptions which he borrows from the *Romaunt de la Rose* Chaucer has surprisingly few examples of women's costumes. However, most of his allusions, even

---

[174] A *Mil. T.*, 3689-3693. Cf. also F *Sq. T.*, 560.
[175] Cf. *supra*, 81.

though they are often fragmentary and incidental, attest the poet's powers of observation in an unusual manner.

I

As has been seen in the discussion of men's costumes, the *Romaunt de la Rose* furnished Chaucer with many elaborately appareled persons. There is no exception as far as women's dress is concerned; there is, indeed, a much larger group of women characters than men in the poem and their garments are described in great detail. All but one or two of the dresses are depicted as being remarkably elaborate and rich.

Ydelnesse, who is described as particularly fair of face, was clothed in a "cote of grene cloth of Gaunt,"[176] a somewhat simple, though probably expensive, garment. She practiced nearly all the arts of adorning herself. Her hair, which was "yelowe of hewe,"[177] as is the nature of women's hair in the romances, had for adornment "a chapelet of fyn orphrays," or gold embroidery,

> And faire above that chapelet
> A rose gerland had she set.
> She hadde (in honde) a gay mirour,
> And with a rich gold tresour
> Her heed was tressed queyntely.[178]

---

[176] Frag. A, 457-461. What was probably the characteristic dress of fourteenth century women was a close-fitting kirtle or loose gown, over which was a mantle, open in front, but held in position by a cord across the breast. Occasionally a third dress was worn over the kirtle. This was either a gown shorter than an under garment, with short sleeves from which depended long lappets, or the sideless cote-hardie, slit up the sides of the skirt, and trimmed with fur or other rich material, but without sides as far as the hips, and without sleeves. Variations of this costume were numerous. Clinch, *op. cit.*, 138; Wilton, *op. cit.*, 58-62.

[177] *Ibid.*, 539-540.

[178] *Ibid.*, 565-569. There were many styles of head dress which medieval English women had adopted at this time. This *tresour* which is mentioned here was probably the caul—a kind of close-fitting cap of silk threads or of metal and often enriched with precious stones. The hair was tightly plaited and bound round the head, then covered with a wimple, or kind of veil, which hung down over the back of the neck; over the wimple the caul was placed. Sometimes the wimple was omitted; in this case the back of the neck was left bare and all the hair was plucked from it. A chaplet of

To complete her costume, Ydelnesse wore fashionably sewed
sleeves and

> . . . to kepe hir hondes faire
> Of glovys whyte she hadde a paire.[179]

Probably the sleeves were of the long, flowing variety, or were
adorned with lappets or long narrow strips of cloth which hung
down sometimes to the ground.[180] Gloves, which at this time
were commonly worn or carried in the hand or thrust beneath the
girdle, sometimes had separate fingers, but frequently did not.
They had long tops and were often decorated with embroidery or
jewels.[181]

Gladnesse, whose hair was also yellow, wore a garland of beautiful orphrays.[182] Her robe was very rich, but is described
briefly:

> And in an over-gilt samyt
> Clad she was, by gret delyt.[183]

Richesse's robe was much more elaborate and described in detail:

> Richesse a robe of purpre on hadde,
> Ne trowe not that I lye or madde;
> For in this world is noon it liche,
> Ne by a thousand deel so riche,
> Ne noon so fair; for it ful wel
> With orfrays leyd was everydel,
> And portrayed in the ribaninges (silk trimmings)
> Of dukes stories, and of kinges.
> And with a bend of gold tasseled,
> And knoppes fyne of gold ameled.[184]
> Aboute hir nekke of gentil entaile
> Was shet the riche chevesaile,
> In which ther was ful gret plentee
> Of stones clere and bright to see.[185]

---

flowers, real or artificial, or a plain circlet of gold was worn sometimes
with this head dress. Cf. Calthrop, *op. cit.*, 133 ff.; Clinch, *op. cit.*, 145-147.

[179] *RR*, Frag. A, 571-572.
[180] Cf. Wilton, *op. cit.*, 58-59.
[181] *Fairholt's Costume*, II, 188; cf. also Clinch, *op. cit.*, 141.
[182] *RR*, Frag. A, 870-872.
[183] *Ibid.*, 873-874.
[184] "Knoppes fyne of gold ameled" seems to mean buds of gold enamel.
Cf. Skeat, *op. cit.*, gloss.
[185] Frag. A, 1071-1084.

The *chevesaile,* or neck-band of the robe, with its jewelled trimmings, was matched by a beautiful girdle, of which the buckle also bore a jewel. This girdle was *barred* or striped with gold:

> Upon a tissu of satyne,
> Ful hevy, greet, and no-thing light,
> In everich was a besaunt-wight.[186]

Upon her hair, Richesse wore a "cercle" or coronet of bright gold, heavily bejewelled with rubies, sapphires, garnets, emeralds, and a fine carbuncle.[187] Altogether, Richesse was attired as a woman of noble rank.

Largesse was gowned in purple "Sarsinesshe,"[188] probably the same as sarcenet—a thin silk used first in the thirteenth century[189]—and the collar of the robe lay open, for Largesse had given away her "broche ful wel wrought." Beneath the dress, as could be seen at the open collar, was a silken smock.[190]

The dress worn by Fraunchyse is referred to first as a "sukkenye,"[191] and later as a "roket."[192] It was probably a kind of loose gown[193] made of fine linen, "not of hempen herdes," or coarse flax, and was "rideled," i. e., plaited or gathered in at the neck or waist, "fetisly."[194] It was white and

> Bitokened, that ful debonaire
> And swete was she that it bere.[195]

This is one of the simplest garments described in the *Romaunt de la Rose*—at least as far as material is concerned—but its fashionable plaits or gathers evidently made it a worthy dress for Fraunchyse.

---

[186] *Ibid.,* 1104-1106. "A besaunt-wight" means besant weight; a besant was a Spanish coin of gold. Robinson, *op. cit.,* gloss.

[187] *Ibid.,* 1107-1128, *passim.*

[188] *Ibid.,* 1187.

[189] *Fairholt's Costume,* II, 357.

[190] *RR,* Frag. A, 1190-1195.

[191] *Ibid.,* 1232.

[192] *Ibid.,* 1240 ff.

[193] Fairholt, *op. cit.,* II, 350.

[194] *RR,* Frag. A, 1233 ff.

[195] *Ibid.,* 1244-1245.

The costumes worn by Avarice and Povert are those of the poorest classes. The former's apparel seems to have been at one time of good quality and probably fashionable. It is the type of clothing which the poor must often have received as a result of their begging:

> And she was clad ful povrely,
> Al in an old torn courtepy,
> As she were al with dogges torn;
> And bothe bihinde and eek biforn
> Clouted (patched) was she beggarly.
> A mantel heng hir faste by,
> Upon a perche, weyke and smalle;
> A burnet cote heng therewithalle,
> Furred with no menivere,
> But with a furre rough of here,
> Of lambe-skinnes hevy and blake;[196]
> It was ful old, I undertake.[197]

Povert also wore patched garments. In fact, like many poor persons of the fourteenth century, no doubt, she had only one gown, and that a wretched one:

> She hadde on but a streit old sak,
> And many a clout on it ther stak;
> This was hir cote and hir mantel,
> No more was there, never a del,
> To clothe her with; . . . .[198]

Like the Plowman's dress, this was evidently a kind of loose garment, perhaps of the same fashion as the tabard. Illustrations of the costume worn by the poor show men's and women's to be very much the same—a long loose gown, generally.

---

[196] *Menivere* (menever), is said to have been the fur on the belly of the squirrel during the winter, just as grys (cf. *supra,* 163) was that of the same animal's back at the same season. *Cal. of Wills,* II, p. 214, n. 4.

In 1351 a law was passed in London which provided that no common or lewd woman of the city or from foreign places residing in London "shall be so daring as to be attired, either by day or by night, in any kind of vesture trimmed with fur, such as menevyr, grey, purree . . . or any other manner of noble budge. . . ." Riley, *Memorials, 267.* It is significant that Avarice wore a coarse coat trimmed, not in menever, but in black lamb-skin.

[197] Frag. A, 219-231.

[198] *Ibid.,* 457-461.

In those poems by Chaucer which are most nearly original, many of the allusions to wearing apparel are fragmentary and conventional. Especially is this so in the poet's consideration of royal or noble women's costumes. He presents occasionally some part of such dress, but he gives no complete picture of it.

Of the garb of Emelye, for example, he says,

> Y-clothed was she fresh, for to devise;
> Hir yelow heer was broyded in a tresse,
> Bihinde hir bak, a yerde long, I gesse.[199]

The yellow hair is, as has been mentioned, a conventional feature of a medieval woman's description. The style of hairdress which Chaucer refers to is only one of many adopted in this period. Young women seem to have been especially prone to wearing their hair long, hanging over the shoulders loose, or braided down the back as Emelye's was. With this style of hairdress the chaplet of flowers, real or artificial, or a plain circlet of gold was frequently worn. When the caul was worn (cf. *supra,* 172), the hair was tightly plaited and bound round the head.[200] It is to be noted that Chaucer is exact in having Emelye gather flowers,

> To make a sotil gerland for hir hede.[201]

Another description of Emelye shows her in hunting costume, "al in grene,"[202] but here again there is no individualizing note.

The Queen of the *Legend of Good Women* and Grisilde of the *Clerk's Tale* are also women whose costumes should represent those of the upper classes. Of the former Chaucer says,

> And she was clad in real habit grene.
> A fret of gold she hadde next hir heer,
> And upon that a whyt coroun she beer
> With florouns smale. . . .
>
> .   .   .   .   .
>
> So were the florouns of hir coroun whyte.
> For of o perle fyne, oriental,
> Hir whyte coroun was y-maked al;

---

[199] A *Kn. T.,* 1048-1050.
[200] Calthrop, *op. cit.,* 133-134; Clinch, *op. cit.,* 145-147.
[201] A *Kn. T.,* 1054.
[202] *Ibid.,* 1686.

> For which the whyte coroun, above the grene,
> Made hir lyk a daysie for to sene,
> Considered eek hir fret of gold above.[203]

The emphasis is again not on the details of the dress, but on the headdress. Somewhat similarly the clothing of Grisilde is conventional and general rather than realistic and concrete:

> And in a cloth of gold that brighte shoon,
> With a coroune of many a riche stoon
> Up-on hir heed, they in-to halle hir broghte.[204]

There are three women in the *Canterbury Tales* whose costumes are strikingly vivid and apparently realistic. These three, representative as they are of only two classes of society, namely the middle class and that of religious women, are the Wife of Bath, the Carpenter's wife in *The Miller's Tale,* and the Prioress.

The Wife of Bath must have attracted much attention by the coverchiefs, or kerchiefs, which she wore on her head. Of them we are told

> I dorste swere they weyeden ten pound
> That on Sunday were upon hir heed.[205]

The coverchief, as a style of headdress, was really not in fashion at this period,[206] but the Wife of Bath, partly because of her own skill at cloth-making,[207] partly because of a desire to attract attention by being different, or possibly because of an independence of spirit in regard to styles, wore them in excess when she wished to appear at her best. More than likely she wore with this elaborate headdress her "gaye scarlet gytes"[208] which she herself refers to in her Prologue:

> Therefore I made my visitaciouns,
> To vigiles and to processiouns,

---

[203] *LGW*, prol., B version, 214-225, *passim*.
[204] E *Cl. T.*, 1117-1119.
[205] A *Gen. Prol.*, 453-455.
[206] Manly, *New Light*, 453.
[207] A *Gen. Prol.*, 447-448.
[208] *Gytes* here probably means garments, particularly gowns. Skeat, *op. cit.*, gloss.

> To preching eek and to thise pilgrimages,
> To pleyes of miracles and mariages,
> And wered upon my gaye scarlet gytes.[209]

That these gytes were frequently worn, she testifies:

> Thise wormes, ne thise motthes, ne thise mytes,
> Upon my peril, frete hem never a deel;
> And wostow why? for they were used weel.[210]

A practical method was certainly hers to keep moths from her garments.

If the Wife was garbed in her red garments on the Canterbury pilgrimage, as she probably was, they were protected by the foot-mantle which she wore about her hips.[211] Evidently a skirt-protector,[212] this article of clothing would keep the dress clean and also keep it from wearing out rapidly. The costume was further enhanced by the fine hose and shoes which the Wife wore:

> Hir hosen weren of fyn scarlet reed,
> Ful streite y-teyd, and shoes ful moiste and newe.[213]

The scarlet hose, tightly fastened, probably by a piece of silk or some other material, just below the knee, were plainly visible through the openings in the low-cut shoes. The shoes must have been of late fashion, for they were new and still pliant.

The Sunday kerchiefs were apparently not worn on the pilgrimage. Rather, the Wife was

> Y-wimpled wel, and on hir heed an hat
> As brood as is a bokeler or a targe.[214]

The wimple, which was a kind of veil of linen or similar material, folded to cover the head, chin, neck, and sides of the face,[215] was usually sufficient in itself as a head-covering. Why the Wife of

---

[209] D 555-559.

[210] *Ibid.*, 560-562.

[211] A *Gen. Prol.*, 472.

[212] *Fairholt's Costume*, II, 170.

[213] A *Gen. Prol.*, 456-457.

[214] *Ibid.*, 470-471.

[215] Robinson, *op. cit.*, gloss.

Bath should have worn her enormous hat on top of it one can not say. Evidently she minded not at all wearing heavy head-dresses; probably she considered herself in the height of fashion with her wimple and hat.

The Carpenter's wife in *The Miller's Tale* was much more tastily dressed than the Wife of Bath. Of her outer garment or robe Chaucer says nothing. With it, however, she wore a "ceint" or girdle barred with silk, and a gored apron, or barm cloth, which was as white as milk. Her white smock, which seems to have been an under garment visible only at the neck, was embroidered at the collar with black silk. Ties on her bonnet or cap were similarly trimmed. Further to adorn her costume was a broad fillet of silk, worn on her head "ful high" so as to reveal her broad brow.[216] A leather purse, tasseled with silk and adorned with little metal buttons or knobs which resembled pearls, hung from her girdle, and

> A brooch she baar up-on hir lowe coler,
> As brood as is a bos of a bocler.[217]

Her shoes, which seem to have been of the high-top variety, were "laced on hir legges hye,"[218] probably, that is, half-way between the ankle and the knee.[219]

There is, as has been suggested, a marked difference between the dress of these two women; yet both women are of the middle class of society and have something in common as far as their respective love affairs are concerned. The difference may be that the Wife of Bath is older than the Carpenter's wife. Like many women the flower of whose youth is gone, the Wife was pitifully eager to make herself attractive without quite knowing how to do so. Lacking sophistication, she flagrantly disported her scarlet dress, her broad hat, and her fine shoes. More subtly the youthful Alisoun studied the ways and means of making herself charming, depend-

---

[216] A 3235-3244.

[217] *Ibid.,* 3310-3311.

[218] *Ibid.,* 3250-3251; 3265-3266.

[219] *Ibid.,* 3267. See *Fairholt's Costume,* II, 68.

ing not only on her dress but also on neatness and "y-pulled" eye-brows[220] and a "shyning" hue.[221]

That Alisoun was a daughter of her times is clearly evidenced by the reference to her plucked eyebrows and broad forehead. It was considered fashionable not only to make one's eyebrows "small" and "bent" by pulling some of the hair from them, but also to make the forehead broad by plucking the hair at the temples and at the top of the forehead. Women are said to have carried small tweezers in their purses for these uses;[222] indeed, the Carpenter's wife may have had such tweezers in her own betasseled purse.

Another one of Chaucer's women characters whose costume is partially described is Criseyde. Although there is hardly enough evidence given by the poet for the reader to form a complete picture in his mind of the clothing which the young widow wore, there are at least in implication some details of a widow's usual garb. The first time Troilus sees Criseyde she is

> In widewes habit large of samit broun.[223]

Later, she is described as wearing a "widewes habite blak,"[224] and again her garments are referred to as "blake wede."[225] Whether brown is actually meant in the first instance is difficult to say; possibly the poet translated a word incorrectly or used "broun" and black in a loose sense, much as we use dark. At any rate, the dress, which seems to be a plainly fashioned garment of full proportions, was of either brown or black.

More distinguishing than her gown was the *barbe* which Criseyde wore and of which Pandarus said,

> Do wey your barbe, and shew your face.[226]

---

[220] A *Mil. T.*, 3245. Much is made of plucked eyebrows in medieval literature. It was something of a convention for heroines to have "bent," "y-pulled," or "narrow" brows.

[221] *Ibid.*, 3310-3311.

[222] See "The Mercer," *Satirical Songs and Poems on Costume,* ed. Frederick W. Fairholt, Percy Soc. Pub., 27 (London, 1849), 12-13.

[223] *TC,* I, 109.

[224] *Ibid.*, I, 171.

[225] *Ibid.*, I, 177.

[226] *Ibid.*, II, 110.

This was "a piece of white plaited linen passed over or under the chin and reaching midway to the waist,"[227] and was generally worn with a long kerchief over the head. It has been said that the "flowing kerchief over the head was the original of the modern 'widow's weeds.'"[228]

Certainly Chaucer's descriptions of women's garb, especially when almost entirely uninfluenced by other literary works, are marked by apparent familiarity with the fashions and practices of the fourteenth century. Unlike the romances which are often most rich in allusions to royal and noble women's costumes,[229] the poet has but little to do with creating the details of the dress adopted by women of rank. Rather, he borrows such descriptions when he needs them, as he does in his earlier works, and gives his attention to the costumes worn by persons of the other classes. In so-doing he has bequeathed to the modern reader interested in the history of costume much information which would hardly be available otherwise. In presenting the Wife of Bath and fair Alisoun, then, Chaucer has rendered a somewhat remarkable service.

II

Just as he knew well the dress of middle class women of the world, so, too, the poet seems fully conversant with the subject of religious women's garb. His consideration of Madame Eglentyne's attire is proof of the accuracy with which he observes details. Besides the garments, which include a wimple which was "ful semely . . . pinched,"[230] and a "ful fetis . . . cloke,"[231] the Prioress is described as carrying an unusually fine rosary:

> Of smal coral aboute hir arm she bar
> A peire of bedes, gauded al with grene;
> And ther-on heng a broche of gold ful shene,
> On which ther was first write a crowned A,
> And after, *Amor vincit omnia.*[232]

---

[227] Robinson, *op. cit.,* 930.

[228] Clinch, *op. cit.,* 179.

[229] It seems superfluous to cite instances of romances in which are found examples of women's dress, for nearly every one of them has some such examples. See Eagleson, *op. cit.,* 339-345.

[230] A *Gen. Prol.,* 151.

[231] *Ibid.,* 157.

[232] *Ibid.,* 158-162.

So much has been written about Madame Eglentyne that it seems almost superfluous to refer to her again; however, to complete as nearly as possible the consideration of Chaucer's treatment of costume it is practically necessary to summarize here the information offered about medieval nuns' dress.

Actually, Madame Eglentyne appears to be somewhat simply dressed. Hers was doubtless the regulation habit worn by Benedictine nuns.[233] The Rule provided that the nuns were to be poorly garbed, having no more clothes than were needed, and which were to be varied according to the climate. Generally a kirtle[234] and a cloak or mantle were considered sufficient, the latter being single in summer and double in winter. An extra kirtle was provided for night wear. Shoes were to be cheap and not the fairest seen. The garments were to be neither too short nor too long, and when they were old were to be given to the poor. The nuns, like the monks, were to have better garments when they went travelling.[235]

With this habit, which is pictured as having a white or undyed tunic with close sleeves and a surcoat of black with wide, flowing sleeves, were worn a veil over the head and a wimple around the neck and up to the chin. The wimple, although sometimes described as having concentric pleats in it,[236] as the wimple or coif of the present-day Benedictine nuns has, is shown in Dugdale[237] and in a reproduction in Gasquet[238] with the pleats arranged longitudinally. This apparently minor point seems significant in relation to Chaucer's allusion to the wimple as being pinched "ful semely." If the pleats were concentric they would probably be held in position by some method of sewing or pinning them; if longitudinal, they would less likely be so held and their remaining

---

[233] The nun seems undoubtedly to have been a member of the Benedictine order. Cf. Robinson, *op. cit.*, 756.

[234] Cf. *supra*, 172, f.n., 176.

[235] *Rule of St. Benet* (Three Middle English Versions), ed. Dr. Ernest A. Koch, EETS OS 120 (London, 1902), 104-105.

[236] Sister M. Madeleva, *Chaucer's Nuns and Other Essays* (New York, 1925), 77.

[237] *Monasticon.*

[238] *English Monastic Life,* facing p. 154.

in good shape would depend much upon how well they had been "pinched." In other words, the Prioress' wimple would look especially neat, with each pleat carefully made and in order.

The Prioress' cloak is described as "fetis," a word which may be interpreted as neat, well-made, graceful, or handsome.[239] That it was new and perhaps a little better than the cloaks ordinarily worn by the nuns is very likely. It may have been provided by the wardrobe mistress of the convent especially for the Prioress' journey to Canterbury. Perhaps Madame Eglentyne would even have had to return it to the common wardrobe after her journey; if so, it behoved her to take particular care of it for the sake of the nun who might wear it next.

There seems no reason to believe that the Prioress was wearing exceptionally fine garments. Surely if her veil or her wimple had been silken, Chaucer would have mentioned it. He does suggest that the veil was worn particularly high when he refers to Madame Eglentyne's forehead as "a spanne brood,"[240] but otherwise there is no indication of it or the wimple as being of unusual quality.

The nun seems to have been meticulously neat rather than vain or extravagant in the matter of dress. She was particularly careful to prevent any food to fall from her lips when she was eating,[241] and one may well believe that she was in every way as tidy as the various difficulties of the journey would permit her to be. Apparently Madame Eglentyne had the happy knack of wearing her religious habit properly and not with veil and wimple askew as religious sometimes unfortunately wear them.

The beads of the Prioress, with their ornamental brooch, have been the subject of much controversial discussion. That such fine ones, of coral with green *gauds* (beads separating the decades of smaller ones)[242] were reprehensible as a possession of one vowed to poverty seems undeniable. They must have been unusual for a religious to carry or Chaucer would probably not have made so much of them. Still, could it not be possible that they

---

[239] Robinson, *op. cit.*, gloss.
[240] A *Gen. Prol.*, 155.
[241] *Ibid.*, 128 ff.
[242] Robinson, *op. cit.*, 756.

had been bestowed on her as a gift and as such were permissible, even though the use of them was not admirable in one of such high ideals as religious are bound by their vocation to have./

The motto, *Amor vincit omnia,* which was engraved on the golden brooch, has been variously regarded by commentators.[243] To one who knows religious life and customs well, there seems absolutely no need for interpreting the motto as having a double significance, even granting that medieval religious were sometimes more interested in the world and its pleasures than they should have been. To consider Madame Eglentyne as being concerned with earthly love[244] seems almost ridiculous and to do so adds nothing to the characterization which the poet gives of her. On the other hand, the interpretation of the motto as being applied to her religious life does in a sense help to understand the character of the nun.

The custom of selecting mottoes still obtains in many religious communities. Sometimes these mottoes are engraved on finger rings, crucifixes, or medals. Their purpose generally is to remind the religious of some virtue which she wishes to acquire and they are chosen by her after some self-examination and in accord with her recognized spiritual needs. If the Prioress is to be regarded as a woman who had tendencies to worldliness, as is indeed suggested by her various characteristics, then surely it is appropriate for her to have selected a motto such as *Amor vincit omnia,* hoping it would remind her of the power of Divine Love to help her overcome her inherent and hitherto unconquered faults. There is, of course, a note of irony in the fact that as yet the Prioress had evidently not acquired sufficient love of God to be above the love of worldly possessions; the motto was conspicuous, but its effective use not so.

To understand how far Madame Eglentyne is from being among the most lax of medieval religious women one has but to glance at some of the records by way of comparison. As early as 1200 a council in London had been obliged to restrain the

---

[243] *Ibid.,* 754-755. Robinson's summary of the numerous comments is fairly complete.

[244] Cf. *Ibid.,* 755.

Black nuns (probably the Benedictines) from wearing coloured headdresses; a later council in Oxford renewed this and added other decrees. Some of the regulations made at this time were as follows: (1) nuns were not to wear silken wimples; (2) they were not to use silver or golden tiring pins in their veils; (3) they were to wear no belts of silk or other fine stuffs; (4) their habits were not to exceed the length of their bodies, and the robe was to reach only to their ankles; (5) only the consecrated (professed?) nun was to wear a ring and was to be content with only one.[245]

Again, in 1237, a synod declared among other things that nuns were "not to use trained and pleated dresses, or any exceeding the length of the body, nor delicate or coloured furs; nor . . . presume to wear silver tiring-pins in their veils."[246] These regulations were repeated almost word for word in 1387 by William of Wykeham in his injunctions to Romesey and Wherwell and similar ones were made by Buckingham in his injunctions to Elstow in that same year.[247]

Frequent charges were brought against nuns for wearing their veils too high on their foreheads. The Prioress of Ankerwyke Priory in 1441 was the subject of many complaints among which was included that

> . . . she carries her veil too high above her forehead, so that her forehead, being entirely uncovered, can be seen of all . . . and she also wears above her veil a cap of estate furred with budge (lambs' wool) . . . .[248]

This prioress admitted many of the charges brought against her, but excused herself for wearing the "cap of estate furred with budge" on the grounds that she suffered "divers infirmities in her head."[249] One may wonder whether Madame Eglentyne could have found a similar excuse for wearing her veil high.

---

[245] Eileen Power, *Medieval English Nunneries* (Cambridge, 1922), 585.
[246] *Ibid.*, 586.
[247] *Ibid.*, 586.
[248] *Visit. of Linc. Diocese*, II, 3-4. The rest of the prioress' dress was as exaggerated as the veil and the cap. See the injunction given by the Visitor, *ibid.*, II, 8.
[249] *Ibid.*, II, 4.

One might repeat numerous examples of the lax observance which marked the attitude of many medieval religious; some of their practices in regard to dress were grave departures from the Rules they professed to follow, but others were of minor importance. Such examples serve to show that Chaucer's nun was after all somewhat conservative in her manner of dress.

Attitude of Moralists and Preachers toward Dress

It has been seen that Chaucer does not show in his works the greatest abuses of the age in respect to costume. The exaggerations so often satirized by writers of the time have but little place in his works, especially in the more original ones. Yet the poet certainly notes the fact that there were many rather serious abuses and further shows the attitude taken by certain preachers and moralists regarding them.

The Wife of Bath cites examples of this attitude, saying:

> Thou seyst also, that if we make us gay
> With clothing and with precious array,
> That it is peril of our chastitee;
> And yet, with sorwe, thou most enforce thee,
> And seye thise wordes in the apostles name,
> 'In habit, maad with chastitee and shame,
> Ye wommen shul apparaille yow,' quod he,
> 'And noght in tressed heer and gay perree,
> As perles, ne with gold, ne clothes riche.'[250]

It is the Parson, however, who fully discusses the question of extravagance and outrageous fashions in dress. It is unnecessary to review all he says, but some of the most forceful of his criticisms are included in the following:

> As to the firste sinne, that is in superfluitee of clothinge, which that maketh it so dere, to harm of the peple; /nat only the cost of embroudinge, the degyse endentinge or barringe, oundinge, palinge, windinge, or bendinge, and semblable wast of clooth in vanitee;/ but ther is also costlewe furringe in hir gounes, so muche pounsinge of chisels to maken holes, so muche dagginge of sheres;/

---

[250] D *WB Prol.*, 337-345.

forth-with the superfluitee in lengthe of the forseide gounes, trailing in the dong and in the myre, on horse and eek on fote, as wel of man as of woman. . . . Upon that other syde, to speken of the horrible disordinat scantnesse of clothing, as been thise cutted sloppes or hainselins. . . . I sey nat that honestetee in clothinge of man or woman is unconvenable, but certes the super-fluitee or disordinat scantitee of clothinge is reprev-able. . . .[251]

Here one notices reference to the custom of using various heraldic devices, suggested in the "endentinge, barringe, oundinge, palinge," and the like. So, too, the use of furs as trimmings, the cutting of the edges of gowns to simulate leaves, the length of garments, and the excessive scantiness of others all come in for their share of the Parson's criticism. There are no harrowing stories of persons who went to hell and suffered terrible torments for their vanity, as there are in the Knight of la Tour Landry's treatment of the subject,[252] but the Parson, without attempting to entertain his

---

[251] I *Pars. T.*, 415 ff.

[252] *The Book of the Knight of La Tour-Landry,* ed. Thomas Wright, EETS, OS 33 (London, 1868), 62-70. One of the knight's stories is of a woman who had at one time possessed more than fourscore gowns, but had eventually died in poverty. After death her face was so hideous that persons could hardly look at it—all because she had been vain and "had popped, painted, plucked, and fared her head."

Another story tells of a woman who was seen in a vision to be in hell. She was being inexpressibly tortured on account of her former vanity:

. . . a develle helde her bi the tresses of the here of her hede, like as a lyon holdithe his praie, in such wise as she might not with her hede remove; and the same develle putte and thruste in her browes, temples, and forhede, hote brenninge alles and nedeles, into the brayne; and the povre woman cried atte everie tyme that he threste in alle or nedille, the whiche was brenninge. And the ermyte asked the aungelle whi the fende dede her suffre that peyne. And the aungelle said for because she hadde, whanne she was on lyve, plucked her browes, front, and forhed, to have away the here, to make herself the fayrer to the plesinge of the worlde; wherefor, in every hole that her here hathe be plucked oute, every day onis the develle thrustithe in a brenninge alle or a nedille into the brayne. . . .

So the knight tried to instruct his daughters. He has many other stories concerning the vanities of the times—the fashions, the use of too few garments, and numerous other phases of costume.

listeners strikes right at the root of the trouble. His discussion is really a summary of the abuses of Chaucer's time, and a summary which is surprisingly comprehensive.

* * * * * * *

There seems no denying the fact that Chaucer's presentation of English medieval costume, though it must be more or less incidental in his works, is remarkably complete. Contrary to most of the romances of his time, the poet's more original characters are chiefly men and consequently their costumes are more amply described than women's. Still, feminine dress is not neglected and there are some excellent views of certain types of it.

Except in works influenced largely by other literary sources, Chaucer has little to do with the dress of men of high social rank. He presents kings as being garbed in robes thickly set with jewels, in an elaborate cote-armure and a short mantle, embroidered with gems of rare brilliancy, or gowns richly ornamented with designs of birds, animals, flowers, and the like. He refers to the custom of slashing the edges of garments; to the use of such materials as samite and Cloth of Tars; and to the styles of hair and head dress, especially to the wearing of garlands of flowers. Summed up, the allusions at least indicate the general characteristics of the dress of men of royal or noble birth.

The lower classes of society appear generally in garments indicative of their various professions or of their social positions. Their costumes are for the most part more concretely depicted than are the foregoing.

Squire, lawyer, physician, merchant, reeve, shipman, miller, plowman—all are described with some details of their dress, hairdress, cut of beard, shoes, and accessories. There is the short gown with wide flowing sleeves, the parti-colored cloak or gown, the surcoat, and tabard; there are beards trimmed and forked, and beards of great length or of unusual width; there are pointed-toed shoes of curious fashions, and hose of various colors. Hats or hoods, some of which are imported from foreign countries, and the inevitable garlands are described as head adornments. In nearly all the views of the costumes worn by these classes of persons one notes particular attention to colors, to materials, and to the names of the various garments.

Military costumes are depicted in two manners, one serious, the other at least partly satirical. From a careful study of all the allusions one learns that there was no one type of armour which was worn at this period; individual caprice often governed the selection of the knight's accoutrement. Generally, however, there seem to have been several pieces of armour which nearly all knights adopted; these included the habergeoun, the gipoun, and the cote-armour.

The habits of religious men are described more fully and realistically than others which Chaucer presents. The characteristic garb of several different orders is considered, usually through a discussion of the disregard shown by certain religious for the regulations which governed their mode of dress.

The allusions to monastic costume show the habit of the Benedictine monks to have consisted of a cope which probably covered a loose-flowing kirtle, a hood, and boots. Departures from this regulation habit are seen in the extra width of the cope, the fine quality boots, and the gold pin which adorned the hood. The Franciscan friars also wore a cope as outer garment, but it was shorter than that of the Benedictines, and evidently heavier. Their hood seems to have had a long tipet hanging from it. The canon's costume consisted of a black gown and surplice, over which was a cloak with hood attached.

Sometimes, it seems, canons wore hats, too. Clerks affected various types of garb. When travelling they wore the courtpy, a type of short cloak, but evidently when in their parishes they wore costumes similar to that of Chaucer's Absolon, namely, a light blue kirtle and surplice. The beautifully cut shoes and the red hose of this Absolon were perhaps not part of the regulation habit.

Besides describing these various types of men's costumes, Chaucer suggests the vanity of men. Generally the marks of vanity, other than fine garments, include combing the hair and making one's self particularly neat and tidy. The chewing of different kinds of herbs to sweeten the breath seems also to be indicative of an attempt to please.

Aside from the descriptions of women's costumes which Chaucer translates from the *Romaunt de la Rose,* there are only a few examples of feminine dress. However, in reviewing all, inclusive of those dependent on the *Romaunt,* it is possible to form a remarkably complete view of the medieval woman's apparel.

The costumes of women of rank are very elaborate. Generally they consist of loose-flowing gowns with wide sleeves and are elaborately embroidered. The headdress is either a caul or a garland of some sort, often of jewels. Silk and fine linen seem to be the materials most widely used for garments.

The poor are pictured as wearing torn and patched clothing. Sometimes they seem to have but one garment and that a very poor one. Apparently they have no fashionable headdresses and no tasseled purses or other accessories.

Certain of Chaucer's descriptions of women's costumes are decidedly conventional in manner. The mention of yellow hair, braided or flowing loosely down a lady's back; the reference to gowns without any concrete details of description; and the vague allusions to dress in general are indicative of the poet's dependence upon other sources.

It is only when he turns to his own created characters that Chaucer becomes realistic in his descriptions of women's dress. He shows the Wife of Bath, a would-be fashionable woman of the world, wearing an elaborate hat and a wimple as headdress. About her hips she wears a skirt protector; on her feet she wears fine shoes and red hose. Probably her dress is also of red, as she insinuates in her prologue.

The Carpenter's wife shows another type of feminine costume. It consists of an apron as white as milk, a white smock trimmed in black silk, and a bonnet with similarly trimmed ties. Her girdle is silk and ornamented with little bars, possibly of contrasting color. On her head she wears a silken fillet, and in her hand she carries a tasseled leather purse. An enormous brooch on her collar completes the costume. Like many women of her times, the Carpenter's wife affects plucked eyebrows.

Further representations of feminine costume include that of a widow and that of a nun. The former dress consists of a long, voluminous black robe and a barbe. The latter's habit is composed of a neatly made cloak and a well-pleated wimple. Undoubtedly the cloak, or mantle, concealed a kirtle, the rather plain garment which the Benedictine nuns of the Middle Ages wore. The nun carries a beautiful rosary of jet, gauded with green and having thereon a brooch or medal with a motto.

Finally, Chaucer's study of dress concludes with a tirade of the Parson, who is like other medieval preachers and moralists in believing dress to have been a cause of much sin. He refers to the fashions, to the exaggerated length of the gowns, to various extravagances in the use of furs and ornamentation, and to the scantness of certain garments.

Surely Chaucer's consideration of English medieval dress, in spite of some deficiencies, is significant in the study of the history of costume. It may be, indeed, that the poet treats of wearing apparel only incidentally; yet he does so with remarkable attention to little details of color, style, material, and the like, and consequently has given his readers the opportunity of observing a wide range of medieval costumes.

CHAPTER V

SPORTS AND PASTIMES

He coude hunte at wilde deer,
And ride an hauking for riveer,
  With grey goshauk on honde;
Ther-to he was a good archeer,
Of wrastling ther was noon his peer,
  Ther any ram shal stonde.
—B *Sir Thopas*, 1926-1931

Medieval English men and women were enthusiastic lovers of "pleye." They hunted in field and forest, went hawking along riversides, participated in brilliant tournaments, danced, wrestled, and tried their skill at archery; in addition, they played at chess, tossed dice in games of chance, played on musical instruments, sang, told stories, and read. Of all these sports and pastimes Chaucer treats, often comprehensively, again only casually. From his poems, which are a treasury of medieval recreational activities, one can understand in part how "Merrie England" has deserved its title.

Sports and Pastimes in General in Chaucer

Almost as an encyclopedist Chaucer gives the details of the two major activities; namely, hunting and the tournament. When compared with other accounts of these sports, those of the poet are seen to be, if not entirely complete, realistic[1] to a surprising degree.

---

[1] Robinson expresses this realism by saying of the hunting scene that it "might be consulted as a document on the practice of the sport." *Chaucer's Complete Works*, 316. Cf. also Oliver F. Emerson, "Chaucer and Medieval Hunting," *Romanic Review*, XIII (April-June, 1922), 150. The description of the tournament also is largely of Chaucer's invention and closely parallels actual tournaments of the fourteenth century. Cf. Robinson, *op. cit.*, 783; Walter H. Schofield, *Chivalry in English Literature* (Cambridge, 1912), 38 ff.

Other recreational pastimes, too, even though described more incidentally, show similar marks of realism. Scattered throughout his poems as are many of the allusions, they indicate the importance of such pastimes in the lives of the different classes of society. Even the most casual allusions, if used merely as figures of speech, generally contribute some specific information concerning the activities themselves or at least concerning the language of sports and pastimes of the Middle Ages.

Hunting and Hounds

Chaucer treats in detail of only one hunting scene, namely, that in the *Book of the Duchess.* Yet he supplements this with numerous other allusions, some of which are fragmentary, both to the sport and the hounds used in it. The frequency, as well as the nature, of his references is proof that at least among the upper classes hunting was the most popular of medieval sports.[2]

The outline of the hunt in the *Book of the Duchess* is vivified by Chaucer's skillful use of hunting terms in their strict sense. From the moment the huntsman blows "t'assaye his horn," that he might know "whether hit were clere or hors of soune," to the

---

[2] Since the dawn of English history hunting had been the chief recreation—the rich hunting for sport alone, the poor for food. In pre-Conquest days the Anglo-Saxons maintained royal preserves of great extent and the country was even in this period famous for its breed of dogs. French methods of hunting and game preservation came in with the Conquest. William the Conqueror, sometimes called "the Father of Modern English Hunting," extended the royal preserves, even at the expense of depopulating villages and destroying property. He and his followers made of the chase a veritable religion. With this encouragement given by the Normans to the sport, hunting became the chief recreational passion of medieval society. "C'était, après la guerre, leur passion, leur vie. . . la chasse était devenue une véritable science, très compliquée, et un métier fort sérieux. . . ." Léon Gautier, *La Chevalerie,* nouvelle édition (Paris, 1883), 173-174. See also James W. Day, *A Falcon on St. Paul's* (London, 1935), 108; Henry L. Savage, "Hunting in the Middle Ages," *Speculum,* VIII (Jan., 1933), 32 ff.; Joseph B. Thomas, *Hounds and Hunting Through the Ages* (New York, 1933), 8 ff.; *An Anonymous Short English Chronicle,* ed. Ewald Zettl, EETS, OS 196 (London, 1935), 37 ff.; *Anglo-Saxon Chronicle,* trans. J. A. Giles (London, 1914), 160-161.

"forloyne,"[3] the progress of the sport is given with almost technical exactness. In view of the air of unreality dominant in the *Book of the Duchess* the striking actuality of the scene is both more apparent and more significant than it would otherwise be.

Alluding to the remarks of the hunters—"how they wolde slee the hert with strengthe,"[4] "howe the hert had . . . so much embosed,"[5] and "that they wolde on huntinge goon,"[6] Chaucer strikes the realistic note even before he begins describing the hunt itself. His references to the hunters and foresters,[7] who with their many relayes (fresh sets or reserves) of hounds and their "lymeres,"[8] all "hyed hem to the forest faste,"[9] are markedly concrete.

With the blowing of three motes or notes on the great horn by the master-huntsman, the hounds are uncoupled[10] and the chase really begins. The blowing of the horn was of special significance in medieval hunting, its two chief uses being to discipline the hounds and to guide the hunters.[11] In this particular instance, the three motes probably indicate that the hart has been sighted, or at least scented by the hounds. According to a medieval explanation the master-huntsman blew his horn for only "three

[3] According to Skeat "the forloyne" was a note for recall. Robinson defines it as a signal that the dogs were far off from the game, and says it was followed by the coupling of the hounds.

[4] *With strengthe,* from the French *à force,* means to kill in regular chase with horses and hounds. Robinson, 883.

[5] To become exhausted. (Lit. "covered with bosses or flecks of foam"). See Emerson, *op. cit.,* 115.

[6] *BD,* 355.

[7] The forester was "an officer of the King (or any other man) that was sworn to preserve the Vert and Venison of the forest. . ." Cf. Emerson, *op. cit.,* 121.

[8] "The lymer was the tracking hound, trained to scent out game for the hunt, to move or start it when hunted, and to gain the scent again if it were lost by the running hounds." Emerson, *op. cit.,* 123. See also the illustration of "The Tufter and the Lymer," from Gaston Phoebus' Ms. painted about 1440, in Wm. A. Baillie-Grohman's *Sport in Art* (London, 1913), 7.

[9] *BD,* 360-362.

[10] *Ibid.,* 376-377.

[11] Savage, *op. cit.,* 39.

males and for one femalle, that is to say, for an hert, the boor, the wolfh male, and alle so for the wolfh female, as wel as to here husbond."[12] The number of motes blown likewise indicated to the hunters what part of the hunt was in progress.

From the uncoupling of the hounds to the forloyn, Chaucer hastens the progress of the action. In few words he pictures the main part of the chase:

> Within a whyl the hert (y)-founde is,
> Y-halowed[13] and rechased[14] faste
> Longe tyme; and at the laste,
> This herte rused[15] and stal away
> Fro alle the houndes a prevy way.
> The houndes had overshote[16] hem alle,
> And were on a defaute[17] y-falle;
> Therwith the hunte wonder faste
> Blew a forloyn at the last.[18]

The manner of blowing the forloyn is described in "Le Venery de Twety." The huntsman explains it thus:

> I shal blowe after one mote, ij motes, and if myn howndes come not hastily to me as y wolde, I shall blow iiij. motes, and for to hast hem to me and for to warne the gentelys that the hert is sene, then shalle I rechace on myn houndis iij. tymes, and when he is ferre from me, than shall y chase hym in thys maner, *Trout, trout, tro ro rot, trout, trout, tro ro rot, trou ro rot, trou ro rot.* Syr hunters, why blowe ye so? For cause that the hert is

---

[12] "Le Venery de Twety," *Reliquae Antiquae,* I, 152.

[13] Emerson explains y-halowed to mean specifically "to set on the dogs with the hallow (halloo)" after the finding. "Chaucer and Medieval Hunting," 127.

[14] Skeat defines rechasing as "headed back," but Emerson believes it to mean, rather, "chased, pursued, hunted fast a long time, the prefix *re*-having here no more force than in receive, request." *Ibid.,* 128.

[15] To ruse is "to make a detour or other movement in order to escape from the hounds." *Ibid.,* 129.

[16] "The running hounds do not at first perceive the deer's change, 'overshoot' the scent, and so lose it for a time." *Ibid.,* 129.

[17] This term, defined as "had a check" means merely that the game is at a standstill. *Ibid.,* 130.

[18] *BD,* 378-386.

seen, an y wot never whedir that myn hundys be become
fro myn meyne.   And what manner of chase clepe ye
that?   We clepe it the chace of the forloyne.[19]

It will be noted that Chaucer's use of the forloyn is essentially
for artistic purposes.[20]   It gives him an opportunity, while the
game is at a standstill, to turn away from the hunt to describe
other adventures which further the progress of the story he is
telling.   No true medieval hunter could have torn himself away
from the scene had the pursuit of the hart been at its height.

Duke Theseus was an enthusiastic lover of the hunt.   He was
indeed so desirous of the sport

> That in his bed ther daweth him no day,
> That he nis clad, and redy for to ryde
> With hunte and horn, and houndes him bisyde.
> For in his hunting hath he swich delyt,
> That it is al his joye and appetyt
> To been him-self the grete hertes bane:
> For after Mars he serveth now Diane.[21]

Troilus participated in various sports, but particularly liked to
hunt:

> In tyme of trewe, on haukinge wolde he ryde,
> Or elles hunten boor, bere, or lyoun;
> The smale bestes leet he gon bi-syde.[22]

Chaucer here shows the courage of the young Trojan; the greater
the beast hunted, the more honor there was to the hunter.   It is
interesting from the point of view of realism that although the
boar was often hunted in England, the bear was not.[23]   Probably
the lion is mentioned to give that touch of local color which
Chaucer so frequently attempts in the *Troilus*.   Both the bear
and the lion also indicate the great strength which Troilus felt
himself to have.   Just as at this particular time he was unusually

----

[19] *Antiquae Reliquae,* I, 152.   Cf. the illustration (Fig. 18) of Gaston
Phoebus instructing his huntsmen how to blow the horn.   *Sport in Art,* 34.
    [20] Emerson, *op. cit.,* 133.
    [21] A *Kn.T.,* 1675-1682.
    [22] *TC,* III, 1779-1781.
    [23] Nicholas Cox, *The Gentleman's Recreation* (London, 1706), 20.

valiant as a warrior, so was he as a hunter. The reason assigned for one answers for the other:

> And this encrees of hardinesse and might
> Cam him of love, his ladies thank to winne,
> That altered his spirt so with-inne.[24]

All his efforts seem to have been well repaid, for

> . . . whan that he com rydinge in-to toun,
> Ful ofte his lady, from hir window doun,
> As fresh as faucon comen out of muwe,
> Ful redy was, him goodly to saluwe.[25]

Under such circumstances, what young lover could not have captured boars, bears, and lions?[26]

Of his Monk, Chaucer writes:

> A Monk ther was, a fair for the maistyre,
> An out-rydere, that lovede venerye.[27]

"Venerye" as used here is generally taken to refer to the Monk's love of hunting in all its aspects. May it not, however, have been meant by Chaucer to indicate a particular liking for hunting

---

[24] *TC*, III, 1776-1778.

[25] *Ibid.*, III, 1782-1785.

[26] In "The Legend of Dido," *LGW*, the lovers and their fellow hunters are not satisfied with hunting the hart, but cry,
> Why nil the leoun comen or the bere,
> That I mighte ones mete him with this spere? 1214-1215.

[27] A *Gen. Prol.*, 165-166. The animals that were hunted were classified as (1) beasts of the forest, or of venery; (2) beasts of the chase; and (3) beasts of the warren. There were said to be four beasts of venery—the hare, the hart, the wolf, and the wild boar; five of the chase—the buck, the doe, the fox, the marten, and the roe; and three beasts of the warren—the grey (possibly the badger), the cat, and the otter. Cf. "Le Venery de Twety," *Reliquae Antiquae*, I, 150. Cox, *The Gentleman's Recreation*, 19; Dame Juliana Berners, *The Booke of St. Albans*, reprint by Gervase Markham (London, 1595), Part I.
In general the distinctions between the groups of animals are vague. The terms probably mean only that certain animals were hunted in one way, and certain others in another; "illegal slaughter of a 'beast of the forest' (since it occupied a higher 'hunting category') brought upon its perpetrator a severer penalty than he would have received had he slain a 'beast of the chase.'" Savage, *op. cit.*, 33.

"beasts of venery?" It is quite in accord with the Monk's character that he would participate in that phase of the chase which involved beasts of the highest category; furthermore, Chaucer mentions specifically that

> Of priking and of hunting for the hare
> Was al his lust, for no cost wolde he spare.[28]

Dame Juliana, the fourteenth century woman sport's writer, says, "The hare is King of al the beasts of Venerie, and in hunting maketh best sport, breedeth the most delight of any other, and is a beast most strange by nature."[29] The hunting of the hart was considered "a princely and royall chace,"[30] and the hart itself "the lightest (swiftest) of beasts and strongest, and of marvellous great cunning;"[31] but the Monk, and oddly enough, Sir Thopas,[32] found their delight in hunting the hare. It will be recalled that members of the royal hunting parties of the Emperour Octovien,[33] of Duke Theseus,[34] and of Dido and Aeneas[35] pursued the hart.[36]

The Monk, under any consideration, showed great disregard for his Rule by hunting. This Rule, which was so strict in relation to the observance of the vow of poverty that it forbade the monks to "give, receive, or keep as their own, anything whatever; neither books, nor tablets, nor pen,"[37] automatically prohibited

---

[28] A *Gen. Prol.* 191-192.

[29] *Booke of St. Albans,* I, 31.

[30] *Booke of St. Albans,* I, 34.

[31] *The Master of Game,* 15; cf. 200, f.n. 47 for complete citation.

[32] B 1946. Sir Thopas likewise hunts the buck. *Ibid.,* 1946.

[33] *BD,* 345 ff.

[34] A *Kn.T.,* 1683 ff.

[35] *LGW,* 1212 ff.

[36] There were certain seasons for the hunting of the different animals. "The fox could be hunted from the Nativity to the Annunciation; the roebuck from Easter to Michaelmas; the roe from Michaelmas to Candlemas; the hare from Michaelmas to Midsummer; the wolf as the fox and the boar from the Nativity to the Purification of our Lady." The season for the hart was in Summer. Note that Chaucer's hunters select May, especially. This may have been the first month of the season for the hart. *The Booke of St. Albans,* I, 34; *The Gentleman's Recreation,* 9; appendix 10.

[37] *Rule of St. Benedict,* Ch. XXIII (Gasquet's ed.), 65; *The Rule of Saint Benet,* ed. H. Logeman, EETS, OS 90 (London, 1888), 63.

the possession of dogs or horses[38] for the purpose of hunting. The Monk, however, was scornful of any restriction on his liberty for,

> He yaf nat of that text a pulled hen,
> That seith that hunters been nat holy men.[39]

His attitude is perhaps typical of that which was rapidly giving rise to great abuses in the monasteries, and which are recorded in large numbers in the Episcopal Visitations, especially in the fifteenth century. Aping the manners of worldly men and participating in all kinds of sports and pastimes, it is little wonder that many of the religious gradually fell into faults such as that of a certain Dom Marmoyne of Dorchester Abbey, who, it was complained, "keeps in the same (house) every week sixteen dogs for coursing, for which he receives two pecks of barley a week besides bran."[40]

The Augustinians at Newnham in one instance complained to the Episcopal Visitor of "the great number of hounds . . . which snatch their meat from the canons' table." The alms of the house were being wasted, they said, in the upkeep of these hounds, and besides, canons often went a-hunting,[41] which was decidedly against their Rule. With wisdom the Visitor commanded in such cases that all dogs for hunting be driven away from the abbeys or priories.[42] With equal wisdom John Myrc in his *Instructions for Parish Priests* wrote,

> Hawkynge, huntynge, and daunsynge,
> Thou muste forgo for any thynge.[43]

The state to which religious had fallen in their fondness for the chase is further suggested by the fact that in the reign of

---

[38] Cf. Oliver F. Emerson, "Some of Chaucer's Lines on the Monk," *Modern Philology,* I (June 1903), 11; Cf. also Dugdale, *Monasticon,* II, 188; Fosbrooke, *English Monachism,* 217, note *a.*

[39] A *Gen. Prol.,* 177-178. Cf. also Emerson, *op. cit.,* 11.

[40] *Lincoln Visitations,* II, part I, 69.

[41] *Ibid.,* III, ii, 234.

[42] See Bishop Gray's injunctions for Caldwell Priory (1421-22), *Linc. Visit.,* I, 27; Bishop Fleming's for St. Frideswide's (1422-23), *ibid.,* 97; the injunction for Kyme Priory (1440), *ibid.,* II, 172.

[43] EETS, ES 31 (London, 1868), p. 2, 11. 41-42.

Richard II civil legislation was enacted to restrain the clergy from the sport. The law provided that

> . . . any priest, or other clerk, not possessed of a benefice to the yearly amount of ten pounds (was prohibited) from keeping a greyhound, or any other dog for the purpose of hunting; neither might they use ferrits, hayes, nets, hare-pipes, cords, or other engines to take or destroy the deer, hares, or rabbits under the penalty of one year's imprisonment.[44]

It will be noted that those clergymen whose social position gave them greater influence were not included in this law. Prelates no doubt still enjoyed the privileges granted them in the Charter of the Forest as granted by Henry III, namely, that under certain restrictions[45] they might hunt even in the King's own preserves.

The medieval gentleman often maintained, even at great cost, a large pack of hounds for the chase.[46] He prized them highly[47]

---

[44] Joseph Strutt, *Sports and Pastimes of the Middle Ages* (London, 1876), 67.

[45] Cf. Cox, *The Gentleman's Recreation,* appendix, 39. The restrictions stated that the prelate must be sent for by the king; that he must be an archbishop or bishop; that he must hunt in view of the forester or must blow his horn to apprise the king or his forester that the deer was not being stolen.

[46] The pack was mixed, the hounds scarcely ever being of one size or breed. There was usually a scenting-hound of the Old Southern type, greyhounds of several kinds, "alaunts" or alans, and many small dogs or kennets. The harrier, the beagle, and the like were also included in some packs. See Savage, *op. cit.,* 36 ff.

[47] It is interesting to note some of the merits ascribed by certain medieval huntsmen to the hound. Edward the Second, Duke of York, in his *The Master of Game,* ed. by Wm. A. and F. Baillie-Grohman, with a foreword by Theodore Roosevelt (London, 1904), 42-44, generously lists these merits, saying:

> . . . an hounde is þe moost reasonable beest and beste knowyng of eny beest þat evere God made, and ʒit in some case I neiþer out take man ne oþer þing . . . An hound is trewe to his lord or to his maystere . . . an hounde is of greet vndirstonding and of greet knowynge, a hound has greet strength and greet bounte, an hounde haþ greet mynde and greet smellyng. . . .

The Master of Game is in large part a translation of a fourteenth century *Livre de Chasse* written by Gaston Phoebus, Comte de Foix. The latter

and took excellent care of them.[48] Usually his hounds accompanied him when he went on journeys or attended social functions. Sometimes, even, they followed him to church, being allowed to wander about after their master, to the great distraction of other worshipers.[49]

Besides the casual references made to the hounds in the *Book of the Duchess* and to those which accompanied Duke Theseus, Chaucer has other allusions which are somewhat more specific. Of the Monk's hounds he writes:

> Grehoundes he hadde, as swifte as fowel in flight.[50]

Greyhounds were dogs of the smooth-coated Italian type, and also of the type represented by Scottish or Irish deerhound, "thin, but rangy, fierce, and shaggy." The former were sometimes known as *petit lévrier pour lièvre,* the latter as *lévrier d'attache.* They hunted by sight rather than by scent and were of best use after the scenting-hounds had driven the animal to within view.[51]

More vividly described than others are the alaunts of Ligurge, King of Thrace. These great dogs, which were probably similar to the modern Great Dane or German boarhound, were powerful,

---

work "still remains unsuperseded in its knowledge of the habits of European game and its insight into the nature of hounds." Savage, *op. cit.,* 32. Since Gaston Phoebus himself had about 800 hounds and "loved dogs above all other animals; and during the summer and winter amused himself much with hunting" (Froissart, *Chronicles,* II, 95), the opinion here expressed as to the nature of the hound bears some importance.

[48] Of the attention accorded them, the Goodman of Paris writes: "Hounds returning from the woods and from the chase be littered before their master and he maketh fresh litter himself before the fire; their feet be greased at the fire with soft grease, they be given sops and be well eased, for pity of their labour. . . " *Goodman of Paris,* 176.

[49] Great abuses arose from this custom, as may be imagined. It was said that often there were many hounds in the church at once. Their barking, the noise of the chains on their necks, and the clapping of the masters' hands as they tried to quiet them were very disturbing. Cf. Alexander Barclay, *The Ship of Fools,* 2 vols. (New York, 1874), I, 220 ff. See also complaints reported at various monasteries or convents, e. g., *Linc. Visit.,* III, part II, 175.

[50] A *Gen. Prol.,* 190.

[51] Savage, *op. cit.,* 38.

aggressive beasts, used chiefly in boar-hunting.[52] Those which Ligurge had were white; there were "twenty and mo, as grete as any steer,"

> And folwed him, with mosel faste y-bounde,
> Colers of gold, and torets fyled rounde.[53]

One cannot help wondering whether these great hounds were among those which Chaucer refers to in his description of the banquet:

> What houndes liggen on the floor adoun.[54]

If they were, and the other guests had several hounds of one kind or another, there must have arisen a great din when bones were tossed to them as they lay under the tables.

It will be observed that Chaucer's allusions to the hounds are of two types, namely to the pack as a whole and to specific kinds of dogs. In nearly every reference there is the suggestion of motion; in the *Book of the Duchess* the hounds are in full action in their pursuit of the hart; the Monk's hounds are "swifte as fowel in flight," and the alaunts of King Ligurge follow after their master's chariot. Describing the hounds in such a fashion the poet gives an unusually realistic impression of them.

Chaucer takes some account of the medieval woman's participation in the chase. His description of Queen Dido in the *Legend of Good Women* has elements of the unreal, but also a touch of actuality which is almost incongruous. Particularly is the reference to Dido herself of a romantic turn:

> Up-on a thikke palfrey, paper-whyt,
> With sadel rede, enbrouded with delyt,
> Of gold the barres up-enbossed hye,
> Sit Dido, al in gold and perre wrye.[55]

---

[52] *Ibid.*, 38.

[53] A *Kn. T.*, 2149-2152.

[54] *Ibid.*, 2205.

[55] 1198-1201. An interesting comparison with this description is to be found in *The Squyr of Lowe Degre*, 738-749.

With the allusion to the hunt, though, Chaucer becomes more realistic:

> The herd of hertes founden is anoon,
> With 'hey! go bet! prik thou! lat goon, lat goon!
> Why nil the leoun comen or the bere,
> That I mighte ones mete him with this spere?'[56]

Evidently, Dido, riding upon the white steed, is in the midst of the enthusiastic crowd of young hunters whose cries ring out in true hunters' fashion.[57]

Only casual reference is made to the fact that Queen Ipolita and Emelye accompanied Duke Theseus on a hunting trip:

> And Theseus, with alle joye and blis,
> With his Ipolita, the fayre quene,
> And Emelye, clothed al in grene,
> On hunting be they riden royally.[58]

That the two women were "clothed al in grene" is an interesting point in the consideration of realism. Generally the women of romance seem to have worn purple and ermine, as did the daughter of the king in *The Squyr of Lowe Degre*,[59] but actual women wore either green or russet. "Phoebus sayth that they ought to be clad in green when they hunt the Hart or Bucke, and in russet when they hunt the Bore, but that it is of no great importance, for I remitte the colour to the fantasies of men."[60] The statue of Diane, on the temple erected to her honor by Duke Theseus, is clothed in green, too:

> In gaude grene hir statue clothed was,
> With bowe in honde, and arwes in a cas.[61]

---

[56] *LGW*, 1211-1213.

[57] Women in participating in the hunt often waited in an enclosure or temporary stand for the game to be driven past there, where they might shoot at it with their arrows. Strutt, *Sports and Pastimes*, 68. See *The Squyr of Lowe Degre,* 764-771; also *TC,* II, 1535-1536:
> "Lo, holde thee at thy triste cloos, and I
> Shal wel the deer un-to thy bowe dryve."

[58] A *Kn. T.,* 1684-1687.

[59] 746-747.

[60] Quoted from Turberville's *Book of Hunting* by Emerson, *op. cit.,* 14.

[61] A *Kn. T.,* 2079-2080. Note that the Yeoman, A *Gen. Prol.,* 57-117, too, is dressed in green.

It is remarkable, perhaps, that Chaucer's allusions to the hunt are on the whole as realistic as they are. With the interest which the poet must have had in the sport to write so exactly as he does in the *Book of the Duchess* it would seem only natural that he should elaborate his scenes and make them more idealistic. The fact that he seldom follows the romances in this matter seems to indicate his recognition of the power that lies in treating of the actual as it is.

Hawking

As much as hunting may have appealed to women of the Middle Ages it probably ranked second to hawking, or falconry, which was more suited to them. This activity was popular with both men and women, for a few persons, rather than a large group, could entertain themselves in a somewhat informal manner. Horses were not required, but were often used. All that was necessary for participation in the sport was to have some kind of hawk,[62] trained to ride on the owner's wrist, to attack fowl, and to return again to the owner.[63]

---

[62] The capture and preliminary taming of a hawk required a certain amount of skill. To catch the bird a net was used. It "must be made of good small threed, which would be died either green or blew," says Dame Juliana Berners, "for feare of the Hawkes espying the same." *The Booke of St. Albans*, 2. As soon as the bird was taken, it was enciled; that is, with needle and thread, its eyelids were drawn closed, the thread being fastened under its beak, or above its head. Then the hawk was taken home and put upon a perch where she was left a night and a day. Of her care at this time Dame Juliana writes:

> . . . on the nexte day towardes evening, take a knife and with great care see you cut the threedes insunder whiche inseele hir, and take them away softly for feare of breaking her eie liddes, then beginne in gentle manner to feede here, and use all the lenitie and meekenesse you can unto her until she will sit quietly upon your fist, for by much striving you shall hurt her wings which were not a little dangerous: and then the same night, after feeding, watch her all night and all the next morrow from any sleepe or rest, which will occasion her to be reclaimed with lesse difficultie: yet note that the first meate which she shall eate be hote, and let her take enough thereof without troubling. *Ibid.*, 2. Cf. also "The Booke of Hawkyng after Prince Edwarde Kyng of Englande," *Reliquae Antiquae*, I, 293.

[63] Part of the bird's training consisted in teaching her by the use of a lure to attack living prey. This lure was bones and muscle wrapped in the feathers of a partridge or some other similar fowl and attached to a cord

All the time she was being trained, the hawk was also learning to submit to wearing a hood of supple brass which followed the form of her head, covering it as far as the neck—the beak and nostrils being left free—and two straps of leather or heavy silk, called jesses, attached to her legs, by which she was carried "on the fist" of her master.[64] The maintenance of hawks was expensive and required much leisure time; consequently the sport was limited to persons of some wealth.[65]

Chaucer alludes frequently, but never in detail, to hawking. Troilus is described as riding "with hauke on hond,"[66] but no reference is made to the kind of hawk it is. Sir Thopas, however, bears a goshawk on his wrist.[67] Sir Walter in the *Clerk's Tale* participates in hawking,[68] but no mention is made of either the bird he uses or the kind of fowl he especially likes to hunt. The King of Inde, that "grete Emetreus" who attends Duke Theseus' tournament, is evidently fond of hawking. He carries "for his deduyt,"

> An egle tame, as eny lilie whyt.[69]

---

which the falconer could swing around his head, allowing the hawk to seize it. When the hawk, after much practice became proficient enough to catch a real bird, she was rewarded by being given a part of it. Gautier, *La Chevalerie*, 180, *notes;* "The Booke of Hawkynge," 297.

[64] Gautier, *op. cit.,* 181, *notes.* The hawk's hood was generally put on after she was enciled. The master was directed to hood and unhood her often, "until she takes no offence at the Hood and will patiently endure handling." *The Gentleman's Recreations,* 34-35. Little bells were also fastened to the hawk's legs by pieces of leather. These were for adornment and for the location of the hawk when out of sight. Various precautions about the bells were observed; for instance, they should not be too heavy, and both of like weight. They were also to be well sounding, but not of one tone. Bells of Milan were considered as among the best. *Booke of St. Albans,* 13.

[65] The very possession of many hawks was considered a sign of affluence. "Faucons sur perche avez, et vair et gris: c'était alors ce que l'on disait des barons qui passaient pour très riches. Posséder des oiseaux de chasse et des fourrures, c'était, comme nous le dirions aujourd'hui, être plusieurs fois millionnaire. Voulait-on faire un riche présent, notamment à une dame? on lui envoyait un faucon. Rien n'était plus galant." Gautier, *op. cit.,* 175.

[66] *TC,* V, 65.

[67] B *Sir Thop.,* 1927-1928.

[68] E 31.

[69] A *Kn. T.,* 2177-2178. This white eagle is said to have been used by Chaucer as an Asiatic touch. Cf. Manly, *Canterbury Tales,* 555.

Naturally, a person who, like this gentleman, had "many a tame leoun and lepart"[70] with him would need the greatest of hawks with which to take other birds of prey, or perhaps even animals such as "an hinde calf, a fawn, a roe, a kidde, an elke. . . ."[71] and the like.

Chaucer is realistic in ascribing certain hawks to different individuals, although as will be noticed he sometimes either mistakes the bird usually assigned a particular class of society or deliberately does so for the sake of irony. It was a curious hierarchy of birds which medieval persons adopted. Each rank of society had a particular type of hawk assigned to it, the order in general being as follows:

> The eagle, the vulture, and the merloun, for an emperour.[72]
> The ger-faulcon, and the tercel of the ger-faulcon for a king.[73]
> The faulcon gentle, and the tercel gentle, for a prince.
> The faulcon of the rock, for a duke.
> The faulcon peregrine, for an earl.[74]
> The bastard, for a baron.
> The sacre, and the sacret, for a knight.
> The lanere, and the laneret, for an esquire.
> The marlyon, for a lady.
> The hobby, for a young man.
> The gos-hawk, for a yeoman.
> The tercel, for a poor man.
> The sparrow-hawk, for a priest.
> The musket, for a holy-water clerk.
> The kesterel, for a knave or servant.[75]

---

[70] *Ibid.*, 2186.

[71] *Booke of St. Albans,* II, 14.

[72] Cf. *supra,* 205.

[73] Cf. F *Sq. T.,* 504 ff.; *PF*, 393 ff.

[74] Canacee's falcon was a peregrine. Cf. F *Sq. T.,* 424 ff.

[75] *The Booke of St. Albans,* 14-16; *The Gentleman's Recreation,* 2-3. There is slight difference of opinion regarding some of these birds, but in general this list is followed. Most of these hawks are described in Gautier, *La Chevalerie,* notes, 178.

Sir Thopas with his grey goshawk—the bird ascribed generally
to a yeoman; King Emetreus, with his eagle; and the allusion to
the Nun's Priest as one who "loketh as a sperhauk with his
yen;"[76] all indicate Chaucer's effective use of the birds to describe
or to emphasize the qualities of certain characters.

More significant references to the hawks themselves are found
in the *Parlement of Foules,* where there are direct descriptive
passages. For example, it is said of the goshawk,

> Ther was the tyraunt with his fethres donne
> And greye, I mene the goshauk, that doth pyne
> To briddes for his outrageous ravyne.[77]

There, too, "the hardy sperhauk" is spoken of as "the quayles
foo,"[78] and the "merlioun" as he

> . . . . that peyneth
> Himself ful ofte, the larke for to seke.[79]

Of the sport of falconry, Chaucer offers but little and that
incidental information. Several times he alludes to the lure used
to teach the birds to attack their prey, but he does so only in a
figurative manner and not in relation to the sport itself. In the
Wife of Bath's Prologue, for instance, he says,

> With empty hand men may none haukes lure,[80]

and in the *Friar's Tale* he employs the following simile:

> This false theef, this Somnour, quod the Frere,
> Hadde alwey baudes redy to his hond,
> As any hauk to lure in Engelond.[81]

Altogether, in spite of the fact that the poet mentions the sport,
one can learn little about it from his allusions. Unlike the hunt,
falcony is not described in progress, which may indicate that

---

[76] B *NPT,* epilogue, 4647.
[77] *Minor Poems,* V, 334-336.
[78] *Ibid.,* 338-339.
[79] *Ibid.,* 339-340.
[80] D 415.
[81] D 1338-1340.

Chaucer considered this activity of relatively little interest or perhaps as having no value for colorful description.

The Tournament

With all their popularity, hunting and hawking must both have been colorless and unexciting in comparison with the tournament. This was sport entailing much physical strength and courage[82]—a martial conflict which served as an excellent preparation for war[83] —and particularly the pastime of knights. It had been introduced into England from France, probably, and had rapidly become popular with the nobility. In the thirteenth and fourteenth centuries it seems to have reached the height of its popularity.

One need look no further than Chaucer's *Knight's Tale* to witness in all its details a medieval tournament. True to his character as a king, Duke Theseus is pleased to avail himself of the opportunity to proclaim a contest between Palamon and Arcite; when he finds them duelling for Emelye's hand, without hesitation he lays before the two knights his proposition:

> And this day fifty wykes, fer ne ner,
> Everich of yow shal bringe an hundred knightes,
> Armed for listes up at alle hightes,
> Al redy to darreyne hir by bataille.[84]

The one who, with his assisting knights, shall slay the other, or drive him from the lists, is to have Emelye for a wife. Theseus himself will have the lists constructed in the place where Palamon and Arcite have been jousting.[85] After hearing these plans, the two knights take their departure to prepare for the combat.

The lists which Theseus constructs for the tournament are very elaborate and not at all like the crude wooden ones which came

---

[82] Francis Cripps-Day, *The History of the Tournament in England and France* (London, 1918), 2-3.

[83] Strutt, *Sports and Pastimes*, 6.

[84] A *Kn. T.*, 1850-1853.

[85] *Ibid.*, 1855-1869.

near being the cause of Queen Philippa's death in 1331.[86] Well might Chaucer boast,

> That swich a noble theatre as it was,
> I dar wel seyn that in this world ther nas.[87]

A mile in circumference, "walled of stoon and diched al withoute," with painted walls and gates, rich sculpturings, and elaborate oratories dedicated to different gods,[88] these lists seem to have been largely the invention of the poet's imagination, although based at least in part on descriptions in Boccaccio's *Teseide,* the source of the poem.[89] Perhaps Chaucer's ability to depict the lists of the *Knight's Tale* was even greater than that required for the construction of actual scaffolds for the two tournaments at Smithfield in 1390—a work of which he had charge.[90]

Certain minor preparations made for the tournament which Duke Theseus is to have are not mentioned by the poet. Medieval customs seem to have provided, however, that soon after the time and place of holding a tournament had been decided upon, heralds, accompanied by trumpeters, visited all the castles and towns nearby. There, in castle yard or market place, the trumpeters sounded their trumpets that the herald might announce the date, the place, and the conditions of the approaching tournament.[91]

In spite of this and perhaps other omissions concerning the minor preparations for the tournament, Chaucer's further description of events is amazingly complete as to details. He tells

---

[86] Stow thus describes this scaffold: ". . . there was a woodden scaffold erected crosse the streete, like unto a Tower, wherein Queene *Philip,* and many other Ladies, richly attyred, ·and assembled from all parts of the realme, did stand to behold the Iustes: but the higher frame in which the Ladies were placed, brake in sunder, whereby they were with some shame forced to fall downe. . . ." Stow, *Survey of London,* I, 268.

[87] A *Kn. T.,* 1885-1886.

[88] *Ibid.,* 1887-2088.

[89] Cf. Robinson, *Chaucer's Complete Works,* 778-779.

[90] As Clerk of the King's Works, a position which Chaucer held from 1389-1391, the poet had as part of his business the duty of constructing these scaffolds for the 1390 tournaments. See Robinson, *op. cit.,* xix; Manly's *Canterbury Tales,* 551.

[91] Dorothy Mills, *The Middle Ages* (New York, 1935), 161.

first of the knights who come to fight both for Palamon and Arcite. It is indeed a noble company,

> For every wight that lovede chivalrye,
> And wolde, his thankes, han a passant name,
> Hath preyer that he mighte ben of that game;
> And wel was him, that ther-to chosen was.[92]

Not long after prime, on that Sunday before the tournament is to begin, the newcomers arrive. They are all taken at once to their inns and are soon enjoying Duke Theseus' feast in their honor.[93] Monday is again spent in festivities,

> But by the cause that they sholde ryse
> Erly, for to seen the grete fight,
> Unto hir reste wente they at night.[94]

In an article discussing Monday as a date for medieval tournaments, Mr. L. A. Vigneras states that "les tournois avaient généralement lieu le lundi."[95] He gives as reason for the popularity of this day the argument that tournaments were usually held in the Spring, at Easter or on Pentecost, and that since the Church disapproved of Sunday for such events, many knights had made vows not to participate in the combats on that day; they waited, then until the next.[96] Mr. Vigneras' description of the activities of Sunday and Monday corresponds in many ways to that given by Chaucer, with the exception that Chaucer mentions no mass:

> . . . Il arrivait que les fêtes commençassent dès le samedi, où l'on célébrait l'arrivée des combattants. . . . Le dimanche se passait en cérémonies religieuses, en fêtes et en danses . . . ; ce jour-là on adoubait aussi un certain nombre de nouveaux chevaliers. . . . Le lundi matin, les jouteurs allaient à l'église entendre la messe du Saint Esprit . . . , puis se rendaient aux lices où l'ouverture du tournoi était officiellement annoncée.[97]

---

[92] A *Kn. T.*, 2106-2109.

[93] *Ibid.*, 2187-2208.

[94] *Ibid.*, 2488-2490.

[95] "Monday as a Date for Medieval Tournaments," *Modern Language Notes*, XLVIII (February, 1933), 80-83.

[96] *Ibid.*, 81-82.

[97] *Ibid.*, 82.

The Christian elements, which Chaucer neglects, have of course no place in the *Knight's Tale,* where homage is paid not to the Christian God but to pagan gods and goddesses. It is characteristic of the poet that, although the character of the tournament is strictly that of fourteenth century England, the religious background is decidedly pagan. There is not even an opportunity for the reader to insert a Sunday mass; the knights are travelling until prime; then they are "inned," and immediately the feast commences. One might wonder, here, why the tournament could not have begun on Sunday. If Vigneras' reasons for the rejection of Sunday are correct, is it not ironical that the pagans of the *Knight's Tale* should follow the Christian practice? At any rate, the curious combination of Athenian local color with English medieval usages is effective and somewhat characteristically Chaucerian.

The main events of the tournament proper occur on Tuesday. Early in the morning everyone busies himself in preparations. Especially around the hostelries is there "noyse and clateringe of hors and harneys."[98] The poet's description of the assembling of folk for the day's activities is particularly vivid and realistic:

> And to the paleys rood ther many a route
> Of lordes, up-on stedes and palfreys.
> Ther maystow seen devysing of herneys
> So uncouth and so riche, and wroght so weel
> Of goldsmithrie, of browding, and of steel;
> The sheeldes brighte, testers, and trappures;
> Gold-hewn helmes, hauberks, cote-armures;
> Lordes in paraments on hir courseres,
> Knightes of retenue, and eek squyeres
> Nailinge the spheres, and helmes bokelinge,
> Gigginge of sheeldes, with layneres lacinge;
> Ther as need is, they weren no-thing ydel;
> The fomy stedes on the golden brydel
> Gnawinge, and faste the armures also
> With fyle and hamer prikinge to and fro;
> Yemen on fote, and communes many oon
> With shorte staves, thikke as they may goon.[99]

---

[98] A *Kn. T.,* 2489-2493.
[99] *Ibid.,* 2494-2509.

At the palace, people stand around in groups of three or more, "holding hir questioun,

> Divyninge of thise Theban knightes two.[100]

They estimate the strength of the opposing sides, some holding with the knights led by Ligurge, others with those under the guidance of Emetreus.[101]

Within the palace, Duke Theseus, awakened by the sound of his minstrels, awaits the appearance of Palamon and Arcite; then after greeting them, he seats himself at a window, where he might be seen by the crowds of people on the outside.[102] With what a mighty roar must not these enthusiastic folk have greeted their sovereign, as they

> . . . presseth thider-ward ful sone
> Him for to-seen, and doon heigh reverence,
> And eek to herkne his hest and his sentence.[103]

To do reverence to the king is important, yes; but to hear what rules are to govern the action of the tournament is probably uppermost in the minds of most of the throng gathered there.

The crowd continues cheering until a herald appears on a platform or scaffold and cries for them to be silent. Gradually the sounds die down,[104] and the herald reads or recites the regulations which Duke Theseus—probably with the assistance of one or more of his heralds[105]—has formulated. They begin with the explanation that Theseus does not wish the tournament to be a death-dealing one; all the rules to be observed are directed toward the preservation of life. Summarized, the regulations are:

1. No kind of "shot," or arrow, no pole-axe, nor short knife is to brought or sent into the lists.
2. No short sword, "with poynt bytinge," is to be used

---

[100] *Ibid.,* 2514-2515.
[101] *Ibid.,* 2516-2522.
[102] *Ibid.,* 2523-2529.
[103] *Ibid.,* 2530-2532.
[104] *Ibid.,* 2533-2535.
[105] "The holder of a tournament, the *challenger,* never thought of drawing up conditions without the assistance of well qualified heralds." Stuart, *Men and Women of Plantagenet England,* 27.

to thrust; neither is it to be worn at one's side.

3. No knight is to ride at his opponent more than one course with a sharpened, or pointed spear.

4. To defend himself, one may thrust on foot.

5. Knights who are vanquished, or are able to be taken, are not to be slain, but brought unto the stake on the opponent's side of the lists. If necessary, force may be used to take the knight to the stake, but once there he cannot leave.

6. If the captain of either side is taken, or if he happens to slay his equal, the tournament is to end at once.[106]

The herald concludes the reading of the regulations with:

> God spede yow; goth forth, and ley on faste.
> With long sword and with maces fight your fille.
> Goth now your wey; this is the lordes wille.[107]

The long-sword, which is the weapon to be used, was about six feet in length;[108] it was the favorite weapon of the medieval tournament. Reference to it here is in the interest of realism.

At the conclusion of the reading, again the cheers of the throng ring out:

> The voys of peple touchede the hevene,
> So loude cryden they with mery stevene:
> 'God save swich a lord, that is so good,
> He wilneth no destruccioun of blood!'[109]

And then, drowning out the cries of the excited people comes the welcome melody of the trumpets,[110] "blowing unto the field."[111]. Here one may imagine the people noisily preparing to start off to the lists—calling to one another, trying to quiet their restless horses, and eventually getting into some kind of order

---

[106] A *Kn. T.*, 2537-2557. Cf. Stuart Robinson, "Elements of Realism in the 'Knight's Tale,'" *Journal of English and Germanic Philology*, **XIV** (April, 1915), 235 ff.

[107] A *Kn. T.*, 2558-2560.

[108] Stuart, *op. cit.*, 29.

[109] A *Kn. T.*, 2561-2564.

[110] In *Le Morte Darthur*, the king himself is described as "blowing to the field," I, 409; again, "there were heralds with trumpets commanded to blow to the field." *Ibid.*, I, 261.

[111] A *Kn. T.*, 2565.

for the procession through the streets. Chaucer hurries over this; he gives no description of "noyse and clateringe," but briefly states,

> And to the listes rit the companye.[112]

The procession of spectators and participants of a tournament in medieval times must have been one of the most colorful scenes of the whole pageant. Stow's record of the famous 1390 tournament held at Smithfield[113] presents such a scene:

> . . . at the day appoynted, there issued forth of the tower, about the third houre of the day, 60. coursers, apparelled for the Iustes, and up-on every one an Esquier of honour riding a soft pace: then came forth 60. Ladyes of honour mounted upon palfraies, riding on the one side, richly apparrelled, and every Lady led a knight with a chayne of gold. Those knights being in the king's party, had their Armour and apparell garnished with white Hartes and Crownes of gold about the Harts neckes, and so they came riding through the streets of London to Smithfield, with a great number of trumpets and other instruments of musicke before them.[114]

It is significant that this real procession is more elaborately described than Chaucer's. The poet practices artistic restraint, leaving to the imagination of the reader the details of color and the like:

> By ordinaunce thurgh-out the citee large,
> Hanged with cloth of gold, and nat with sarge.
> Ful lyk a lord this noble duk gan ryde,
> Thise two Thebanes up-on either syde,
> And after rood the quene, and Emelye,
> And after that another companye
> Of oon and other, after hir degree.[115]

Evidently the poet considered "ful lyk a lord" sufficient indication of the splendor of the scene. With such colorful and

---

[112] A *Kn. T.*, 2566.

[113] Cf. *supra*, 209, f.n. 86.

[114] *Survey of London*, II, 30. Cf. also *A Chronicle of London*, anon. (London, 1827), 76-77, and the detailed account of the tournament in Froissart's *Chronicles*, II, 477 ff.

[115] A *Kn. T.*, 2566-2573.

picturesque aids as the golden chariot drawn by four white bulls,[116] in which Ligurge had come to Duke Theseus' palace, the twenty or more alaunts which followed beside the chariot,[117] the gorgeously trapped steed of Emetreus,[118] and many tame leopards and lions, what an opportunity Chaucer let pass. He might have presented a procession which would easily have surpassed even the one made to Smithfield. However, it would no doubt have seemed less realistic than the one he has given, and besides, would have too long deferred the tournament itself.

It is not yet prime when the company arrive at the lists. The spectators, with Theseus, Ipolita, Emelye, and other ladies according to their degree, occupy the seats of honor; the other people crowd into the remaining space in the lists. The two groups of knights, led by Arcite and Palamon, respectively, ride into the gates at opposite sides of the field:

> And west-ward, thurgh the gates under Marte,
> Arcite, and eek the hundred of his parte,
> With baner reed is entered hight anon;
> And in that selve moment Palamon
> Is under Venus, est-ward in the place,
> With baner whyt, and hardy chere and face.[119]

Once on the field, the two groups of knights take their places in two ranks.[120] It was customary for a trumpet or horn to be sounded as each knight entered the lists; then one of the heralds in attendance declared what were his armorial insignia, which was called "blazoning his arms."[121] Chaucer seems not to refer to this practice, however, unless the reading of the names is substituted because of the large number of combatants. He tells us "that hir names rad were everich oon,"[122] that there might be

---

[116] *Ibid.,* 2137-2138.

[117] *Ibid.,* 2148.

[118] *Ibid.,* 2157-2159.

[119] *Ibid.,* 2575-2586.

[120] *Ibid.,* 2594.

[121] Stuart, *op. cit.,* 29.

[122] A *Kn. T.,* 2595.

no treachery on either side. The gates are then closed, and with
a loud cry of

"Do now your devoir, yonge knightes proude!"[123]

the actual conflict is ready to begin.

The heralds now stop riding up and down the field, and the
trumpets sound the beginning of the first round, as one might
call it. It is said that with the sounding of the trumpets, the
heralds usually shouted, "Laissez les aller, laissez les aller, les bons
chevaliers!"[124] but of this Chaucer makes no reference.

The poet hastens the action of the conflict, itself, and in extremely vivid fashion notes the noise and flash of a fiercely
fought tournament:

In goon the speres ful sadly in arest;
In goth the sharpe spore in-to the syde.
Ther seen men who can juste, and who can ryde;
Ther shiveren shaftes up-on sheeldes thikke;
He feleth thurgh the herte-spoon the prikke.
Up springen speres twenty foot on highte;
Out goon the swerdes as the silver brighte.
The helmes they to-hewen and to-shrede;
Out brest the blood, with sterne stremes rede.
With mighty maces the bones they to-breste.[125]

No matter now the rich array of the combatants, or the fine
trappings of the horses, for horses stumble and knights are
plunged into the dust. Even

The stronge king Ligurge is born adoun;
And king Emetreus, for al his strengthe,
Is born out of his sadel a swerdes lengthe.[126]

The tournament concludes with the capture of Palamon by Arcite;
the duke himself "cries a Ho!"[127] and declares Arcite the victor.

---

[123] *Ibid.,* 2598.

[124] Stuart, *op. cit.,* 28. In *Le Morte Darthur,* II, 422, is a description of a
conflict between Sir Lavaine and Sir Launcelot, "and right as the heralds
should cry: Lesses les aller, right so came in Sir Launcelot. . ."

[125] A *Kn. T.,* 2562-2611.

[126] *Ibid.,* 2644-2646.

[127] *Ibid.,* 2655. "Hola" seems to have been the usual cry for stopping a
tournament. Cripps-Day, *op. cit.,* 25.

With the sound of trumpets and other musical instruments, accompanied by the joyous shouts of his friends, the successful knight dons his helmet, mounts his horse, and rides before the stands where Emelye and the other ladies are seated.[128]

The tournament is indeed concluded, but it has left in its wake physical injuries which must receive attention. Not to mention the tragic fall received by the victorious Arcite, which occasions but little alarm until after the three days' feast held by Theseus,[129]

> Al were they sore y-hurt, and namely oon,
> That with a spere was thirled his brest-boon.
> To othere woundes, and to broken armes,
> Some hadden salves, and some hadden charmes;
> Fermacies of herbes, and eek save
> They dronken, for they wolde hir limes have.[130]

As gallant in defeat and injury as they had been on the field, these medieval sportsmen are undaunted, and under the hospitable roof of the duke, "made revel al the longe night."[131] What mattered a few dislocated shoulders, broken arms, and wounds from spears? Chaucer himself explains it thus:

> For soothly ther was no disconfiture,
> For falling his nat but an aventure;
> Ne to be lad with fors un-to the stake
> Unyolden, and with twenty knightes take
> O persone allone, with-outen mo,
> And haried forth by arme, foot, and to,
> With footmen, bothe yemen and eek knaves,
> It nas aretted him no vileinye,
> Ther may no man clepen it cowardye.[132]

Distinctly good losers, with a philosophical outlook on their defeat, are these battered knights who had set out so confidently for the lists that morning before prime.

The conclusion of a tournament seems to have been celebrated always by a feast. Generally, too, the prizes were awarded then

---

[128] *Ibid.*, 2671-2679.
[129] *Ibid.*, 2684-2699; 2736 (the reference to the feast); 2743 ff.
[130] *Ibid.*, 2709-2714.
[131] *Ibid.*, 2717.
[132] *Ibid.*, 2721-2730.

to the knights who had especially distinguished themselves on the field. Such a feast and the rewards made at it are described by John Gower:

> And whan they were set and served
> Than after, as it was deserved
> To hem, that worthy knightes were
> So as they setten here and there,
> The prise was yove and spoken out
> Among the heralds all aboute.[133]

At one of the tournaments in Arthur's court, the guests returned from the lists, unarmed themselves, went to evensong and then to supper. The prizes were awarded after supper in the garden.[134].

Sometimes, there was one great prize, awarded to the knight who was proclaimed by the judge to be the victor. This might be "a rich circlet of gold worth a thousand besants,"[135] such as the Lady de Vawse offered at a great tournament which she announced. Again, one might win a gerfalcon and a white steed trapped with gold, as Sir Uwaine did when he smote down thirty knights in a combat.[136] None of these rewards, however, would Arcite—or Palamon—have accepted in preference to the prize offered by Duke Thesus, namely, the fair Emelye. As if this were too great a reward to be kept until the feast, Duke Theseus gives the young lady to Arcite immediately after the victory,

> I wol be trewe juge, and no partye.
> Arcite of Thebes shal have Emelye.[137]

Later, at the feast, he shows his great generosity to the other knights,

> And yaf hem yiftes after hir degree.[138]

The nature of these latter gifts is not mentioned by Chaucer; apparently he considers "after hir degree" is sufficient information concerning them.

---

[133] *Confessio Amantis*, ed. Reinhold Pauli, 3 vols. (London, 1857), I, 127.
[134] *Le Morte Darthur*, I, 19.
[135] *Ibid.*, I, 143.
[136] *Ibid.*, I, 145.
[137] A *Kn. T.*, 2657-2658.
[138] *Ibid.*, 2735.

As noncommittal as the poet is about the rewards, so is he concerning the three days spent in feasting and entertainment after the tournament, saying only:

> And fully heeld a feste dayes three;
> And conveyed the kinges worthily
> Out of his toun a journee largely.
> And hoom wente every man the righte way.[139]

Chaucer shows, as he frequently does, good judgment in describing this part of the festivities briefly. Arcite's serious injuries are about to cause his death; in view of such a sad event, the poet's failure to elaborate on pleasures is particularly effective and fitting.

The tournament herein described is, then, that medieval spectacle as Chaucer must have known it. In an age when "strength, not learning, was man's ideal."[140] when love of display and excitement were dominant in the lives of many, small wonder is it that "as a sport of knights it had no rival throughout the Middle Ages."[141] The striking realism of treatment in the *Knight's Tale*[142] enables the modern reader to visualize that great pageant which in many respects is a synthesis of all the color, all the romance, and all the sportsmanship in medieval chivalry.

Dancing

Hunting, hawking, and the tournament were by their very nature practically restricted to the upper classes of society. However, there was one pastime in which all persons, even the poorest of the poor, could and did participate. This was dancing, an activity of which one author has written:

> They danced in the streets whenever it was possible, which was one of the reasons why May-day was so joyous a festival . . . they danced together singing minstrels' songs; they danced in the garden, they danced in the meadow, they went out at night to dance with tapers in their hands; they danced to beautiful music played by an orchestra. . . .[143]

---

[139] *Ibid.,* 2736-2739.
[140] Cripps-Day, *op. cit.,* 6.
[141] *Ibid.,* 6.
[142] Robertson, "Elements of Realism," 235 ff.
[143] Walter Besant, *Medieval London,* 2 vols. (London, 1906), I, 311-312.

This seems hardly exaggerated; one has only to survey Chaucer's allusions to dancing to observe the part which this pastime played in the lives of various persons belonging to different classes of society.

It is to be expected that the characters in *The Romaunt de la Rose* enjoy dances which are of French origin. Chaucer, in his translation, pictures them as participating in the caroles:

> Tho mightest thou caroles seen,
> And folk (ther) daunce and mery been,
> And make many a fair tourning
> Upon the grene gras springing.[144]

This is a somewhat dignified and stately kind of dance, accompanied by the playing and singing of "floutours, minstrales and even jogelours." There are also many female timbrel-players, or tambourine-players, and dancers who leap high when performing—"timbesteres" and "saylours,"[145] Chaucer calls them—who add gaiety to the dance. Graceful and dexterous, the joyful "fair folk so lyk to angels," disport themselves with all the abandon of happy, light-hearted youth:

> The timbres up ful sotilly
> They caste, and henten (hem) ful ofte
> Upon a finger faire and softe,
> That they (ne) fayled never-mo.
> Ful fetis damiselles two,
> Right yonge, and fulle of semlihede,
> In kirtles, and non other wede,
> And faire tressed every tresse,
> Had Mirthe doon, for his noblesse,
> Amidde the carole for to daunce;
> But her-of lyth no remembraunce,
> How that they daunced queyntely.
> That oon wolde come al prively
> Agayn that other: and whan they were
> Togidre almost, they threwe y-fere

---

[144] Frag. A, 759-762. See also Gaston Vuillier, *A History of Dancing*, sec. ed. (New York, 1918), 382; Salzman, *English Life in Middle Ages*, 98. Many English folk-songs are derived from these old caroles. *Ibid.*, 180.
[145] *Ibid.*, 763-771.

> Hir mouthes so, that through hir play
> It seemed as they kiste alway;
> To dauncen wel coude they the gyse;
> What shulde I more to you devyse?[146]

Particularly interesting is the figure dance here; side to side, now back to back, and casting glances over their shoulders, or lifting their faces to their partners, so that "it semed as they kiste," the dancers appear to interpret the music in their own way, and to dance accordingly. It may be a dance similar to this which Chaucer refers to in *The Hous of Fame,* when he lists "love-daunces:"

> Ther saugh I famous, olde and yonge
> Pypers of the Duche tonge,
> To lerne love-daunces, springes,
> Reyes, and these straunge thinges.[147]

Perhaps the dancers of fairy-land, who

> Daunced ful ofte in many a grene mede,[148]

according to the Wife of Bath, were executing the carole when the knight "happed hym to ryde . . . under a forest-syde," and

> . . . . saugh up-on a daunce go
> Of ladies foure and twenty, and yet mo.[149]

What kind of dance it was the knight himself could probably not have told, for as he approached near to the women,

> Vanisshed was this daunce, he niste where.[150]

---

[146] *Ibid.,* 773-790.

[147] III, 1235-1236. The *reye* mentioned here is supposed to have been "the Hay," a dance of which little is known, except that it was probably danced in a ring. Reginald St. Johnston, *A History of Dancing* (London, 1906), 53. A dance known in Germany during medieval times, called the *reie,* is said to have been one in which the "couples formed in a row and danced across the meadow." Cf. Sister Catherine Teresa Rapp, *Burgher and Peasant in the Works of Thomasin von Zirclaria, Freidank, and Hugo von Trimberg,* [diss.] (Washington, D. C., 1936), 27.

[148] D *WB,* 860.

[149] *Ibid.,* 990-992.

[150] *Ibid.,* 996.

Absolon, the parish-clerk of *The Miller's Tale,* must have known nearly all the steps in medieval dancing:

> In twenty manere coude he trippe and daunce
> After the scole of Oxenforde tho,
> And with his legges casten to and fro,
> And pleyen songes on a small rubible.[151]

The carole, the roundel, the hay, besides numerous variations of each, would probably have been ordinary dances in this gay young man's repertoire. The Morris, too, though it was much more elaborate than the others, and characterized by complicated figures executed by dancers carrying staves in their hands,[152] would no doubt have given him an excellent opportunity both to show off his agility and his beautiful shoes, "with Powles window corven"[153] on them. The costuming often used in the Morris would have appealed to Absolon, although he might have objected to having his face blackened.[154] At any rate, wherever persons of his acquaintance assembled for jollity, especially to enjoy dancing, there was Absolon, with his "gitern" (a kind of guitar):

> In al the toun nas brewhous ne taverne
> That he ne visited with his solas.[155]

But there was at least one person who may have outdanced Absolon. This was the "propre short felawe" of *The Cook's Tale,* of whom Chaucer writes:

> Dauncen he coude so wel and jolily,
> That he was cleped Perkin Revelour.[156]

This young man seems especially to have liked to "singe and

---

[151] A 3328-3331.

[152] Salzman, *op. cit.,* 98; Evelyn Sharp, *Here we go Round* (New York, 1928), 49.

[153] A *Mil. T.,* 3318.

[154] Sharp, *op. cit.,* 49.

[155] A *Mil.T.,* 3334-3335; "Solas" is defined as joy-giving powers, i.e., playing, singing, dancing. See D. Brown, *"Solas in 'The Miller's Tale',"* *MLN,* XLVIII (June, 1933), 370.

[156] *Ibid.,* 4370-4371.

hoppe" at weddings, which he always attended.[157]   The medieval
bride customarily danced with anyone who asked her,[158] and one
may believe that Perkin would not have hesitated to request more
than one such dance..

Indeed, in the interest he had in dancing, Perkin often neglected to do his work.   When there were tournaments or processions and the streets were filled with people intent upon
celebrating in the gayest manner, the young apprentice thought no
more of his duties:

> Out of the shoppe thider wolde he lepe.
> Til that he hadde al the sighte y-seyn,
> And daunced wel, he wolde nat come ageyn.[159]

Like his modern prototype, Perkin was not content to enjoy such
occasions by himself:

> And gadered him a meinee of his sort
> To hoppe and singe, and maken swich disport.[160]

Evidently his master could not help liking this jolly apprentice,
for he retained him in his employ a long time, considering that
he could not depend much on his assistance when pleasure inter-
fered.   Had Perkin been less skillful in games of chance,[161] however, his employer's affection might have been less.

Sometimes professional dancers entertained medieval Englishmen.   One of the favorite dances performed by them was that
known as the sword-dance, the performer balancing himself,
head downward, feet up, on swords or other things.[162]   In illustrations of banquets of the times one often sees representations
of this feat.[163]   Doubtless the professional dancers travelled from

---

[157] *Ibid.*, 4375.
[158] Salzman, *op. cit.*, 254.
[159] A *Cook's Tale*, 4378-4380.
[160] *Ibid.*, 4380-4381.
[161] *Ibid.*, 4385-4386.
[162] Jusserand, *English Wayfaring Life*, 219.   This sort of dance had been
in vogue since ancient times, having been popular among the Greeks and
Romans.
[163] Cf. *The Babees Book*, Plate V.

place to place, being paid for their services as entertainers;[164] royal and noble households particularly must have employed such performers for their great feasts. In two allusions, somewhat casually made, Chaucer seems to refer to this type of dancer. In the *Pardoner's Tale,* for example, the poet mentions "tombesteres fetys and smale,"[165] by whom he may mean professional dancing women. Again, in the *Merchant's Tale* is reference to Venus, who

> . . . with hir fyrbrond in hir hand aboute
> Daunceth biforn the bryde and al the route.[166]

This is probably not the sword dance to which the poet alludes, but it is apparently some sort of solo dance designed to attract attention.

Many, perhaps even most of Chaucer's allusions to the dance are general rather than specific. They convey but little information other than this, that medieval folk loved the pastime and spent many hours at it. It has already been noted of Duke Theseus' guests that "al that Monday justen they and daunce,"[167] and that there was dancing at the feast given in honor of the knights before the tournament was held.[168] Of the rich merchants in the *Introduction to the Man of Law's Prologue* it is said,

> At Cristemasse merie may ye daunce![169]

This bears the suggestion that persons of wealth had lighter hearts than those persons who were so poor that "alle thy freendes fleen fro thee,"[170] but the reference to the poor widow, whose dancing was not hindered by the gout,[171] indicates that the poor were by no means deprived of that spirit which impelled them to dance.

---

[164] Jusserand, *op. cit.,* 220.
[165] C 477.
[166] E 1727-1728.
[167] See *supra,* 210.
[168] A *Kn. T.,* 2202.
[169] B 126.
[170] *Ibid.,* 121.
[171] B *NPT,* 4030.

The Wife of Bath boasts of her former ability at this pastime. When she was "young and ful of ragerye, . . . and joly as a pye," she says,

> Wel coude I daunce to an harpe smale,
> And singe y-wis, as any nightingale,
> Whan I had dronke a draughte of swete wyn.[172]

This one-time jolly woman may have belonged to as lively a group of young folk as the "Flaundres companye," who

> . . . haunteden folye,
> As ryot, stewes, and tavernes,
> Wher-as, with harpes, lutes, and giternes,
> They daunce and pleye at dees bothe day and night,
> And ete also and drinken over hir might.[173]

One notices that the dance as Chaucer describes it has two distinct characters. It is in one case aesthetic—graceful, dignified, and artistic; and in the other, riotous—accompanied by drinking, gambling, and loose living in general. There were, of course, variations in the two types of dances, but the groups were nevertheless distinct. The former kind seems to have furnished enjoyment for knights and ladies particularly[174] and is described by Chaucer in those poems which depend most largely upon sources. The latter generally amused the lower classes and provided entertainment in public houses; in his later and more realistic poems, and especially those which are least edifying, Chaucer describes this type.

The riotous kinds of dancing were heartily condemned by medieval writers on occasion. Chaucer's Pardoner, it will be recalled, refers to it along with singing and other forms of riotousness as "the verray develes officeres

> To kindle and blowe the fyr of lecherye,
> That is annexed un-to glotonye.[175]

---

[172] D *WBP,* 455-459.

[173] C *Pard. T.,* 463-468.

[174] An interesting description of such a dance, in which knights and ladies participate, is found in "Sir Launfal," Ritson, II, 22-23, 11. 638 ff.

[175] C *Pard.T.,* 476-482.

A similar attitude is expressed in a later medieval work, *The Ship of Fools:*

> He God displeasyth, which doth suche foly hate
> Suche lese theyr tyme in vayne and oft therin
> Are many hurtis: and cause of dedely sin.[176]

Regardless of condemnation, however, medieval dancers kept up this pleasant pastime with probably little or no temptation to abandon it.

Archery

It is singular that archery, which later played such an important part in English sports, should have played so little a rôle in Chaucer's age. In military life it was most significant, but as a sport it was so rarely enjoyed that both Edward III and Richard II are said to have found it necessary to make regulations forcing people to engage in it. Edward III complained to the sheriffs of London that skill in shooting with arrows had been almost totally laid aside for useless and unlawful games. He commanded them to prevent the latter practices within the city and liberties of London, and to see that leisure time on holidays was spent in recreation with bows and arrows. The penalty for disregard of the king's command was imprisonment at the king's pleasure.[177] This and similar regulations made later by Richard II had no permanent effect. For the time being, archery as a sport was doomed to comparative neglect.

Although Chaucer might have made picturesque use of archery in various of his poems, he is enough of a realist not to have done so. While he presents several views of the equipment[178] used in the pastime, there is no effort to show anyone participating in it. His one direct allusion is to Sir Thopas, of whom he says:

> Ther-to he was a good archeer.[179]

There is perhaps much significance in the fact that this doughty knight engages in a sport which most of his fellowmen seem to

---

[176] Barclay, I, 291.

[177] Strutt, *Sports and Pastimes,* 117.

[178] Cf. RR. 923-936; 941-948; 973-974, etc.; A *Gen. Prol.,* 104 ff.

[179] B *Sir Thopas,* 1929.

have deigned unworthy of their notice. It is interesting also to observe that Sir Thopas is one of the most versatile of Chaucer's sportsmen. Like the people of the upper social classes, he goes hunting and hawking and participates in the tournaments; like those of the middle and lower classes, he enjoys archery and wrestling :

> He coude hunte at wilde deer,
> And ryde an hauking for riveer,
>> With grey goshauk on honde;[180]

. . . .

> Al of a knyght was fair and gent
> In bataille and in tourneyment.[181]

. . . .

> Of wrastling was ther noon his peer,
> Ther any ram shal stonde.[182]

Undoubtedly, if Sir Thopas had ever won his tournament there would also have been a feast and entertainment, at which Sir Thopas would surely have demonstrated that he could "sing and hoppe," too, as well as anyone.

Wrestling

The medieval wrestling match seems to have had a strong appeal to persons of the lower classes. In its roughness and the frequent quarreling and consequent physical injuries which it entailed,[183] this sport had some elements of the tournament. But it was without the color and romance of the more knightly pastime, and entertained the masses of a less refined type.

---

[180] *Ibid.,* 1926-1928.

[181] *Ibid.,* 1905-1906.

[182] *Ibid.,* 1930-1931.

[183] Besant, *Medieval London,* I, 312. From the coroners' records of the period one learns something of this matter. For example, a certain Peter de Huntingdon and Andrew Prille, growing weary of drinking in a tavern, agreed to wrestle. Within a short time, Andrew's clothes were so badly torn that he declared he would discontinue. But Peter had not had enough of the sport, and persuading Andrew to take his vest (wardecors), the wrestle was resumed. The final result was that Peter's right leg was broken—an injury from which Peter later died. *Calendar of the Coroners' Rolls of the City of London,* ed. R. R. Sharpe (London, 1914). 20-21.

Like other sports, wrestling was not necessarily harmful. Often it was among the activities which youths enjoyed on holy days in the summer months.[184] The usual prizes awarded to the winner of a match were rams[185] or cocks[186]—which seem to have been selected almost as symbols of the sport, whether wittingly or unwittingly.

The status of wrestling may be understood from Chaucer's references to it. The Miller of the Canterbury pilgrims, the miller in the *Reeve's Tale,* and Sir Thopas are the characters who engage in the sport. The first-named, it will be recalled, was "a stout carl, big of braun, and eek of bones,"[187] so strong that

> Ther nas no dore that he nolde Heve of harre,
> Or breke it, at a renning, with his heed.[188]

His character matched his physical appearance; he "was most of sinne and harlotryes,"[189] dishonorable in his dealing with others,[190] and, in short, a low-type individual. This great brawny man was such a marvel at wrestling that

> . . . he wolde have alwey the ram.[191]

Like this Miller, Simkin in the *Reeve's Tale* was also a dishonest man:

> A theef he was for sothe of corn and mele,
> And that a sly, and usaunt for to stele.[192]

---

[184] Stow, *Survey of London,* I, 92-93. "In the holy dayes all the Sommer, the youths are exercised in leaping, dancing, shooting, wrastling, casting the stone, and practicing their shields: the Maidens trip in their Timbrels, and daunce as long as they can see."

[185] Strutt, *Sports and Pastimes,* 148; Besant, *op. cit.,* I, 312.

[186] Strutt, *op. cit.,* 148. See in Strutt the illustration on p. 148 of a wrestling match. A cock seems to be the prize.

[187] A *Gen. Prol.,* 545.

[188] *Ibid.,* 550-551.

[189] *Ibid.,* 561.

[190] *Ibid.,* 562-563.

[191] *Ibid.,* 548.

[192] A 3939-3940.

He had several accomplishments, among which was that of wrestling:

> Pypen he coude and fisshe, and nettes bete,
> And turne coppes, and wel wrastle and shete.[193]

Both rascals, both millers, and both wrestlers—these two were perhaps rather typical of those persons who most enjoyed a sport as rough as wrestling. Although their opposite in nearly every way, Sir Thopas, nevertheless, was an expert at the same sport.[194] The note of incongruity here sounded is effective in Chaucer's characterization of the pseudo-knight. Who knows but that the poet deliberately selected his three "wrastlers?"

Probably one of the most realistic touches in Chaucer's mention of wrestling is that in which he alludes to the comments of the persons watching the match. Each is satisfied that the wrestlers could do better by changing their methods of attack and defense. The crowd is singularly like any modern one watching a contest of strength:

> But natheles, al-though that thou be dulle,
> Yit that thou canst not do, yit mayst thou see;
> For many a man that may not stonde a pulle,
> Yit lyketh him at the wrastling for to be,
> And demeth yit wher he do bet or he.[195]

Perhaps the spectators were of somewhat higher mental calibre than the wrestlers were, but even though they were not, they considered themselves very capable of suggesting to the others what to do.

Of the foregoing sports and pastimes which demanded physical activity, Chaucer generally offers enough information that one can glean accurate knowledge of them—of their popularity, the persons who engaged in them, sometimes the rules which governed them, and the attitude of the people toward them. There are a few others, more or less participated in by all persons, such as leaping, running, casting of darts or of stones, and different

---

[193] *Ibid.*, 3927-3928.
[194] Cf. *supra*, 227.
[195] *PF*, 162-166.

kinds of ball-playing. To these Chaucer makes only passing reference.

Chess and Tables

Chess, which is often referred to as the royal pastime,[196] had for a century or two been popular in England. The origin of the game is not known, although numerous interesting stories are told of it. One of these stories relates that chess was devised for the reproval and correction of a certain King Evilmerodach, a man so cruel that he "did hewe his faders body in three hondred pieces and gaf it to ete and devoure to three hondred byrdes that men calle vultress."[197] The inventor of the game, a Greek philosopher called Philometor, or Xerxes, so successfully diverted the king from his evil habits that thereafter chess was popular with royalty.[198]

This tale is of particular interest here, for Chaucer's reference to the invention of the game indicates his familiarity with this or a similar tale. "Athalus," the poet tells us, "made the first game of the ches."[199] Athalus, or Attalus III, King of Pergamos, is no other than the Philometor mentioned above; the source of information is probably the *Romaunt de la Rose*.[200]

Chaucer's most significant use of the game is in an allegorical sense. The poet compares the death of Blanche, Duchess of Lancaster, to the loss[201] of the Fers or Queen in a game played with Fortune:

> Atte ches with me she gan to pleye:
> With hir false draughtes divers

[196] Strutt, *op. cit.*, 405.

[197] J. Cessolis, *The Game of the Chesse*, Caxton's ed., re-edited by Vincent J. Figgins (London, 1860), ch. I.

[198] *Idem.*

[199] *BD*, 663.

[200] Robinson, *op. cit.*, 884.

[201] The manner of playing chess appears to have been similar to that used at the present time, but with fewer problems. There were two systems of nomenclature for the pieces: the first, characteristic of Spanish chess, included King, Fers, Aufin, Knight (Horse), Rook, and Pawn; the second, characteristic of the German game, included King, Queen, Bishop (Sage, Count, Fool), Knight, Rook (Margrave), and Pawn. As used in England, these two systems eventually overlapped and became confused. Gautier,

> She stal on me, and took my fers
> And whan I saw my fers aweye,
> Alas! I couthe no lenger pleye,
> But seyde, "farwel, swete, y-wis,
> And farwel al that ever ther is!"[202]

Willard Fiske, discussing the poet's use of the Fers, says that Chaucer's knowledge of the game is apparent here; that "many people since his time have found it difficult to play after losing their 'fers!'"[203] However that may be, the game is soon ended for,

> Therwith Fortune seyde "chek here!"
> And "mate!" in mid pointe of the chekkere
> With a poune erraunt, allas![204]

Fortune, or Death, which it here represents, as saying checkmate, is a natural metaphor quite commonplace in medieval literature. Chaucer's use of it seems to have been derived from the *Romaunt*

La Chevalerie, 653, note 1; Harold J. R. Murray, *A History of Chess* (Oxford, 1913), 425.

The chessmen were made of ivory, walrus-ivory, bone, rock-crystal, jasper, ebony, and other hard woods. Wealthy persons sometimes had ones that were elaborately carved. Many of these chessmen have been preserved and are of great interest to antiquarians. Certain ones kept in the royal treasury of St. Denis, near Paris, are said to have belonged to Charlemagne. Only fifteen pieces and one pawn are remaining of the set. They are of ivory, very much yellowed by time, and have crude inscriptions at their bases. The largest piece represents a king sitting on a throne. It is about twelve inches high and eight broad, and is very clumsily carved. The pawn is about three inches in height, and is the image of a dwarf with a large shield. Murray, *op. cit.,* 758-763; Richard Twiss, *Chess* (London, 1781), 3; *Good Companion,* ed. James F. Magee, Jr. (Florence, 1916).

The boards upon which medieval chess was played were larger and more massive than those now in use. They were sometimes magnificent, being made of silver, gold and ivory, and other fine materials. The field of play was surrounded by an elaborately decorated raised edge or border. Louis XIII of France is said to have had a board quilted with wool, the chessmen having pointed bases. Thus the king could play when riding in a carriage, sticking the men in the cushion. Murray, *op. cit.,* 756; Cessolis, *op. cit.,* ch. IV; Twiss, *op. cit.,* 5.

[202] *BD,* 652-658.
[203] *Chess Tales and Chess Miscellanies* (New York, 1912), 183.
[204] *BD,* 659-661.

de la Rose.[205] This same term is used by the poet in a slightly different fashion in *Troilus and Criseyde,* where Criseyde says,

> Shal noon housbonde seyn to me "chekmat"![206]

There is little or nothing original in Chaucer's frequent allusions to chess. As a royal game it was almost an essential element in the romances.[207] Much more complete than any reference in Chaucer's works is the description of the game in the *Tale of Beryn.* Beryn, the hero of the tale, is a champion player. On one occasion he plays with a Burgess; in part, the game is described thus:

> The Ches was al of yvery, the meyne fressh and newe
> I-pulsshid, and I-pikid, of white, asure and blewe.
> .   .   .   .
> The meyne were I-set up; they gon to pley (e) fast.
> Beryn wan the first, þe second, and þe þird;
> And atte fourth (e) game, (right) in the ches a-myd,
> þe Burgeyse was I-matid; but þat lust hum(ful) wele.[208]

Beryn, seeing that the game is one-sided, wishes to stop playing. But the Burgess wants another game, for a wager. The mated man is to do the victor's bidding, or drink all the salt water in the sea. Not realizing that he is falling into a trap, Beryn agrees to this, and the game continues:

> The Burgeyse toke a-visement long on every drauȝte;
> So within an houre or to, Beryn he had I-cauȝte
> Som what oppon the hipp, þat Beryn had þe wers.[209]

The climax of the game comes not long after this:

> The Burgeyse, whils þat Beryn was in hevy þouȝte,
> The next drauȝt aftir, he toke a roke for nauȝte.[210]

---

[205] Murray, *op. cit.,* 751.
[206] Bk. II, 754.
[207] See, for example, "The Lay of Eliduc," *Lays of Marie de France,* 41; "A Story of Beyond the Sea," *ibid.,* 182; *Le Morte Darthur,* I, 379-380, etc.
[208] Pp. 53-54, ll. 1733-1752, *passim.*
[209] *Ibid.,* p. 55, ll. 1779-1781.
[210] *Ibid.,* p. 56, ll. 1811-1812.

Beryn is in great distress, for he sees that he is losing the game. The Burgess calls to his sergeants,

> . . . comyth nere! ye shul se þis man
> How he shall be matid, with what man me list!
> He drouȝte, and seyd "Chek mate!" þe Sergauntis were ful prest
> And sesid Beryn by the scleve. . . .[211]

It will be observed that here the game serves the plot of the tale and is consequently an important device. In other romances it is merely one of the hero's accomplishments or it serves a moral or an allegorical purpose.

Chaucer professes no special fondness for playing chess. Rather, he prefers reading romances. On one occasion when he cannot sleep, he seeks diversion:

> Upon my bedde I sat upright,
> And bad oon reche me a book,
> A romaunce, and he hit me took
> To rede and dryve the night away;
> For me thoghte it better play
> Than pleyen either at chesse or tables.[212]

The suggestion that chess and tables sometimes furnished the medieval gentleman such relaxation that they induced sleep is evidence of the games' distracting or absorbing qualities.

Tables, referred to here, was the game now called backgammon. It was similar to chess in that it was played on a board and with pieces. The board was composed of two tables (hence the name of the pastime) united by hinges, on which there were twelve points, six opposite six, precisely the same as at present. Each player had fifteen pieces, and the game could be played in a variety of ways. Two, four, or six persons could engage in it at once.[213]

> Then dauncen, and they pleyen at ches and tables.[214]

---

[211] *Ibid.*, p. 56, 11. 1820-1823.

[212] *BD*, 46-51.

[213] John Neale Dalton, *The Collegiate Church of Ottery St. Mary* (Cambridge, 1917), 189.

Tables is one of the games which Dorigene's friends played with her to amuse her in Arveragus' absence,

> Then dauncen, and they pleyen at ches and tables.[214]

With the exception of one or two casual allusions similar to this, Chaucer does not mention this pastime. It seems not to have been of great popularity, at least as a literary device.

Gambling

All games in which dice were used seem to have been particularly popular with medieval persons. Often they were played for money or other stakes rather than for the mere sake of pastime, with the result that gambling and the vices attendant on it created no small number of difficulties.

Chaucer's chief gambler is Perkin Revelour. This young man seems to have been very proficient at casting dice:

> . . . in the toune nas ther no prentys,
> That fairer coude caste a paire of dys
> Than Perkin coude, and ther-in he was free
> Of his dispense, in place of privetee.[215]

That Perkin sometimes stooped to dishonest practices at his play is not to be wondered at. Not only was he sometimes "snibbed" or rebuked for this, but he was also

> . . .somtyme lad with revel to Newgate.[216]

Was Perkin, like Robert Scot, a certain fourteenth century *hosyere,* found guilty of cheating with false dice? If so, was he perhaps fined a sum of money, put upon the pillory for an hour, with the false dice around his neck, as was Robert, and then taken to Newgate, "and from thence, on the two following days, with trumpets and pipes, . . . taken again to the said pillory, there to remain for one hour each day, the false dice being hung around his neck?"[217] Whatever may have been Perkin's punishment, it is certain that it had but little permanent effect on him. One may believe that after his dismissal by his master he con-

---

[214] F. *Fkl. T.,* 900.
[215] A *Cook's T.,* 4385-4388.
[216] *Ibid.,* 4401-4402.
[217] Riley, *Memorials,* 457.

tinued in his old practices, spending much of his time in a fashion similar to that of the young folk described by the Pardoner. These rioters danced, and played at dice both day and night.[218]

The Pardoner preaches at length of the evils of gambling, or "hasardy :"

> Hasard is verray moder of lesinges,
> And of deceite, and cursed forsweringes,
> Blaspheme of Crist, manslaughtre, and wast also
> Of catel and of tyme ; and furthermo,
> It is repreve and contrarie of honour
> For to ben holde a commune hasardour.
> And ever the hyer he is of estaat,
> The more is he holden desolaat.
> If that a prince useth hasardye,
> In governaunce and policye
> He is, as by commune opinioun,
> Y-holde the lasse in reputacioun.[219]

To illustrate his point, the Pardoner tells of Stilbon, a wise embassador from Lacidomie, who was sent to Corinth to make an alliance with the Corinthians. It happened

> That alle the grettest that were of that lond
> Pleying atte hasard he hem fond,[220]

so Stilbon refused to make the alliance ; he would not so defame himself or his country as to ally himself with hasardours.[221]

The Parson, too, berates people for gambling. He says that from it

> . . . comth deceite, false othes, chydinges, and alle
> ravines, blaspheminge, and reneyinge of god, and hate
> of his neighbores, wast of godes, misspendinge of tyme,
> and somtyme manslaughtre. Certes, hasardours ne mowe
> nat been with-outen greet sinne whyles they haunt that
> craft.[222]

---

[218] C. *Pard. T.*, 467.
[219] *Ibid.*, 591-602.
[220] *Ibid.*, 603-608.
[221] *Ibid.*, 610-619.
[222] I *Pars. T.*, 793-794.

From this and other condemnations, it appears that dicing was
generally a cause of evil.[223]

Music and Reading

The part played by music and reading in medieval English social
life can hardly be overestimated. However, since both subjects
have recently been treated in special studies,[224] it seems sufficient
to present here only a cursory view of the most significant of
Chaucer's allusions. Medieval gentlemen were required to learn
the use of some musical instrument as part of their education.[225]
It is not surprising, then, that the poet frequently alludes to music
and instruments.

Instrumental music alone sometimes provided entertainment;
often, however, it accompanied singing and dancing. In the
House of Fame "alle maner of minstrales" and performers on
numerous types of instruments are mentioned. Harpers, who were
perhaps the most common kind of musicians of the times, are
listed; but more significant, because less familiar in literature,
are the many other players:

> Tho saugh I stonden him bihinde,
> . . . .
> Many thousand tymes twelve,
> That maden loude menstralcyes
> In cornemuse (bagpipe), and shalmyes (shawms, reed pipes),
> And many other maner pype,
> That craftely begunne pype

---

[223] In literature there is probably no greater addict to dicing and gambling
than Beryn. Often, we are told, "he cam home al nakid," having lost even
his clothes in losing the game. So fond was he of his pleasure that when
a damsel came to him with the news of his mother's death, he became violently angry that his game was disturbed. His mother's body lay in a
leaden coffin for four weeks, but Beryn was so much absorbed in his dicing
that he didn't go near to see her. Nor did he repent of his harshness.
Later, his step-mother, Rame, complained that he had come home fifteen
times in one month without clothes, and that she had had to reclothe him.
Tale of Beryn, pp. 30-39, 11. 923 ff.

[224] Fletcher Collins, *Chaucer's Understanding of Music*, unpublished dissertation, Yale University, 1934. Also, Ruth Crosby, *Chaucer and the Custom
of Oral Delivery*, unpublished dissertation, Radcliffe College, 1929. I have
not seen either of these works.

[225] Besant, *Medieval London*, I, 313. Among the instructions given for the
education of Horn in the romance, "King Horn," was included:

> Both in doulcet (dulcet, sweet-sounding pipe) and in rede,
> That ben at festes with the brede;[226]
> And many floute and lilting-horne,
> And pypes made of grene corne.[227]

In addition to these, there are also players on trumpets, clarions, and the like.[228]

As has been suggested, the harp was a very popular medieval instrument. Gentlemen usually learned to master it, and took great interest in performing on it both publicly and privately. Romance writers made especially good use of it in their works, as only a brief glance at some of the romances will reveal.[229] That there were some players who showed lack of skill, or at least of good judgment, is seen in a significant allusion in the *Troilus*. Referring to the letter which Troilus was to send to Criseyde, Pandarus warns him of repetition, comparing it to "harping on a single string:"

> For though the beste harpour upon lyve
> Wolde on the beste souned joly harpe
> That ever was, with alle his fingers fyve,
> Touche ay o streng, or ay o werbul harpe,
> Were his nayles poynted never so sharpe,
> It shulde maken every wight to dulle,
> To here his glee, and of his strokes fulle.[230]

It is perhaps significant that in his works which are most independent of literary sources, Chaucer's characters play on in-

---

> And tech him to harpe
> Wiþ his nayles scharpe.

Middle Eng. Met. Romances, p. 32, ll. 231-232; cf. also *Le Morte Darthur,* I, 282.

[226] This allusion to the use of the dulcet at feasts with the *brede,* or roast meats is interesting in regard to customs at meals. It suggests that different instruments may have been played by the minstrels according to the part of the meal in progress.

[227] Book III, 1197 ff.

[228] *Ibid.,* III, 1240 ff.

[229] "Sir Orpheo," Ritson, *op. cit.,* III, pp. 10-11. "King Horn," pp. 25-70, *passim; Le Morte Darthur,* 1, 381, *The Squyr of Lowe Degre,* ll. 1069 ff.

[230] II, 1030-1036.

struments other than the harp. The Friar, for instance, could play on the harp, but he was also familiar with the *rote*,[231] a kind of fiddle with three strings.[232] Nicholas, the scholar of the *Miller's Tale,* "made a nightes melodye" on the *sautrye,*[233] or psaltery, a kind of harp. Absolon, the parish clerk, mentioned in the same tale, entertained his friends by playing "songs on a small *rubible*"—a lute or fiddle[234]—or on his *gitern,* a kind of guitar.[235] Besides these instruments, Chaucer refers several times to the organ. He compares the voice of Chaunticleer to it, saying,

> His vois was merrier than the mery orgon
> On messe-dayes that in the chirche gon.[236]

Again, in the *Second Nun's Tale,* he alludes to organs,

> And whyl the organs maden melodye,
> To god alone in herte thus sang she.[237]

The allusions here selected are, it is true, the purely obvious ones made to instrumental music in Chaucer's works. There are others, most of which merely name the instruments and thus offer but little additional information on the subject. Brief though the review here given is, it shows that persons of nearly every class of society participated in playing and that a variety of instruments was known and used.

Besides playing, nearly all medieval persons delighted in singing, sometimes alone and frequently accompanied by other persons or by musical instruments. The Squire could sing or play the flute;[238] the Friar sang to the accompaniment of his own playing

---

[231] A *Gen. Prol.,* 236.

[232] Skeat, *Student's Chaucer,* gloss. See also Charles Burney, *A General History of Music,* with critical and historical notes by Frank Mercer, 4 vols. (New York, 1789), I, 594, 661.

[233] A 3213-3215.

[234] *Ibid.,* 3331. Burney, *op. cit.,* 662.

[235] *Ibid.,* 3333. Skeat, gloss.

[236] B *NPT,* 4041-4043. Cf. also Burney, *op. cit.,* 663.

[237] G 134-135. The use of the plural is especially to be noted here. See Burney, *op. cit.,* 663.

[238] A *Gen. Prol.,* 91.

on the rote or on the harp;[239] Nicholas, the scholar, sang to the melody he played on the sautrye:

> And *Angelus ad Virginem* he song;
> And after that he song the Kinges note;
> Ful often blessed was his mery throte.[240]

Absolon, whose accomplishments included playing on the rubible, sang "ther-to . . . som-tyme a loud quinible;"[241] or he took his gitern and went out to serenade the carpenter's wife:

> He singeth in his vois gentil and smal,
> 'Now, dere lady, if thy wille be,
> I preye yow that ye wol rewe on me,'
> Ful wel acordaunt to his giterninge.[242]

Even more interesting than instrumental accompaniment to singing mentioned by Chaucer is that of another voice or voices. The Summoner and the Pardoner, for instance, sang together.

> Ful loude he song, 'Com hider, love, to me.'
> This Somnour bar to him a stif burdoun,
> Was never trompe of half so greet a soun.[243]

The Pardoner's voice is described as one "as smal as hath a goot;"[244] the Summoner's was evidently low and deep.[245] The song they sang was probably one that was popular in Chaucer's day.

Further evidence of harmonized singing is given in Chaucer's

---

[239] *Ibid.*, 236; 266-267.

[240] A *Mil.T.*, 3213-3218. For an explanation of *the Kinges note* see Fletcher Collins, "The Kinges Note," *Speculum*, VIII (April, 1933), 195-197; George L. Frost, "The Music of the Kinges Note," *Speculum*, VIII (Oct., 1933), 526-529.

[241] A *Mil. T.*, 3331-3332. Frank Mercer, in his notes to Burney's *History of Music*, says of the quinible, "It seems as if this good clerk had preserved the ancient manner of singing by fifths, expressed by the verb *Quintoier*." I, 662.

[242] A *Mil.T.*, 3360-3363.

[243] *A Gen. Prol.*, 672-674.

[244] *Ibid.*, 688.

[245] Burney, *op. cit.*, 661.

translation of the *Romaunt de la Rose,* although the poet is writing of birds rather than of men:

> Ful fair servyse and eek ful swete
> These briddes maden as they sete.
> Layes of love ful wel sowning
> They songen in hir jargoning;
> Summe highe and summe eek lowe songe
> Upon the braunches grene y-spronge.[246]

How much of this part singing was actually done in medieval times is not known. It is said that "no English music in parts is preserved, so ancient as the time of Chaucer,"[247] yet the allusion quoted certainly suggests it.

Singing as related to the Church is treated in several of the passages in our poet's works. The Prioress is described as singing the divine office "entuned through hir nose ful semely."[248] Then, as now, the high key of the chant used for the office required a nasal quality for the best rendition.[249]

The Pardoner is said to have sung the offertory of the Mass with special fervor, not because of his religious nature, but

> . . . wel he wiste, whan that song was songe,
> He moste preche, and wel affyle his tonge,
> To winne silver, as he ful well coude;
> Therefore he song so meriely and loude.[250]

This is a depressing picture of the churchman whose attention was not attracted to the offertory, but to the silver which would be collected immediately afterwards.

On the whole, music, instrumental and vocal, seems to have interested Chaucer. His many references show his familiarity with the instruments used and several of these allusions are definite contributions to our knowledge of the history of music.

---

[246] Frag. A, 713-718.
[247] Burney, *op. cit.,* 665.
[248] A *Gen. Prol.,* 122-123.
[249] Robinson, *op. cit.,* 775. Cf. also Sister M. Madeleva, *Chaucer's Nuns and Other Essays,* 11.
[250] A *Gen. Prol.,* 710-713.

Because of the scarcity of books in medieval England, the pastime of silent reading was limited to relatively few persons. Chaucer describes himself as being greatly devoted to this means of entertainment.

> On bokes for to rede I me delyte,
> And in myn herte have hem in reverence;
> And to hem yeve swich lust and swich credence,
> That ther is wel unethe game noon
> That from my bokes make me to goon,
> But hit be other up-on the haly-day,
> Or elles in the joly tyme of May.[251]

As a matter of fact, it is evident from the poet's numerous references to other literary works and his use of them as sources that he spent many hours at reading. His sixty books, which he mentions and partially lists,[252] and doubtless many others, were read by him:

> For whan thy labour doon al is,
> And hast y-maad thy reckeninges,
> In stede of reste and newe thinges,
> Thou gost hoom to thy hous anoon;
> And, also domb as any stoon,
> Thou sittest at another boke,
> Til fully daswed is thy loke.[253]

Besides silent reading which seems to have been done in the quiet seclusion of one's own chamber, it was customary in Chaucer's time for reading to be done aloud by one person of a group, for the entertainment of all. Pandarus, it will be recalled, found Criseyde and two other ladies sitting in a pave parlour,

> . . . and they three
> Herden a mayden reden hem the geste
> Of the Sege of Thebes, whyl hem leste.[254]

---

[251] *LGW*, prol., A version, 30-36.

[252] *Ibid.*, 273 ff.

[253] *HF*, 652-658.

[254] *TC*, II, 82-84. For a general discussion of the practice of reading aloud see Ruth Crosby, "Oral Delivery in the Middle Ages," *Speculum*, XI (Jan., 1936), 88-100. Cf. also Froissart's *Chronicles*, II, 94, in which the author describes how he read to the Count Gaston Phoebus de Foix every evening.

The telling of tales is closely related to the pastime of reading. One finds many allusions to it in Chaucer's works. The device used for the *Canterbury Tales* is evidence sufficient of the popularity of this pastime. However, the poet contributes other information concerning it. In *Troilus and Criseyde,* for example, the telling of tales, together with playing and singing is referred to as follows:

> He song; she pleyde; he tolde tale of Wade.[255]

In the *Reeve's Tale* the miller and his guests are described as spending a long time in entertainment of various sorts.

> They soupen and they speke, hem to solace,
> And drinken, ever strong ale atte beste.[256]

Possibly the speaking of which the poet writes is concerned at least partly with telling stories. At any rate, the miller and his guests "aboute midnight went . . . to reste."[257]   There is no need to multiply the allusions to the pastime of story-telling; it is sufficient to note that Chaucer himself is so skillful a master at this art that the tales he told have lived for over five hundred years.

*   *   *

There is hardly any other subject which Chaucer treats with such completeness and consistent realism of detail as he does the sports and pastimes with which the people of England entertained themselves. His frequent and meaningful allusions impress one with the light-heartedness of medieval men and women and give to the poet's works a charming lightness of touch.

Hunting was a sport especially popular among persons of high rank. Men and women "a grete route" assembled with horses and hounds to spend hours in pursuing one or other animal. With the blowing of the horn by the master huntsman the hounds were uncoupled and the sport began. As soon as the animal pursued was scented the master-huntsman blew his horn to apprise the

---

[255] III, 614.
[256] A *Rv.T.,* 4146-4147.
[257] *Ibid.,* 4148.

other hunters of the fact. At this point the pursuit began in earnest, all of which action is given in detail by Chaucer in terms applicable only to the sport. When the hounds lost the scent of the animal and could no longer distinguish the direction of its course, the huntsman blew a "forloyn," that is, a signal to recall the hounds. Beyond this, the poet does not describe further the action of the chase.

Among the animals which medieval folk hunted were the hare, the hart, the wolf, and the boar. Chaucer includes also the lion and the bear, neither of which was probably hunted in England at that period. He may have introduced them for the effect of Trojan local colour.

Practically all classes of persons participated in the chase. Noble men, having both leisure and money for the sport, devoted much of their time to it. So, too, monks and priests, even though forbidden to do so, participated in hunting, often to the scandal of other persons. Women, sometimes as actual hunters and again as interested onlookers, accompanied men on the chase. Chaucer refers to them, usually describing their hunting garb as being of green, but saying little of their part in the sport.

As has been seen, the poet's allusions to the hunt are exceptionally realistic and inclusive. In addition to the information given about the sport itself, he refers to several kinds of hounds—greyhounds and alaunts being specifically mentioned—and others suggested. Hounds accompanied their masters every place they went. At feasts they lay on the floor beneath the tables, waiting for bones and other food which might be thrown to them. In a brief reference the poet suggests the dogs so lying on the floor of the great hall.

Hawking was almost as popular with medieval English men and women as hunting was; yet Chaucer alludes to it in only incidental fashion. The kinds of hawks are named and at least partially described. Besides telling of the appearance of some of the hawks, the poet refers to such facts as the preference of the sparrow-hawk for quail and the merlin for larks. He indicates, too, the custom of assigning certain birds to men of different classes of society. Altogether, the hawks rather than the actual progress of the sport are significant in Chaucer's works.

Perhaps no pastime of the Middle Ages was so characteristic of the spirit of the times or so colorful as the tournament. It entailed great physical strength and courage and was the chief sport of knights. Excuses for holding a contest of this kind were eagerly sought; often a lady's favor instigated it, as in the *Knight's Tale*. Great crowds of onlookers—the royal family, lords and ladies, and other persons—assembled a day or two before that which had been previously announced as the one on which the tournament was to be held. They began the festivities with feasts and dancing. Then, on the actual day of the tournament, after a reading of the rules to be observed on the occasion, all went in procession through the gaily decorated streets to the *lists,* or arena, where the contest was to be held.

Heralds blew their trumpets to mark the beginning of the combat, and the knights on horseback rushed into the arena and commenced their battle. Urged on by the spectators, who sat in seats erected nearby, the knights fought bravely. The clash of swords, the clatter of the spears against shields, the unhorsing of riders—all was exciting to the crowd, which cheered lustily when one side or the other gained an advantage. Before long the contest was ended and the victorious combatants rode from the arena, while the leader donned his helmet, mounted his horse, and rode before the stands where the ladies, particularly the lady of his choice, were. All this, together with allusions to the numerous injuries the knights received and the feasting and gaiety which followed the tournament, Chaucer presents in realistic fashion and in detail.

Dancing engaged much of the medieval person's leisure time, too. Everyone could participate in it, and practically everyone did. Persons of the upper classes of society seem to have liked such dances as the carole. Lords and ladies, dressed in their finest garments, met in gardens or on village greens and there, accompanied by music and singing, they gave themselves to the enjoyment of the carole or other dances which Chaucer does not specify.

There were other less courtly dances; Absolon, the parish-clerk, is said to have known twenty ways of varying his steps. Again, however, Chaucer gives no exact information, and the reader is left to his own imagination to understand them. Perhaps the morris, the roundel, the hay, and similar ones were in his repetoire. He may also have imitated professional dancers in performing such feats as dancing on his hands with his feet extended in the air, or carrying a firebrand in his hand and executing various fancy steps.

Persons of lower class seem often to have enjoyed riotous dancing. The Wife of Bath, for instance, tells us that she could dance her best when she had drunk wine. So, too, the young folk of whom the Pardoner writes. They ate and drank much; and they danced. Medieval preachers and moralists objected strenuouly to such riotous pastimes. They condemned especially those young persons who spent hours in public houses engaged in the pursuit of pleasure.

Archery, which was most important to the English army at this time, was hardly recognized as a worthwhile pastime. A few little allusions to the equipment necessary for it are scattered throughout Chaucer's poems, but not one of them is of significance except insofar as it indicates that archery could have been more popular than it was.

Wrestling appealed to the lower classes of society as much as the tournament did to the upper ones. It was a sport without color and romance, its claim to popularity being the test of strength of each participant. Rams were usually offered as prizes to the winners. Chaucer's references to wrestling are interesting particularly because they are concerned rather with the persons engaged in it than with the sport itself. Likewise, a single allusion to the comments made by spectators is given. It shows the crowd offering advice to one or other of the contestants as to how to change his method so he could win.

Of the pastimes which required less activity than the foregoing sports, the most popular among the upper classes was chess. The game was played very much as it is today, except that it presented fewer problems. As a literary device, chess was frequently employed by medieval writers, from whose allusions much information is offered. Chaucer, following traditional uses, refers to the origin of chess and also allegorically to a game between Fortune and a lover. Incidentally, the language and something of the method of playing are given, too. It is apparent that the poet was well acquainted with the game and had perhaps often enjoyed it. However, there is not much that is original in his treatment of it, nor in the similar pastime called tables, which he mentions several times in passing.

The love of games of chance often led medieval folk into the vice of gambling, and although preachers and moralists objected violently to the practice, it persisted. Even though the participation in gambling sometimes resulted in one's being led to Newgate or in being placed in the pillory and suffering other punishments, many persons were hazardous enough to indulge in it. Chaucer presents not only the gambler, but also and especially the arguments of the preachers against the vice.

Music, both instrumental and vocal, reading, and story-telling provided medieval English folk with entertainment just as they provide the modern English man and woman with it today. As a part of his education every gentleman learned to use a musical instrument of some kind; often he mastered several. Chaucer refers to persons playing at least one of these: the flute, the harp, the bagpipe, the reed pipe (shawm), the dulcet, the trumpet, the clarion, the rote, the psaltery, the rubible, the gitern, and the lute. He also alludes several times to the organ.

Vocal music was generally accompanied by an instrument. Sometimes, too, several persons sang in harmony. To sacred and profane music, to solos and to choruses, to accompanied and unaccompanied vocal selections Chaucer alludes, thus furnishing interesting and worthwhile information on the subject.

To silent reading, which could not be universally enjoyed on account of the scarcity of books, Chaucer makes allusions which show especially his own love for it. He says he reads when he cannot sleep at night, and that no other pastime gives him so much pleasure. Perhaps the poet's attitude toward silent reading was unusual in the Middle Ages; still, one may believe that all persons who enjoyed the luxury of a few volumes found pleasure similar to his. Those persons who could not or for some reason did not wish to read silently were sometimes entertained by hearing books read aloud. This delightful custom must have been especially appropriate in households where books were scarce and a large group of persons wished to enjoy them. As a pastime it seems to have been superseded occasionally by the telling of tales largely of the teller's invention.

As a source of information regarding the sports and pastimes of medieval England, Chaucer's works are probably more fertile than those of any other single author of the period. The comprehensive treatment, the accuracy of detail, and the number of references found in his volume testify to the poet's unusual powers of observation, his ability to reproduce faithfully what he saw, and his appreciation of the spirit of play which was so dominant in the English man and woman of the fourteenth century.

GENERAL SUMMARY AND CONCLUSIONS

I

In retrospect we see that in comparison with other sources of social history Chaucer's literary works afford one of the best means of studying the daily life of the people in fourteenth century England. There is apparently no other single volume of poetry or prose which embodies more references to English domestic life of the times than his does. His allusions, whether casual or direct, conventional or strongly individualized, faithfully reflect the civilization of his own age and country to the extent that even in those poems with ancient or foreign settings the background generally becomes in his hands distinctively fourteenth century and English.

The English home, as seen by a brief review, was in Chaucer's age rapidly assuming more domestic aspects than it had formerly possessed. In allusions varying from the vaguely suggestive to the specific, the poet presents four types of homes, namely, the castle, the manor, the town house, and the cottage. He shows particularly well the exterior arrangement and architectural details of the castle. Although in the *Hous of Fame* he describes it as of beryl, with walls, floors, and roofs of gold set with jewels, in somewhat conventional fashion, the general outline of the structure is realistic.

There is no well-defined, distinctive picture of the exterior of the manor or the town-house given by Chaucer. Various indirect and casual references suggest their existence, but evidently neither had as yet begun to rival the castle as a subject for literature, although history attests the importance of both in the development of domestic life. The cottage, on the other hand, is somewhat specifically pictured, although there is only one good view, and that not from the standpoint of architectural details.

Rooms are again and again referred to. Some of the allusions to them are informative, but many of them are mere hints without any special significance. Only slight information is given regarding the general layout of the house, and that by implication rather than directly. Fairly accurate are the descriptions of the great hall. From all the allusions to this room one is able to obtain some idea of it, with its raised platform or dais across one end, whereon the table dormant occupied the important position in houses of the wealthy, its windows with seats in the recesses, the stairs which led up from the hall, and its walls adorned with painted scenes or rich hangings. Its uses as dining hall, living room, bed room, and perhaps even chapel are suggested, too. Still, as one observes by studying social histories, there are some omissions; Chaucer does not refer to the tables on trestles, to the fireplace in the center of the room, to the minstrels' gallery, to the screens, or to the rushes which generally covered the floor of the hall.

The chamber is never alluded to by the poet as the solar, yet that seems to have been the common name for it in the fourteenth century. However, the chamber is used frequently as the scene of action in his poems, and is described with some degree of accuracy. Its location in reference to other rooms is implied; so also is its size. Otherwise, the details which make the chamber seem real are the furnishings and hangings. One of the most striking descriptions is of a student's room; the selection of concrete details makes it particularly vivid.

The lady's chamber, so often elaborately drawn in other medieval literature, is scarcely more than mentioned by Chaucer. At least there is no view of it, and only the vaguest suggestions as to its furnishings. Ordinarily the furniture in a medieval house was scarce; it is not surprising, then, that there are not many articles mentioned in the poems. A few allusions to beds, a perch for clothing, chests, and benches help one to form only a rather general idea of the furnishings of the chamber.

Rooms other than the hall and bower or chamber are only incidentally mentioned. A chapel is perhaps implied; a study, a counting-room, and the kitchen and other houses of office are merely referred to in passing. Yet in spite of these and similar omissions the composite view obtainable from the allusions as a whole is fairly satisfactory.

In some respects the garden is less realistically described than the house. The elaborate picture in the *Romaunt de la Rose,* with its lists of trees and birds, seems to have furnished a kind of standard from which Chaucer had difficulty in breaking away, save perhaps in his latest creative period. This resulted in the use of the conventional method to the extent that the impression of realism often had to be sacrificed. There are however, several of the poet's gardens briefly delineated, which are effective. The views are enhanced by several individualizing objects, such as the new benches of freshly cut turves, and the railed alleys.

In a period when the useful garden was still important to the medieval housewife, it seems a little strange that Chaucer is concerned chiefly with pleasure gardens. He has only incidentally recorded herbs and vegetables, and save the listing of trees, barely alludes to fruits. On the whole, though, his concern is with the social significance of the garden; hence his apparent indifference to kitchen plots. It will be noted that there is always someone in the gardens he pictures; often it is a merry company of folk who walk and chat or sing; sometimes it is a smaller group, leaping, casting darts, or discussing weighty matters of state; again, it is a party of picnickers. The garden scenes may indeed seem to lack originality of treatment; yet fundamentally they are of fourteenth century England exclusively.

Surprisingly numerous are Chaucer's references to food, meals, serving, and table etiquette. The time of taking dinner, with casual allusions to the evening meal; the description of various feasts; the names of particular dishes; the indirect suggestions of cookery; and hints of over-indulgence are among the most significant phases of the subject treated.

In satirizing the table manners of the times, the poet indicates both the negligence of people in general and the refinement of certain persons. Even though the description of Madame Eglentyne's manners has been taken largely from another source, the very fact that the poet included it in his portrait of the nun is significant. Convents and monasteries of the period seem often to have been centers of culture and refinement.

Omitted in Chaucer's allusions to foods and meals are the daily menu, the medieval housewife, a complete meal, and the kitchen.

The medieval appetite, suggested rather than described, has often been pictured in a gross fashion by other authors of the time. Here it is impossible to form any idea of it, other than by inference. Despite all omissions, however, there is on the whole much realism in the references. Chaucer contributes materially to our knowledge of medieval food and its serving.

Of the various types of costume worn in the fourteenth century the poet includes practically all. Sometimes they are pictured after the manner of the romances, by an extravagant use of details; more frequently, perhaps, they are described with restraint and in a strikingly concrete manner. Some evidence is given of the wearing apparel of nearly every class of society; there are the noble and wealthy men and women in richly embroidered silks, fashionably trimmed and cut; there are the middle class persons in motley or parti-coloured garments, stylishly made; there is the poor man in his shabby tabard; and the knight in armour. Besides costumes of monks and nuns, described with many of the exaggerations not approved by their rules, or as being carelessly worn and cared for, there are suggestions of the habit worn by widows and of the huntsman's garb. Of special interest is the fact that Chaucer's characters are usually clothed in garments which indicate their characteristics, their position in life, or the general attitude of the times.

Marks of vanity in both men and women are recorded. There are hints of curled and dyed hair, of an over-solicitousness concerning dress and the neatness of it, of painted cheeks, plucked brows, and attractive accessories. Lastly, there is a medieval sermon on the exaggerated fashions, costly materials, and the immodestly cut garments.

Much evidence is given of the sports and pastimes enjoyed. The most popular of sports, hunting, is described in detail, and in the language of the chase. There is information as to the popularity of the sport, of the animals hunted, of the hounds used, and of the persons participating in it. Hawking, probably more popular with women than with men, is alluded to only incidentally and without any exact information being contributed to our knowledge of the sport itself. The tournament, distinctively medieval, is very concretely and completely depicted. Realistic in effect, there are nevertheless many hints of literary tradition in the description. The love of dancing is shown by the large number of characters participating in it. Every class enjoys the pastime, which is seen to have been of two types—the one aesthetic and the other riotous. Archery, wrestling, and other sports are alluded to in varying degrees of directness. The games merely mentioned as well as those of which more information is given all attest the medieval love of physical activity.

The pastimes of a more quiet nature, probably enjoyed in the winter especially, include chess, dicing, tables, story-telling, reading, music, and the like.

II

The foregoing investigation of Chaucer's use of the domestic life and amusements of his own times as social background reveals several significant facts. First of all, one is amazed that so much of social history should be faithfully represented in works which are at best only incidentally concerned with it. Even excepting the many aspects of manners and customs which are not treated in this work, one is impressed by the completeness of the panoramic view which stretches out before him as he summarizes the poet's scattered references.

Secondly, the startling relation there is between the methods of description used by Chaucer and the resulting representations of life, is clearly shown. We have already noted that the poet's earlier works depended largely upon other literary sources and were consequently often marked by conventionality. Like the writers whom he imitates or translates, he presents in this period of his development as a poet a highly romantic or idealistic view of life. His characters are of the upper ranks of society; they dwell in castles or other spacious mansions; their gardens are extremely wide and full of luxuriant foliage; they are not concerned with the necessities of life, not even meals; their garments are generally of finest quality materials elaborately decorated with jewels; their pleasures are sought in dancing, singing, music, chess, and similar quiet pastimes. They occupy themselves sometimes in promenading in gardens where they are attended by gaily attired knights and ladies. This is the traditional life of poetry; it is in a sense characteristic of the kind of life led by persons of high rank and for that reason is significant in the consideration of English domestic life.

Fortunately for his readers, Chaucer was not content to see through the eyes of others. The result is that in his later works he transcribes the social manners and customs of his age with unwonted realism. He no longer paints the idealistic, but the actual. He has become an older, wiser man, and although he retains much of the robust optimism so characteristic of his early works, he is now impressed at times with harsh realities. He is seldom, if ever, a reformer, however, but merely records the different phases of life as they appear. He is no longer especially concerned with royalty and the nobility, but depicts persons of all classes of society and in their proper milieu. By selecting salient features—a table dormant, a fat swan loved best of any roast, kerchiefs which weigh ten pounds, pies twice cooked, and a wimple pinched "ful semely"—the poet in many instances breaks away entirely from his contemporaries. His departure from the traditional method of description it is as much as anything else which makes him great and eternal. The universality of such immortal characters as the Wife of Bath, the Squire, the Monk, and the Prioress, for instance, is achieved largely by the accuracy with which the poet records details of description and indicates the various elements which constitute these characters' environment. Certainly one must agree that if only the *Canterbury Tales,* including the Prologue, remained to represent his literary efforts, Chaucer's contribution to English social history would be generous and significant.

APPENDIX

I

The Goodman of Paris records in detail several feasts of his time. A dinner given by M. (the abbé) de Lagny for Mons. de Paris, the President, the Procureur and the Avocat du Roy and the rest of the Council was one of these. It provided for eight covers, that is, for sixteen persons, two using each plate. The preparations entailed among other things procuring tablecloths for the tables, vessels for the dining hall and the kitchen, branches, and greenstuff to set on the table, cups with feet, two comfit dishes, silver salt cellars, and bread two days old for toast and trenchers. For the kitchen, two large pails, two washing tubs, and two brooms were needed. The Mons. de Paris had three esquires of his own to serve him and he was served apart with covered dishes. Mons. the Pres. had one esquire and was served apart, but not with covered dishes. At the request of Mons. the Pres., the Procureur du Roi was seated above the Avocat du Roi.[1] After the meal, the guests washed, said Grace, and went to the withdrawing room, and then the servants dined, and·immediately afterwards served wine and spices.[2]

More elaborate were the preparations for the wedding feast of Jehan de Chesne, at which forty persons were to be served at dinner and twenty at supper.[3] The officers needed for this feast included (1) for the kitchen: a clerk or varlet to purchase supplies such as greenery, violets, chaplets, certain foods, logs, coal, salt, vats and washing tubs; a cook and his varlets; two knife-bearers; one or two water-carriers; "a big and strong sergeant to guard the portals";[4] two esquires of the kitchen and two helpers; (2) for the dining hall: two esquires to give out and collect spoons and cups, and to pour the wine; two other esquires for the wine cellar; two honest and skilled esquires to accompany the bridegroom and to go with him before the dishes; two stewards to seat the guests; and a sewer and two servants for each table, "who shall serve and take away, throw the remnants into the baskets and the sauces and broths into the buckets and pails and receive and bring the dessert dishes to the esquires of the kitchen. . . ."[5] A woman chaplet-maker was also engaged to make and deliver garlands on the wedding eve and on the wedding day. The women of the household were to make provisions for tapestries, "to order and spread them and in especial

---

[1] *Goodman of Paris*, 236.
[2] *Ibid.*, 238.
[3] *Ibid.*, 238.
[4] *Ibid.*, 242.
[5] *Ibid.*, 242-244.

to dight the chamber and the bed that is to be blessed."[6] Likewise, a laundress was needed for folding[7] (sheets?), and the ministrels were hired.[8] The Goodman seems to have forgotten no details of the preparations, which must have been carried out with great efficiency.

II

Royal feasts and those held in the homes of noblemen were of particularly great proportions, as has already been indicated by the number of servants employed in their households and by the preparations necessary. The dinner given by M. (Abbé) de Lagny, for instance, at which only sixteen persons were served, consisted of the following courses and dishes:

. . . two quarts of (wine of) Grenache, to wit (allowing) two persons to the half-pint (but that is too much, for a half-pint between three suffices, and let the seconds have some). Hot cracknels and ruddy apples roast with white comfits thereon, a quarter lb.; ripe figs roast, five quarters; sorrel, cress and rosemary.

Pottages, to wit a salemine of six salmon and six tench, green porray, and white herring, a quarter (lb.); six fresh-water eels salted the day before, and three stockfish soaked for a night.

For the pottages: almonds, 6 lbs.; ginger powder, ½ lb.; saffron, ½ oz.; small spices, 2 oz.; cinnamon powder, ¼ lb.; comfits, ½ lb.

Sea fish: soles, gurnard, congers, turbot, salmon. Fresh-water fish: luce, two Marne carps, bream.

Entremets: plaice, lamprey à la boe. Roast: and more towels be needed and likewise sixteen oranges, porpoise in its sauce, makerel, soles, bream, chad à la cameline, or with verjuice, rice with fried almonds thereon; sugar for rice and apples, 1 lb.; little napkins.

For dessert: compost with white and red comfits spread thereon; rissoles, flawns, figs, dates, raisins, filberts.

Hippocras and wafers are the issue. . . .[9]

This dinner, let it be noted, was held during Lent and for that reason was less extravagant than it might have been. Fish, rather than meat, was the chief food of the day.

---

[6] *Ibid.,* 244. It is interesting to observe that "if the bed be covered with cloth, there is needed a fur coverlet of half vair; but if it be covered with serge, not so."

[7] *Ibid.,* 244.

[8] *Ibid.,* 247. The minstrels were to be paid eight francs, "without the spoons and other gratuities; and they will play on the wedding eve and the acrobats (likewise)."

[9] *Goodman of Paris,* 236-238.

The wedding feast of Jehan de Chesne, at which forty persons were served dinner and twenty supper, appears modest in comparison to Duke Lionel's feast of thirty courses. The Goodman summarizes the foods served at the former feast. His comments are especially naïve:

Service: Butter, none, because it is a feast day.

Item, cherries, none, because none were to be had; and for this course nought.

Pottages: Capons with blankmanger, pomegranates and red comfits thereon.

Roast: On each dish a quarter of a kid; a quarter of a kid is better than lamb; a duckling, two spring chickens and sauce thereto; oranges, cameline, verjuice and fresh towels and napkins therewith.

Entremets: Crayfish jelly, loach, young rabbits and pigs.

Dessert: frument and venison.

Issue: Hippocras and wafers.

Sally-Forth: wine and spices.

Supper for twenty persons

Cold sage of the halves of chickens, little ducklings, and a vinaigrette of the same meats for the said supper in a dish. A pasty of young hares and two peacocks (although some say that at the bridals of free folk there ought to be darioles), and in another dish minced kids with the heads halved and glazed.

Entremets: jelly as above.

Issue: Apples and cheese without hippocras, because it is out of season.

Dancing, singing, wine and spices, and torches for lighting.[10]

Some idea of the cost of such a feast as the foregoing may be obtained from the Goodman's account, too. Almost to tediousness he lists the purchases to be made:

10 dozen flat white loaves, baked the day before—1 penny apiece.

Trencher bread—3 dozen, ½ ft. wide and 4 in. high, baked four days before and let it be brown, or let Corbeil bread be got.

Wine cellar: 3 cauldrons of wine.

---

[10] *Ibid.,* 238-239. It is interesting to compare this menu with one given for a bridal feast in "The Boke of Nurture," *Babees Book,* 375-377:

1. Boar's head and a Device of Welcome.
2. Venison and custard with a Device of Meekness.
3. Venison, crane, baked meat, and a Device of Gladness and Loyalty.
4. Sweets and game (Creme of Almondys, losynge in Syruppe, betoure, partrich, plover, snyte, pouder-veal, leche veal, etc.,) Device of Thankfulness.
5. Cheese, payne-puff, freynes (cheese-cakes), hot bread, and a Device of Child-Bearing and a Promise of Babies.

From the butcher: ½ mutton, to make sops (soups?) for the guests and a quarter of bacon to lard them; the master bone of a leg of beef to cook with the capons, so as to have broth to make blankmanger; a fore quarter of veal to serve for blankmanger. The seconds a hind quarter of veal or calves feet, to have liquid for jelly. Venison, a foot quartered.

From the wafer-maker: first, for the bride's service, 1½ doz. cheese *gauffres*, 3s; a dozen and a half of *gros batons*, 6s., 1½ doz. *portes*, 18 d.; 1½ of *estriers*, 18d.; 100 sugared *galettes*, 8d., etc.

From the poulterer: 20 capons at 2s. Parisis (Paris money) apiece; 5 kids, 4s. Parisis; 20 ducklings, 3s. Parisis apiece; 50 chickens, 12d. Parisis apiece; that is—forty roasts for the dinner, five for the jelly, and five at supper for the cold sage. 50 young rabbits—40 for dinner, which shall be roast, and 10 for the jelly, and they shall cost 12d. Parisis apiece. A lean pig for the jelly, 4d. Parisis apiece; 12 pigeons for the supper, 10d. Parisis the pair.

In the market, bread for the trenchers, 3 doz. (loaves).

Pomegranates for blankmanger, three.

Oranges, 50.

Six green cheeses and one old cheese and 300 eggs.

Sorrel to make verjuice for the chickens, sage and parsley to make the cold sage, 200 apples.

. . . .

From the saucemaker—three half pints of cameline for dinner and supper and a quart of sorrel verjuice.

From the spicer: 10 lbs. almonds, 14 d. per lb.—3 lbs. hulled corn, 8d the lb.—1 lb. ginger, 5s.—cinnamon, rice, sugar, saffron, cloves, pepper, mace, galingale, bay leaves—2 lbs. of large and small candles —Torches—flambeaux—3s. a lb. when purchased and the ends to be taken back at 6d. less per lb. Spices for the chamber: orange peel, citron, red anise, rose-sugar, white comfits, etc.

Sum total of this spicery—12 francs—½ franc per cover.

At the milk-market—good milk, neither curdled nor watered, to make frumenty.

100 Bergundy faggots, 13s—2 sacks of coal, 10s.

. . . .

100 crayfish, ½ pint loach, etc.[11]

Besides these expenses were 4½ francs for the cook and his helpers; 1 franc for the porter, 4 francs to the concierge of Beauvais; 5 francs for tables, trestles, *et similia;* 15 francs to the chaplet-maker, 20 shillings for water; 8 shillings for greenery; 7 francs for kitchen vessels, towels, cloths, and glasses; 4 francs for pewter pots, and the aforementioned 8 francs for minstrels.[12]

---

[11] *Ibid.,* 239-241.
[12] *Ibid.,* 247.

III

One of the outstanding English medieval feasts was that for the Installation of Ralf de Born, Prior of St. Augustine's in Canterbury, in 1309, at which 6,000 persons were served. The itemized list of what was used at this feast follows:

	£	S
53 qrs. of wheat	19	
58 qrs. of malt	17	
11 tuns of wine	24	
20 qrs. of oats	24	
spices	28	
300 lbs. wax	8	
500 lbs. almonds		18
30 oxen	27	
100 hogs	16	
200 muttons	30	
1,000 geese	16	
500 capons and hens	6	5
473 pullets	3	14
200 pigs	5	
24 swans	7	
600 rabbits	15	
16 brawn	15	
Partridge, mallards, bitterns, larks	18	
Fish, cheese, milk, onions, etc.	2	10
9,600 eggs	4	10
Saffron and pepper	1	4

Besides these items there were 1,000 earthen pots, nine quarters of salt, 1,400 mugs or wooden cans to drink from, 3,300 dishes and platters, or trenchers, 300 ells of caneum, canvas, or flax, the making of trestles, tables, and dressers, and the wages of the musicians, of the cooks and their boys to be paid for. The sum total of the expense was 287 pounds 7 shillings, which is equivalent to about $20,000 of our money.[13]

IV

Whatever may have been the results of the attempts to restrict the great feasts and banquets of the fourteenth century, however great may have been the feasts held, most people of the times must have lived in the periods between the feasts somewhat moderately. There appear to be no records of excessive extravagance in these ordinary repasts; still judging from the general temper of the times, persons of rank must have enjoyed plenty.

[13] Bishop Fleetwood, *Chronicon Preciosum* (London, 1745), 67-71. Bishop Fleetwood says that at the time of this feast prices were unusually high.

It is of interest to note that in the household of Edward IV's mother, Princess Cecill, that the daily meals were of no great delicacy. They seem, indeed, to have lacked variety, with their apparently invariable menus:

Uppon Sondaye, tuesdaye, and thursdaye, the househoulde at dynner is served with boyled beefe and mutton, and one roste; at supper leyched (sliced) beefe and mutton roste.

Uppon mondaye and wensdaye at dynner, one boyled beefe and mutton; at supper, ut supra.

Uppon fastinge dayes, salte fysche, and two dishes of fresh fishe; if there come a principall feaste, it is served like unto the feaste honorablye.

If Mondaye or wensdaye be hollidaye, then is the household served with one roste, as in other dayes.

Uppon satterdaye at dynner, saltfyshe, one freshfishe, and butter; at supper saltfishe and egges.[14]

Probably the menu was varied a little by the use of bread, wine, spices, and fruits or other desserts; still, the principal courses of meat or fish were of a sameness which would certainly discourage any modern person.

Dame Alice de Bryene's household[15] fared better than this, as far as variety was concerned, at least. An entry in Dame Alice's household book, selected almost at random, indicates the type of meals served daily. Besides, the number of persons served and in many cases the prices of the purchases are included. The account for September 29, 1412, is as follows:

Meals: Breakfast 8, dinner 20, supper 20. Sum 48 (persons)

Pantry—40 white loaves and six black loaves; wine from what remained; ale from stock. Kitchen—one quarter of bacon, one joint of mutton, one lamb, and 32 pigeons. Purchases in companage, 2d. Provender—hay from stock for 7 horses of the Lady and of the company; fodder for the same one bu. of oats.[16]

---

[14] *A Collection of Ordinances and Regulations for the Government of the Royal Household,* Society of Antiquaries (London, 1790), 38.

[15] This household was evidently that of a manor. Most of the entries in the household book seem to be for foods and other provisions which could not be procured from the land itself; consequently, one must bear in mind that there was probably garden produce to supplement what is here given.

[16] *Household Book of Dame Alice de Bryene,* 1.

On Friday, September 30, 1412, the items include fish instead of meat. The sum of persons present for the three meals is 40; the provisions are:

Pantry—46 white loaves and 6 black loaves. Wine from what remained; ale from stock. Kitchen—half a saltfish and one stockfish. Purchases—100 white herrings, 18d.[17]

Dame Alice's account book furnishes an idea of what the cost of food in her time was; not so much does it tell of individual items as it does of the sum total. For the years 1412-1413 the records are as follows:

Sum paid for victuals for the year _____	£44	23½d
Sum of all purchases for the year _____	£23	7½d

Sum total   £67   2s   7d[18]

These figures probably include purchases listed in fragmentary memoranda also; that is, foods such as cheese, almonds, salt, figs, raisins, dates, and the like. If to obtain the relative evaluation of the pound in the Middle Ages one must multiply the present value of it by ten or fifteen,[19] then the cost of the purchases in present-day figures would amount to about 3,500 dollars. There were in one month, October, over 1,400 persons served at meals, so the relative cost of the food is very small. Likewise, when one summarizes the amount of food purchased for this same month, it is found that for so many persons it is not great:

wheat baked, 6 quarters
wine——
barley or drage malt brewed, 10 qrs. 5 qrs. drage malt.
beef—one carcase and 2 quarters
pork—one pig and 2 quarters
one swan
one goose
mutton—5 joints
6 lambs
4 chickens
4 conies
5 partridges
275 pigeons
8 salt fish
6 stock fish
Loaves of bread: approximately 1565 (white)
                       197 (black)[20]

---

[17] *Ibid.*, 1.

[18] *Ibid.*, 102.

[19] Mead, *The English Medieval Feast*, 34, 227.

[20] These figures were obtained from the accounts given in the household book and are subject to error, but they may give some idea of the quantity of foods used.

Of interest is the fact that on the day when the swan was served there were 62 persons present for the dinner. For these guests, besides the swan, there were one lamb, 4 conies, 5 partridges, 23 pigeons: the other purchases were mutton and pork, milk and "crem."[21]

Dame Alice's larder had to be stocked with fish for Lent. On Ash Wednesday, March 8, 1413, the sum of persons served meals was 26. For the pantry there were 36 loaves of white bread and eight of black; wine and ale were from the stock. The kitchen supplies included:

> 50 red herrings, 40 white herrings, half a salt fish, one stock fish. Purchases—200 oysters, 11 plaice, 2 haddocks, 200 whelks, etc.[22]

V

In spite of the apparent lack of restraint in feasting, various rules and regulations had been made from time to time in medieval England to limit the people to some kind of moderation. Edward II, realizing that

> . . . by the outrageous and excessive multitude of meats and dishes, which the great men of the kingdom used in their castles, and by persons of inferior rank imitating their example beyond what their stations required, and their circumstances could afford, many great evils had come upon the kingdom, the health of the King's subjects had been injured, their property consumed, and they had been reduced to poverty,[23]

had ordained, with the consent of his Great Council, that certain rules should be observed. In general they were as follows:

> That the great men of the kingdom should have only two courses of flesh meats served up to their tables, each course consisting only of two kinds of flesh meat: except Prelates, Earls, Barons, and the great men of the land, who might have an intermeat (delicacies), of one kind of meat if they pleased. On fish days they should only have two courses of fish, each consisting of two kinds, with an intermeat of one kind of fish, if they thought fit. And those who should transgress this ordinance should be severely punished.[24]

Evidently very little attention was paid to the regulations, for again, later, the excess in banqueting was so great that King Edward III was obliged "to establish certain rules, forbidding any common man to have dainty dishes at his table, or costly drink."[25]

---

[21] *Household Book,* 8.

[22] *Ibid.,* 45.

[23] *A Collection of Ordinances,* intro., viii.

[24] *Ibid.,* viii-ix.

[25] Hartshorne, *Ancient Metrical Tales,* notes to "Piers of Ffulham," 331-332; Andrews, *History of Great Britain,* 439.

Works on Chaucer

1. texts

The Complete Works of Geoffrey Chaucer. Edited by Fred Norris Robinson. New York, 1933.

The Canterbury Tales. Edited by James M. Manly. New York, 1928.

The Student's Chaucer. Edited by Walter W. Skeat. Oxford, 1929.

Troilus and Criseyde. Edited by Robert Kilburn Root. Princeton, 1926.

2. special studies

Babcock, Robert W. "Medieval Setting of Chaucer's Monk's Tale," *Publications of the Modern Language Association,* 46 (March, 1931), 205-213.

Brown, David. "Solas in the Miller's Tale," *Modern Language Notes,* 48 (June, 1933), 369-370.

"Chaucer's World," *Living Age,* 227 (Dec. 1, 1900), 580-583.

Collins, Fletcher. "The Kinges Note," *Speculum,* 8 (April, 1933), 195-197.

———, *Chaucer's Understanding of Music.* Unpublished dissertation. New Haven, 1934.

Cook, Albert S. "The Last Months of Chaucer's Earliest Patron," *Transactions of the Connecticut Academy of Arts and Sciences,* 21 (December, 1916), 1-144.

———, "The Historical Background of Chaucer's Knight," *Transactions of the Connecticut Academy of Arts and Sciences,* 20 (Feb., 1916), 161-240.

———, "Beginning the Board in Prussia," *Journal of English and Germanic Philology,* 14 (July, 1915), 375-389.

Coulton, George G. *Chaucer and His England.* London, 1908.

Curry, Walter C. *Chaucer and the Medieval Sciences.* New York, 1926.

Ellesmere Manuscript. Produced in facsimile. Manchester, 1911.

Emerson, Oliver F. "Chaucer and Medieval Hunting," *Romanic Review,* 13 (April-June, 1922), 115-150.

———, "Some of Chaucer's Lines on the Monk," *Modern Philology,* 1 (June, 1903), 105-115.

Fansler, Dean S. *Chaucer and the Roman de la Rose.* New York, 1914.

French, Robert D. *A Chaucer Handbook.* New York, 1929.

Frost, George I. "The Music of the Kinges Note," *Speculum,* 8 (October, 1933), 526-529.

Gerould, Gordon Hall. "The Social Status of Chaucer's Franklin," *Publications of the Modern Language Association,* 41 (June, 1926), 262-279.

Getty, Agnes K. "The Medieval-Modern Conflict in Chaucer's Poetry," *Publications of the Modern Language Association,* 47 (June, 1932), 385-402.

Griffin, Nathaniel E. "Chaucer's Portrait of Criseyde," *Journal of English and Germanic Philology,* 20 (Jan., 1921), 39-46.

Hinckley, Henry B. *Notes on Chaucer.* Northampton, 1906.

————, "The Grete Emetreus the King of Inde," *Modern Language Notes,* 48 (March, 1923), 148-149.

Ives, Doris V. "A Man of Religion," *Modern Language Review,* 27 (April, 1932), 144-148.

Karpinski, Louis C. "Augrim-Stones," *Modern Language Notes,* 27 (Nov., 1912), 206-209.

Kirby, Thomas A. "Note on Troilus II, 1298," *Modern Language Review,* 29 (Jan., 1934), 67-68.

Kittredge, George L. *Chaucer and His Poetry.* Cambridge, Mass., 1915.

————, "Chaucer and Some of His Friends," *Modern Philology,* 1 (June, 1903), 1-9.

Koellreuter, Maria. *Das Privatleben in England nach den Dichtungen von Chaucer, Gower und Langland.* Dissertation. Halle, a. S., 1908.

Lawrence, William W. "Satire in Sir Thopas," *Publications of the Modern Language Association,* 50 (March, 1935), 81-91.

Linn, Irving. "The Arming of Sir Thopas," *Modern Language Notes,* 51 (May, 1936), 300-311.

Linthicum, M. Channing. " 'Faldyng' and 'Medlee,' " *Journal of English and Germanic Philology,* 34 (Jan., 1935), 39-41.

Looten, le Chanoine. *Chaucer, ses Modèles, ses Sources, sa Religion.* Lille, 1931.

Lounsbury, Thomas R. *Studies in Chaucer.* 3 vols. London, 1892.

Lowes, James L. *Geoffrey Chaucer and the Development of His Genius.* New York, 1934.

Madeleva, Sister M. *Chaucer's Nuns and Other Essays.* New York, 1925.

Manly, James M. *Some New Light on Chaucer.* New York, 1926.

————, "Sir Thopas; A Satire," *Essays and Studies,* 13 (Oxford, 1928), 52-73.

Originals and Analogues. Edited by Frederick J. Furnivall and others. New York, 1926.

Patch, Howard R. "Chaucer and the Common People," *Journal of English and Germanic Philology,* 29 (July, 1930), 376-384.

Rands, William B. *Chaucer's England.* 2 vols. London, 1869.

Robertson, Stuart. "Elements of Realism in 'The Knight's Tale,' " *Journal of English and Germanic Philology,* 14 (April, 1915), 226-256.

Root, Robert Kilburn. *The Poetry of Chaucer.* Boston, 1922.

Schramm, Wilbur L. "The Cost of Books in Chaucer's Time," *Modern Language Notes,* 48 (March, 1933), 139-145.

Sedgwick, Henry. *Dan Chaucer.* New York, 1934.

Schlauch, Margaret. *Chaucer's Constance and Accused Queens.* New York, 1927.

Slaughter, E. E. "Allas! Allas! that ever Love was sinne," *Modern Language Notes*, 49 (Feb., 1934), 83-86.

Snell, Frederick. *The Age of Chaucer*. London, 1901.

Sypherd, Wilbur O. *Studies in Chaucer's Hous of Fame.* Chaucer Society Publications. London, 1907.

Tatlock, John S. P. "The Epilog of Chaucer's Troilus," *Modern Philology*, 18 (April, 1921), 625-659.

Thompson, William H. "The Chaucer Garden," *Living Age*, 7 (Nov. 3, 1900), 379-383.

Tupper, Frederick. "Chaucer's Sinners and Sins," *Journal of English and Germanic Philology*, 15 (Jan., 1916), 56-106.

———, "Chaucer and the Seven Deadly Sins," *Publications of the Modern Language Association*, 29 (Jan., 1914), 93-128.

———, "The Quarrels of the Canterbury Pilgrims," *Journal of English and Germanic Philology*, 14 (April, 1915), 256-271.

———, "Wilful and Impatient Poverty," *Nation* (N. Y.), 99 (July, 1914), 41.

Wainwright, Benjamin B. "Chaucer's Prioress Again: an Interpretive Note," *Modern Language Notes*, 48 (Jan., 1933), 34-87.

Watt, Francis. *Canterbury Pilgrims and their Ways*. London, 1917.

Winstanley, Lillian. *The Prioress's Tale. The Tale of Sir Thopas*. Cambridge, 1922.

Works on Medieval Social Life

1. original sources

Account Rolls of the Abbey of Durham. 3 vols. Surtees Society Publications, 99, 100, 103. Durham, 1898, 1900.

Accounts of the Obedientiars of Abingdon Abbey. Edited by Richard Edward G. Kirk. Camden Society Publications, 51. London, 1892.

Ancient Metrical Tales. Edited by Charles H. Hartshorne. London, 1829.

Anglo-Saxon and Norse Poems. Edited by Nora Kershaw Chadwick. Cambridge, 1922.

The Anglo-Saxon Chronicle. Edited by John Allen Giles. London, 1914.

An Alphabet of Tales. Edited by Mary M. Banks. EETS OS 126, 127, London, 1904, 1905.

An Anonymous Short English Metrical Chronicle. Edited by Ewald Zettl. EETS OS 196. London, 1935.

Antiquitates Culinariae. Edited by Richard Warner. London, 1791.

Arnold's Chronicle. London, 1811.

Barclay, Alexander. *The Ship of Fools*. Edited by T. H. Jamieson. 2 vols. Edinburgh, 1874.

Bede. *Vita S. Cuthberti*. Migne PL, XCIV. Col. 729-790.

Berners, Dame Juliana. *The Gentleman's Academie, or The Booke of St. Albans*. Reprint by Gervase Markham. London, 1595.

The Book of the Knight of La Tour-Landry. Edited with notes and introduction by Thomas Wright. EETS OS 33. London, 1868.

Boorde, Andrew. *Introduction and Dietary.* EETS ES 10. London, 1870.

Le Bréviaire Grimani à la Bibliothèque Marciana de Venise. Edited by Ferd. Ongania. Venice, 1903.

Calendar of the Close Rolls. (Richard II, vol. I, A. D. 1377-1381). London, 1914.

Calendar of the Coroners' Rolls of the City of London. Edited by Reginald Robinson Sharpe. London, 1914.

Calendar of Letters from the Mayor and Corporation of the City of London. A. D. 1350-1370. Edited by Reginald Robinson Sharpe. London, 1885.

Calendar of the Liberate Rolls. (Henry III, 1226-1240). London, 1916.

Calendar of Select Pleas and Memoranda Rolls of the City of London. Edited by Arthur H. Thomas. London, 1926.

Calendar of Wills. Edited by Reginald Robinson Sharpe. 2 vols. London, 1889.

Les Cent Nouvelles Nouvelles. Edited by Paul L. Jacob. Paris, 1858.

Chapters of the Augustinian Canons. Edited by Herbert E. Salter. Canterbury and York Society. London, 1933.

A Chronicle of London from 1089-1483. London, 1827.

A Collection of Ordinances and Regulations for the Government of the Royal Household. Society of Antiquaries. Edited by J. Nichols. London, 1790.

Collectanea Anglo-Premonstratensia. Edited by Cardinal Gasquet. Camden Society Publications. Third series, 6, 10, 12. London, 1904-1906.

Compotus Rolls of the Obedientiaries of St. Swithun's Priory, Winchester. Edited by George W. Kitchin. Hampshire Record Society Publications. London, 1892.

Cook, Albert S. and Chauncy Tinker. *Translations from Old English Prose.* Boston, 1908.

Documents Illustrating the Activities of the General and Provincial Chapters of the English Black Monks, 1215-1540. Camden Society Publications. Third Series, 45. Edited by William Pantin. London, 1933.

Early English Romances in Verse: Done into Modern English by Edith Rickert: Romances of Friendship. London, 1908.

Ellis, George. *Specimens of the Early English Poets.* 3 vols. London, 1845.

English Cookery Five Hundred Years Ago. Privately printed. Totham, 1849.

The English Works of Wyclif. Edited by Frederick D. Matthew. EETS OS 74. London, 1880.

The Exeter Book. Edited and translated by Israel Gollancz. EETS OS 104. London, 1894-1895.

A Fifteenth Century Courtesy Book and Two Franciscan Rules. Edited by Raymond Wilson Chambers. EETS OS 148. London, 1914.

The Fifty Earliest English Wills. Edited by Frederick J. Furnivall. EETS OS 78. London, 1882.

The Forme of Cury, a Roll of Ancient Cookery, compiled about 1390, by the Master-Cooks of King Richard II. Edited by Samuel Pegge. London, 1780.

French Medieval Romances from the Lays of Marie de France. Translated by Eugene Mason. Second edition. London, 1924.

Froissart, *Chronicles of England, France, Spain and Other Countries.* Edited by Thomas Johnes. 2 vols. London, 1844.

Godstow Nunnery Records. Edited by Andrew Clark. EETS OS 129, 130. London, 1905, 1906.

The Gorleston Psalter. Described by Sydney Cockerell. London, 1907.

Gower, John. *Confessio Amantis.* Edited by Reinhold Pauli. 3 vols. London, 1857.

Graesse, John G. Th. *Jacobi a Voragine Legenda Aurea.* Lipsae, 1850.

Guilford, Everard L. *Select Extracts Illustrating Sports and Pastimes in the Middle Ages.* New York, 1920.

Hammond, Eleanor P. *English Verse Between Chaucer and Surrey.* Duke University Press, 1927.

Hardy, William. *A Collection of Chronicles and Ancient Histories of Great Britain.* Edited by John de Wavrin. London, 1864.

Heures de Turin. Quarante-cinq feuillets à peintures provenant des très belles Heures de Jean de France, duc de Berry. Paris, 1902.

The Household Book of Dame Alice de Bryene. Translated by Marian K. Dale and edited by Vincent Redstone. Ipswich, 1931.

The Lay of Havelok the Dane. Edited by Walter W. Skeat. Oxford, 1902.

Leechdoms, Wortcunning, and Starcraft of Early England. Collected and edited by Oswald Cockayne. Rolls series. 2 vols. London, 1864, 1865.

Libeaus Desconus. Edited by Max Kaluza. Leipzig, 1890.

Liber Albus. Edited by Henry T. Riley. London, 1861.

Liber Custumarum. Edited by Henry T. Riley. 2 vols. London, 1860.

The Master of Game. Edited by William A. and F. Baillie-Grohman, with a foreword by Theodore Roosevelt. London, 1904.

Medieval Lore. Edited by Robert Steele. London, 1893.

Le Ménagier de Paris. 2 vols. Paris, 1846.

Memorials of London and London Life. Edited by Henry T. Riley. London, 1868.

Middle English Metrical Romances. Edited by Walter H. French and Charles B. Hale. London, 1930.

Monumenta Franciscana. Edited by Richard Hawlett. 3 vols. London, 1882.

Malory, Sir Thomas. *Le Morte Darthur.* 2 vols. London, 1903.

Myrc, John. *Instructions for Parish Priests.* EETS OS 31. London, 1868.

Napier, Mrs. Alexander. *A Noble Boke off Cookry.* London, 1882.

Neckam, Alexander. *De Naturis Rerum.* Edited by Thomas Wright. London, 1863.

Nicolas, Sir Nicholas H. *Testamenta Vetusta.* 2 vols. London, 1826.

Nichols, John. *Illustrations of the Manners and Expences of Antient Times in England . . . from the Accompts of Churchwardens,* etc. London, 1797.

Old English Riddles. Edited by Sir Arthur Wyatt. Boston, 1912.

An Old English Miscellany. Edited by Richard Morris. EETS OS 49. London, 1872.

Partonope of Blois. Edited by a Trampe Bödtker. EETS ES 109. London, 1912.

The Paston Letters. Edited by James Gairdner. 6 vols. London, 1904. I, II.

Phoebus, Gaston (Comte de Foix). *Livre de la Chasse.* Paris, 1909. (Reproduction Réduite des 87 miniatures du manuscrit français 616 de la Bibliothèque Nationale.)

Pierce the Ploughman's Crede. Edited by Walter W. Skeat. EETS OS 30. London, 1867.

Piers Plowman. Edited by Walter W. Skeat. (Texts B and C.) EETS OS 38, 54. London, 1869, 1873.

Piers Ploughman's Vision and Creed. Edited by Thomas Wright. 2 vols. London, 1887.

Political, Religious, and Love Poems. Edited by Frederick J. Furnivall. EETS OS 15. London, 1866.

Political Poems and Songs. Edited by Thomas Wright. Rolls series. London, 1850.

Power, Eileen. *The Goodman of Paris.* (Translation of Le Ménagier de Paris). London, 1928.

The Promptorium Parvalorum. Edited by Anthony Mayhew. EETS OS 102. London, 1908.

Queen Mary's Psalter. Introduction by George Warner. London, 1912.

Reliquae Antiquae. Edited by Thomas Wright and James O. Halliwell. 2 vols. London, 1845.

Rhodes, Walter E. "An Inventory of the Jewels and Wardrobe of Queen Isabella." *English Historical Review,* 12 (July, 1897), 517-521.

Richard the Redeless. Edited by Walter W. Skeat. EETS ES 54. London, 1873.

Ritson, Joseph. *Ancient English Metrical Romances.* 3 vols. Revised by Edmund Goldsmid. Edinburgh, 1884.

The Romance of Emaré. Re-edited by Edith Rickert. Chicago, 1907.

Royal and Noble Wills. Edited by John Nichols. London, 1780.

The Rule of St. Benet. (Three Middle English Versions.) Edited by Ernest A. Koch. EETS OS 120. London, 1902.

The Rule of St. Benedict. Translated and edited by Cardinal Gasquet. London, 1925.

Satirical Songs and Poems on Costume. Edited by Frederick W. Fairholt. Percy Society Publications, 27. London, 1849.

Sir Beues of Hamtoun. Edited by Eugene Kölbing. EETS ES 46. London, 1885.

Sir Gawayne and the Green Knight. Edited by Richard Morris. EETS OS 4. London, 1864.

Spencer, Sylvia. *Up from the Earth.* A Collection of Garden Poems 1300-1935. Boston, 1935.

The Squyr of Lowe Degre. Edited by William E. Mead. Boston, 1904.

The Stonor Letters and Papers. 1290-1483. Edited by Charles L. Kingsford. Camden Society. Third Series, 29, 30. London, 1919.

Supplementary Stonor Letters and Papers. Edited by Charles L. Kingsford. Royal Historical Society Publications. (Camden Miscellany, 13.) London, 1924.

The Tale of Beryn, with a Prologue of the Merry Adventure of the Pardoner with a Tapster at Canterbury. Edited by Frederick J. Furnivall and W. G. Stone. EETS ES 105. London, 1909.

The Tale of Gamelyn. Printed from Walter W. Skeat's edition. New Rochelle, 1901.

Thirty-two Miniatures from the Book of Hours of Joan II Queen of Navarre. 2 parts. Roxborough Club Publications. London, 1899.

Two Fifteenth-Century Cookery-Books. Edited by Thomas Austin. EETS OS 91. London, 1888.

Visitations of Religious Houses in the Diocese of Lincoln. Edited by Alexander H. Thompson. 3 vols. Canterbury and York Society Publications. London, 1919-1927.

William Thorne's Chronicle of St. Augustine's Abbey Canterbury. Translated by Alfred H. Davis. Oxford, 1934.

2. SECONDARY WORKS

Abram, Annie. *English Life and Manners in the Later Middle Ages.* London, 1913.

Addy, Sidney Oldall. *The Evolution of the English House.* Revised and enlarged from the author's notes by John Summerson. London, 1933.

Andrews, James Pettit. *The History of Great Britain.* London, 1794.

Ashdown, Charles H. *Armour and Weapons in the Middle Ages.* London, 1925.

Ashton, John. *The History of Gambling in England.* London, 1898.

Baillie-Grohman, William A. *Sport in Art.* London, 1913.

Barrow, Sarah F. *The Medieval Society Romances.* New York, 1924.

Bede, His Life, Times, and Writings. Alexander H. Thompson. Oxford, 1935.

Belloc, Hilaire. *The Book of the Bayeux Tapestry.* New York, 1914.

Benham, Canon and Charles Welch. "Medieval London," in *The Portfolio,* 42. London, 1921.

Bennet, Henry S. *The Pastons and Their England.* Cambridge, 1922.

Besant, Sir Walter. *Medieval London.* 2 vols. London, 1906.

Boas, Ralph P. and Barbara Hahn. *Social Backgrounds of English Literature.* Boston, 1930.

Boissonnade, Prosper. *Life and Work in Medieval England.* Translated by Eileen Power. London, 1927.

Brandon, Leonard G. *A Short Economic and Social History of England.* London, 1930.

Brett, Edwin J. *A Pictorial and Descriptive Record of the Origin and Development of Arms and Armour.* London, 1894.

Burney, Charles. *A General History of Music,* with critical and historical notes by Frank Mercer. 4 vols. New York, 1789. Vol. I.

British Museum Guide to the Medieval Room. Oxford, 1907.

Britton, John. *A Dictionary of the Architecture and Archeology of the Middle Ages.* London, 1838.

The Buke of the Order of Knyghthood. Translated by Sir Gilbert Hay. Edited by Beriah Botfield. Edinburgh, 1847.

Butler, Cuthbert. *Benedictine Monachism.* London, 1924.

Byrne, Sister Mary of the Incarnation. *The Tradition of the Nun in Medieval England.* Dissertation. Washington, 1932.

Calthrop, Dion C. *English Costume.* 4 vols. London, 1906.

Camden, William. *Britannia.* 2 vols. London, 1753. Vol. I.

Campbell, James Marshall. "Patristic Studies in the Literature of Medieval England," *Speculum,* 8 (Oct., 1933), 465-478.

Capes, William W. *The English Church in the Fourteenth and Fifteenth Centuries.* New York, 1900.

Cecil, Mrs. Evelyn. *A History of Gardening in England.* Third edition. London, 1910.

Cessolis, Jacobus. *The Game of the Chesse.* Caxton's edition. Re-edited by Vincent Figgins. London, 1860.

Chadwick, Dorothy. *Social Life in the Days of Piers Plowman.* Cambridge, 1922.

Chambers, Edmund K. *The Medieval Stage.* 2 vols. Oxford, 1903.

Cheyney, Edward P. "Village Life in Medieval England," *Lippincotts,* 68 (Sept., 1901), 365-373.

Chivalry. Edited by Edgar Prestage. New York, 1928.

Clinch, George. *English Costume from Prehistoric Times to the End of the Eighteenth Century.* London, 1909.

Cockaine, Sir Thomas. *A Short Treatise of Hunting.* London, 1591. Roxborough Club, 1897.

Collingwood, John. *The Bayeux Tapestry Elucidated.* London, 1856.

Collins, Ross W. *A History of Medieval Civilization in Europe.* Boston, 1936.

Cooper, Charles. *The English Table in History and Literature.* London, 1929.

Coulton, George G. *Five Centuries of Religion.* 3 vols. Cambridge, 1923.

———, *Social Life in Britain.* Cambridge, 1918.

———, *Life in the Middle Ages.* Second edition. New York, 1930.

———, *The Medieval Village.* Cambridge, 1925.

———, *The Medieval Scene.* Cambridge, 1930.

———, *A Medieval Garner.* London, 1910.

Cox, J. Charles. *The Royal Forests of England.* London, 1905.

Cox, Nicholas. *The Gentleman's Recreation.* London, 1706.

Craik, George L. and Charles MacFarlane. *Pictorial History of England.* 8 vols. London, 1849.

Cranage, David H. S. *The Home of the Monk.* Cambridge, 1934.

Cripps-Day, Francis. *The History of the Tournament.* London, 1918.

Crisp, Sir Frank. *Medieval Gardens.* 2 vols. London, 1924.

Crosby, Ruth. "Oral Delivery in the Middle Ages," *Speculum,* 11 (Jan., 1936), 88-110.

Cutts, Edward L. *Scenes and Characters of the Middle Ages.* New edition. London, 1925.

Dale, Edmund. *National Life and Character in the Mirrour of Early English Literature.* Cambridge, 1907.

Dalton, John Neale. *The Collegiate Church of Ottery St. Mary.* Cambridge, 1917.

D'Aussy, Le Grand. *Histoire de la vie Privée des Français.* 3 vols. Paris, 1782.

D'Auvergne, Edmund B. F. *The English Castles.* New York, 1926.

Davis, Henry W. C. *Medieval England.* A new edition of Barnard's *Companion to English History.* Oxford, 1924.

Dawson, C. B. *The Mirror of Oxford.* London, 1912.

Day, James W. *A Falcon on St. Paul's.* London, 1935.

Dillon, Harold A. *Fairholt's Costume in England.* 2 vols. London, 1896.

Dixon, William H. *Fasti Eboracenses.* Edited and enlarged by James Raine. London, 1863.

Dolby, Anastasia. *Church Vestments: Their Origin, Use, and Ornament.* London, 1868.

Dugdale, Sir William. *Monasticon Anglicanum.* Second edition. 8 vols. London, 1846.

———, *Monasticon Anglicanum.* 3 vols. London, 1718-1723.

Eagleson, Harvey. "Costume in the Middle English Metrical Romances," *Publications of the Modern Language Association,* 47 (June, 1932), 339-345.

Eckenstein, Lina. *Woman Under Monasticism.* Cambridge, 1896.

Emden, Alfred B. *An Oxford Hall in Medieval Times.* Oxford, 1927.

Evans, Joan. *Life in Medieval France.* Oxford, 1925.

Evans, Mary. *Costume Throughout the Ages.* Chicago, 1930.

Feasey, Henry J. *Monasticism.* London, 1898.

Fiske, Willard. *Chess Tales and Chess Miscellanies.* New York, 1912.

Fleetwood, Bishop. *Chronicon Preciosum: or, An Account of English Gold and Silver Money, The Price of Corn and Other Commodities . . .* London, 1745.

"Food Hygiene of the Middle Ages," *London Quarterly Review,* 153 (Jan., 1930), 40-52.

Forbes, Duncan. *The History of Chess.* London, 1860.

Formoy, Beryl E. R. *The Dominican Order before the Reformation.* London, 1888.

Fosbroke, Thomas D. *British Monachism.* Third Edition, with additions. London, 1843.

Franklin, Alfred. *La Vie Privée d'Autrefois.* 23 vols. Paris, 1888.

    I. Les Soins de Toilette.

    III. La Cuisine.

    VI. Les Repas..

    VIII. Variétés Gastronomiques.

––––––, *La Vie au Temps des Premiers Capétiens.* 2 vols. Paris, 1911.

Gardner, John Starkie. *Armour in England from the Earliest Times to the Reign of James the First.* London, 1897.

Gasquet, Cardinal. *English Monastic Life.* London, 1904.

––––––, *Parish Life in Medieval England.* Chicago, 1906.

––––––, *Monastic Life in the Middle Ages.* London, 1922.

Gautier, Léon. *La Chevalerie.* Paris, 1883.

Gerarde, John. *The Herball, or General Historie of Plantes.* London, 1597.

Goatley, H. D. "History of Hunting: Some Medieval Literature," in *British Hunts and Huntsmen.* 4 vols. London, 1908. I, 1-18.

Good Companion. Edited by James F. Magee, Jr. Florence, 1910.

Gotch, John. *The Growth of the English House.* Second edition, revised and enlarged. London, 1928.

Gothein, Marie Luise. *A History of Garden Art.* Edited by Walter P. Wright and translated from the German by Mrs. Archer-Hind. 2 vols. London, 1928.

Grose, Francis. *Military Antiquities Respecting a History of the English Army from the Conquest to the Present Time.* Second edition. 2 vols. London, 1812.

Hartley, Dorothy. *Medieval Costume and Life.* New York, 1931.

Hayward, Charles H. *English Rooms and their Decorations at a Glance.* New York, 1926.

Hecker, Justus F. C. *The Epidemics of the Middle Ages.* London, 1844.

Hefener-Alteneck, J. H. de. *Costumes du Moyen-Age Chrétien.* 3 vols. Frankfort, 1850-54.

Helm, William H. *Homes of the Past.* London, 1921.

Home, Gordon and Edward Foord. *Medieval London.* London, 1927.

Hill, O'Dell Travers. *English Monasticism.* London, 1867.

Huizinga, Johan. *The Waning of the Middle Ages.* London, 1924.

Hulton, Samuel F. *Rixae Oxonienses.* London, 1892.

Hyll, Thomas. *A Most Briefe and Pleasaunt Treatyse, Teachynge how to Dress, Sowe, and Set A Garden.* First edition. London, 1565.
———, *The Profitable Art of Gardening.* Third edition. London, 1579.
Jameson, Anna Murphy. *Sacred and Legendary Art.* Second edition. London, 1850.
Joret, Charles. *La Rose dans L'Antiquité et au Moyen Age.* Paris, 1892.
Jusserand, Jean Jules. *English Wayfaring Life in the Middle Ages.* Translated by Lucy T. Smith. New edition. New York, 1931.
de Lewenhaupt, Count C. A. C. *Sport Across the World.* London, 1933.
Longman, William. *The History of the Life and Times of Edward III.* 2 vols. London, 1869.
Lyte, Henry. *A New Herbal.* London, 1619.
Macklin, Herbert W. *The Brasses of England.* London, 1907.
Macquoid, Percy and Ralph Edwards. *The Dictionary of English Furniture.* 3 vols. New York, 1924.
Madden, Dodgson H. *A Chapter of Medieval History.* London, 1924.
Mallet, Sir Charles Edward. *A History of the University of Oxford.* London, 1924.
Mead, William E. *The English Medieval Feast.* London, 1931.
"Mr. Bull at Home in the Middle Ages," *Household Words,* 4 (Nov. 1, 1841), 121-126.
Murray, Harold J. R. *A History of Chess.* Oxford, 1913.
Nichols, Rose Standish. *English Pleasure Gardens.* New York, 1902.
"Old English Cookery," *Quarterly Review,* 178 (January, 1894), 82-104.
Oliver, Basil. *The Cottages of England.* New York, 1929.
Our English Home. (Anonymous). London, 1860.
Owst, Gerald R. *Literature and Pulpit in Medieval England.* Cambridge, 1933.
Painter, Sidney. "Monday as a Date for Medieval Tournaments," *Modern Language Notes,* 48 (Feb., 1933), 80-83.
Parker, John H. *Some Account of Domestic Architecture.* 2 vols. London, 1859.
Parkyns, George J. *Monastic and Baronial Remains.* 2 vols. London, 1816.
Pendrill, Charles. *London Life in the Fourteenth Century.* London, 1925.
———, *Wanderings in Medieval London.* London, 1928.
Planché, Joseph R. *A Cyclopedia of Costume.* 2 vols. London, 1876, 1879.
———, *History of British Costume.* London, 1843.
Power, Eileen. *Medieval People.* London, 1924.
———, *Medieval English Nunneries.* Cambridge, 1922.
Powicke, Frederick M. *Medieval England.* London, 1931.
Quennell, Marjorie and C. H. B. *A History of Everyday Things in England.* New York, 1922.
———, *Everyday Life in Anglo-Saxon, Viking, and Norman Times.* New York, 1927.

Racinet, Albert C. *Le Costume Historique.* 6 vols. Paris, 1876-1888. III, IV.

Rait, Robert S. *Life in the Medieval University.* Cambridge, 1912.

Rapp, Sister Catherine Teresa. *Burgher and Peasant in the Works of Thomasin von Zirclaria, Freidank, and Hugo von Trimberg.* Dissertation. Washington, D. C., 1936.

Rogers, James, E. Thorold. *A History of Agriculture and Prices in England.* 1259-1499. Vol. II. Oxford, 1866.

———, *Six Centuries of Work and Wages.* New York, 1914.

Rohde, Eleanour S. *The Story of the Garden.* Third edition. Boston, 1936.

———, *The Scented Garden.* Fourth edition. Boston, 1936.

Sabine, Ernest L. "Butchering in Medieval London," *Speculum,* 8 (July, 1933), 335-353.

Salzman, Louis F. *English Life in the Middle Ages.* London, 1921.

———, *Medieval Byways.* New York, 1913.

———, *More Medieval Byways.* London, 1926.

Saunders, Herbert W. *An Introduction to the Obedientiary and Manor Rolls of Norwich Cathedral Priory.* Norwich, 1930.

Savage, Henry L. "Hunting in the Middle Ages," *Speculum,* 8 (Jan., 1933), 30-41.

Schofield, William H. *Chivalry in English Literature.* Cambridge, Mass., 1912.

Seton, William. "Pen Picture of English Life in the Fourteenth Century," *Catholic World,* 76 (Jan., Feb., 1903), 531-42; 636-44.

Sharp, Evelyn. *Here we go Round.* New York, 1928.

Singleton, Esther. *The Shakespeare Garden.* New York, 1931.

Snape, Robert Hugh. *English Monastic Finances in the Later Middle Ages.* Cambridge, 1926.

Snell, Frederick. *The Customs of Old England.* London, 1911.

Sparrow, Walter S. *The English House.* New York, 1909.

Stevenson, John J. *House Architecture.* 2 vols. London, 1880.

St. Johnston, Reginald. *A History of Dancing.* London, 1906.

Stow, John. *Survey of London.* Edited by C. L. Kingsford. 2 vols. Oxford, 1908.

Strickland, Agnes. *Lives of the Queens of England.* 16 vols. Philadelphia, 1902. II, III.

Strutt, Joseph. *The Regal and Ecclesiastical Antiquities of England.* London, 1842.

———, *Sports and Pastimes of the Middle Ages.* London, 1876.

———, *A Complete View of the Dress and Habits of the People of England.* 2 vols. London, 1842.

Stuart, Dorothy M. *Men and Women of Plantagenet England.* London, 1932.

Tatlock, John S. P. "Middle Ages: Romantic or Rationalistic." *Speculum,* 8 (July, 1933), 295-304.

Taunton, Ethelred L. *The English Black Monks of St. Benedict.* 2 vols. London, 1898.

Taylor, Henry Osborn. *The Medieval Mind.* 2 vols. London, 1911.

Thomas, A. H. "Illustrations of the Medieval Municipal History of London," in *Transactions of the Royal Historical Society.* Fourth series, 4 (London, 1921), 81-102.

Thomas, Joseph B. *Hounds and Hunting Through the Ages.* New York, 1933.

Thompson, James W. *An Economic and Social History of the Middle Ages.* New York, 1928.

Thorndike, Lynn. *History of Magic and Experimental Science.* New York, 1923.

————, "Sanitation, Baths, and Street-Cleaning in the Middle Ages and Renaissance," *Speculum,* III (April, 1928), 192-204.

Tipping, Henry Avray. *English Homes.* Period I. London, 1921.

Trevelyan, George. *England in the Age of Wycliffe.* New edition. London, 1904.

Tullock, W. W. "Manners and Meals in Olden Times," *Belgravia,* 14 (March, 1871), 118-129.

Tupper, Frederick. *Types of Society in Medieval Literature.* New York, 1923.

Turner, Hudson. *Some Account of Domestic Architecture of the Middle Ages.* 12-14 century. 2 vols. Oxford, 1853.

————, "Usages of Domestic Life in the Middle Ages," *Archaeological Journal,* II (1845), 173-180; 258-266.

Twiss, Richard. *Chess.* London, 1781.

Vigneras, L. A. and Sidney Painter. "Monday as a Date for Medieval Tournaments," *Modern Language Notes,* 48 (Feb., 1933), 80-83.

Viollet-le Duc. E. *Dictionnaire Raisonné de L'Architecture Française du* XI and XVI siècle. 9 vols. Paris, 1858-1868.

————, *Dictionnaire Raisonné du Mobilier Français, de L'Epoque Carlovingienne à la Renaissance.* 6 vols. Paris, 1914.

Vuillier, Gaston. *A History of Dancing.* Second edition. New York, 1918.

Warton, Thomas. *The History of English Poetry.* 3 vols. Second edition. London, 1840.

Wethered, Herbert N. *A Short History of Gardens.* London, 1933.

Wilton, Mary M. *The Book of Costume.* London, 1846.

Wright, Richardson L. *The Story of Gardening.* New York, 1934.

Wright, Thomas. "Medieval Manners," *The Art Journal,* 12 (Jan., 1, 1860), 45-47.

————, *The Homes of Other Days.* London, 1871.

INDEX

Absolon, 159, 160
Ale, 48, 49, 70, 95, 105, 114, 134, 135
Alison, 134, 171, 179, 180, 181
Aniseed, 151
Antigone, 83
Apron, 179
Arbour, 86, 88. See also Trees
Archery, 192, 226, 227, 245, 252
Arcite, 37, 208, 210, 212, 216, 217, 218
Armour, 155, 158, 159, 160, 189, 215, 251
Arveragus, 85, 234
Avarice, 175

Bacon, 104, 105
Backgammon, 233, 234, 246, 252
Balcony, 119
Bartholomaeus Anglicus, 55
Beans, 105
Beard, 150, 151, 152, 154, 160, 188
Beds, 15, 20, 21, 27, 36, 37, 38, 39, 40, 45, 46, 51, 121, 170, 249
Benches, 17, 21, 28, 29, 31, 40, 41, 51, 63, 65, 88, 90, 249, 250
Birds, 41, 42, 43, 55, 58, 61, 83, 86, 90, 144, 188, 240, 250
Bird Cages, 42, 43, 52
Blackmanger, 115, 136
Blessed Virgin, 63, 88
Boccaccio, 209
Book of the Duchess, 7, 26, 33, 193, 194, 201, 202, 203
Books, 21, 36, 43, 44, 169, 198, 241, 246
Boots, 151, 163, 189
Bower, 14, 19, 37, 50, 89, 137, 249
Brass, 154, 205
Bread, 48, 49, 95, 101, 104, 105, 106, 107, 109, 126, 136
Le Bréviaire Grimani, 19
Bridle, 165
Buttery, 18
Buttercups, 56

Cabbage, 105
Cambinskan, King, 7, 21, 25, 26, 32, 95, 120, 121, 124, 135, 141
Canacee, 41, 42, 43, 52
Candles, 29, 41

The Canon (Augustinian), 167, 189
Canterbury Tales, 9, 140, 146, 177, 242, 253
Canticle of Canticles, 63, 64, 88
Carnation, 77
Caroles, 220, 221, 244
Carts, 45, 46
Carpenter, 14, 15, 18, 34, 36, 48, 50, 52, 68, 70, 71, 81, 154, 179, 190, 239
Castle, 2, 3, 4, 8, 9, 11, 17
Cattle. See Kine
Ceiling, 36
Cellars, 15, 17
Cetewale, 80
Chairs. See Benches
Chamber, 12, 13, 15, 18, 20, 21, 30, 31, 32, 34, 44, 51, 67, 89, 97, 249
Chapel, 15, 16, 50, 95, 249. See also Oratory
Chaunticleer, 82, 238
Cheese, 105
Chess, 230-234, 245, 252
Chickens, 19, 110, 114, 136
Chimneys, 8, 17
Chivalry, 156
Clerk of Oxenford, 168, 169
Clerk's Tale, 11, 96, 176, 205
Cloths, 36, 37, 154, 155
Clove-gilliflower, 78, 89
Coat, 145, 152, 154
Coat-of-arms, 143
Coif, 148, 182
Cope, 163, 165, 166, 170, 189
Cottage, 18, 19, 20, 22, 50, 248
Counting-house, 15, 18, 44, 50, 249
Counting-stones, 36
Cowl, 163
Cupid, 143
"Court," 10, 11, 12, 49. See also Hall
Cradle, 15, 20
Criseyde, 28, 30, 31, 32, 37, 46, 62, 67, 79, 83, 84, 85, 92, 93, 98, 134, 180, 232, 237, 241
Cristofre. See St. Christopher

Dais, 23, 25, 50, 121, 122, 126, 249
Daisies, 56, 74, 75, 84, 88, 89
Dame Pertolote, 82

275

Damian, 32, 124, 127, 170
Dance, 58, 83, 90, 119, 134, 135, 137, 192, 219-226, 236, 244, 245, 252
Daun John, 86, 93, 110, 133
Deiphebus, 62, 67, 93
De Naturis Rerum, 55
De Proprietatibus Rerum, 55
Dinner, 92, 93, 94, 95, 96, 135, 250
Diomede, 134
Ditch, 19, 50
Dogs. See Hounds
Doorway, 12, 25
Dorigene, 85, 234
Drawbridge, 12
Dyer, 154

Eggs, 104, 118
Eglentyne, Madame. See Prioress
Eleyne, 62
Ellesmere Manuscript, 147, 148, 149, 158
Emelye, 7, 37, 68, 79, 84, 175, 208, 215, 217, 218
Emetreus, King of Inde, 75, 142, 143, 205, 207, 212
Ermine, 145
Evilmerodach, King, 230
Eyebrows, 180, 190, 251

Falcon, 19, 207, 218
Fennel, 80
Filostrato, 83
Fire, 20, 50
Fireplace, 12, 37, 41, 137, 249
Fish, 105, 106, 118, 136
Flanders, 151, 155
Floor, 19, 21, 25, 35, 46, 80, 119, 243
Flute, 238, 346
Fountains, 59, 60, 65, 88
Franklin, 25, 101, 102, 103, 104, 105, 132, 149
Franklin's Tale, 7, 43
Friar, 10, 40, 106, 107, 108, 110, 145, 166, 238
Friar's Tale, 154, 207
Froissart, 20, 24, 77
Fur, 51, 146, 148, 149, 170, 185, 187, 190

Gambling, 234-236, 246
Garden, 11, 35, 53-90, 218, 244, 250, 252, 253
Garlands, 84, 85, 90, 143, 144, 145, 155, 173, 188, 190
Garlic, 66, 81, 89, 112, 171

Garret, 18, 20, 46
Gateway, 9
Gates, 4, 5, 46, 49, 63, 216
Gille, 35
Gipoun (jupon), 157, 158, 189
Girdle, 148, 149, 153, 154, 173, 174, 179, 190
Gloves, 173
Gold, 5, 21, 26, 27, 42, 57, 142, 143, 144, 149, 160, 163, 172, 174, 175, 184, 185, 189, 216, 218
Goodman, 131
Goodman of Paris, 27, 42, 78, 110
Goose, 49, 95, 117
Geese, 105, 128
Graynes, 81
Grisilde, 19, 26, 28, 82, 121, 176, 177
Grocer, 18, 28, 151

Haberdasher, 154
Habergeoun, 156, 157, 158, 160, 189
Hair, 142, 143, 147, 153, 154, 169, 170, 171, 172, 175, 188, 189, 190
Hall, 14, 15, 16, 17, 19, 21, 22, 23, 24, 25, 26, 27, 28, 29, 30, 32, 46, 50, 93, 97, 98, 120, 123, 135, 136, 137, 249. See also Court
Harpers, 5, 236, 237, 238, 246
Hart, 195, 196, 198
Hat, 147, 150, 154, 155, 168, 179, 188
Hauberk, 157
Hawking, 192, 203-208, 227, 243, 251
Heralds, 212, 215, 244
Herons, 100
Herrings, 112
Honey, 70
Honeysuckle, 62, 88
Hood, 146, 148, 149, 152, 153, 154, 163, 165, 166, 169, 167, 188, 189
Hood (hawking), 205
Horn, 193, 215, 242
Horses, 51, 96, 143, 147, 199, 213, 215, 216, 217, 242, 244
Hose, 146, 148, 152, 154, 155, 169, 178, 188, 189, 190
Hosteler, 46, 47, 52
Host, 95, 161, 168
Hounds, 194, 195, 199, 200, 201, 202, 242, 243, 251
House of Fame, 4, 9, 221, 236, 248

Inns, 46, 95, 96, 210
Ipolita, 215
Ivory, 160

Jailer, 6, 68
Jack of Dover, 116, 136
Jambeux, 160
January, 10, 11, 21, 32, 62, 63, 71,
    86, 94, 97, 120, 121, 124, 127,
    134, 135
Jesters, 5
Jewels. See Precious stones
John of Gaunt, 24
Josephus, 23
Josian, 123
Juno, 37

Keep, 3
Kenilworth Castle, 24
Kerchiefs, 177, 178, 181, 253
Kine, 19, 20, 100, 137, 215
Kirtle, 153, 169, 182, 189, 190
Kitchen, 14, 15, 17, 44, 50, 135, 137,
    138, 249, 250
Knight of la Tour Landry, 187
Knight's Tale, 6, 24, 68, 69, 119,
    208, 209, 211, 219, 244
Knives, 149, 152, 154, 155

Langland, 20, 125
Larder, 17, 91, 102, 136
Leeks, 66, 81
"Legend of Ariadne," 6
Legend of Good Women, 6, 9, 57,
    176, 202
Licorice, 80
Ligurge, King of Thrace, 142, 201,
    202, 212
Lilies, 54, 63, 75, 88, 89, 160
Linen, 45, 51, 159, 174, 178, 181, 190
Lionel, 100
Liver, 107
Lydgate, 42, 64, 65, 164, 165
Lyte, Henry, 74

Malle, 19
Man of Law's Tale, 7, 224
Man of Law, 148, 149, 155
Manor, 9, 10, 11, 12, 13, 18, 22, 49,
    104, 248
Mantle, 143, 146, 155, 165, 166, 182,
    188, 190
Marigolds, 79, 89
Marriage Feast, 94, 96, 120, 121, 133,
    223
Marshall, 124, 125, 126, 128, 137
Mass, 16, 17, 22, 93, 94, 210, 211, 240
May, 10, 32, 62, 63, 64, 86, 94, 121,
    170
Merchant's Tale, 32, 121, 224

Mew, 41, 52
Milk, 104
Miller, 32, 48, 49, 51, 52, 95, 151,
    152, 188, 228, 242
Miller's Tale, 14, 18, 34, 48, 68, 70,
    169, 177, 179, 222, 238
Minos, King, 6
Minstrels, 32, 83, 119, 120, 121, 126,
    236, 249
Mint, 79
Moat, 3, 4, 11, 12, 19, 49, 50
Monk, 161, 162, 163, 164, 197, 198,
    202, 253
Morpheus, 37
Morris (dance), 222, 245
Mortar, 4
Musical instruments, 4, 36, 119, 192,
    217, 220, 236, 238, 240, 246

Neckam, Alexander, 55
Nero, 141
Nicholas, 14, 34, 35, 36, 37, 40, 48,
    68, 238, 239
Nine Worthies, 27
Nun's Priest's Tale, 18, 46, 65, 82
Nun's Priest, 207
Nutmeg, 80

Oatmeal, 105
Onions, 66, 81, 89, 112, 171
Oratory, 15. See also Chapel
Organ, 238, 246
Ox-stall. See Kine

Palamon, 68, 156, 208, 210, 212, 216,
    218
Palmer, 123
Pandarus, 28, 31, 32, 40, 84, 85, 92,
    98, 99, 180, 237, 241
Pantaloons, 148
Pantry, 15, 18, 125
Parapets, 12
Pardoner, 113, 131, 169, 225, 235,
    239, 240, 245
Pardoner's Tale, 224
Parsley, 105, 117
Partridge, 105
Parlement of Foules, 57, 61, 67, 69,
    73, 83, 207
Parson, 132, 140, 170, 186, 187, 190
Periwinkle, 60, 79, 88, 89
Persia, 154
Philippe-Auguste, 3
Philometer. See Xerpes
Physician, 133, 148, 149, 155, 188
Picnic, 85, 90, 250

Piers the Ploughman's Crede, 165
Pies, 115, 116, 253
Pigs, 19, 105, 107
Pigsnie, 79
Platter, 130
Plowman, 104, 105, 152, 153, 155, 175, 188
Porch, 17
Povert, 175
Precious stones, 42, 148, 160, 173, 174, 188, 190, 248, 252
Priest, 47, 52
Primrose, 79
Prioress, 65, 129, 177, 181, 182, 183, 184, 185, 240, 250, 253
Prison, 6

Queen Dido, 99, 202, 203
Queen Isabella, 150

Raisins, 112
Romaunt de la Rose, 2, 5, 9, 55, 56, 57, 65, 66, 67, 69, 72, 79, 83, 87, 140, 143, 171, 172, 174, 190, 220, 230, 231, 240, 250
Reeve, 19, 188
Reeve's Tale, 15, 32, 48, 152, 228, 242
Rice, 115
Richard II, 24, 100, 143, 200, 226
Richard Toky, 18, 28, 44, 151
Robe, 144, 148, 154, 173, 185, 188, 190
Robin, 35
Roof, 14, 50, 217
Rosary, 181, 183, 190
Roses, 54, 62, 63, 71, 72, 73, 74, 88, 89, 144, 145, 149
Rufus, William, 24

Salmon, 112
St. Benedict, 109, 163, 164, 165
St. Bernard, 130
St. Christopher, 154
St. Francis, 165
St. Julian, 136
St. Richard of Chichester, 168, 169
Satin, 38
Second Nun's Tale, 76, 238
Sewer, 17
Sheep, 19, 112
Shipman, 134, 152, 153, 188
Shoes, 145, 146, 147, 148, 149, 154, 155, 163, 169, 170, 178, 179, 182, 188, 189, 190, 222
Silks, 21, 51, 144, 148, 150, 159, 174, 178, 179, 183, 185, 190

Silver, 149, 154, 240
Simkin, 15, 18, 152, 228
Simon de Canterbury, 17
Sir Beves of Hamtoun, 123
Sir Gawayne, 8, 145
Sir John Bishopsden of Lapworth, 12
Sir Launfal, 145
Sir Mirth, 143, 144
Sir Thopas, 80, 138, 152, 154, 158, 159, 160, 161, 198, 205, 207, 226, 227, 228
Sleep, 120
Sleeves, 144, 149, 152, 157, 163, 173, 182, 188, 190
Solar, 14, 15, 17, 18, 30, 35, 40, 51, 249
Soups, 100, 114
Sows. See Pigs
Spices, 59, 61, 65, 77, 79, 88, 89, 96, 112, 114, 118, 129, 134, 136, 171
Squire, 147, 188, 238, 253
Squire's Tale, 41, 43, 99
Squyr of Lowe Degre, 36, 100, 128, 203
Stable, 14, 17, 50, 68
Stairs, 31, 67
Steward, 124, 125, 137
Stockings. See Hose
Story-telling, 242, 246, 252
Sturgeon, Nicholas, 27
Sugar, 70, 115, 118
Summoner, 81, 106, 239
Summoner's Tale, 10, 26, 39, 106
Supper, 94, 95, 96, 135
Swans, 100, 110, 128, 253

Tabard (Inn), 48, 175
Tabard (Jacket), 153, 188, 251
Table of Honor, 122, 123
Tables, 17, 21, 25, 26, 29, 50, 51, 119, 126, 130, 202, 249
Tableware, 138
Tale of Beryn, 65, 232
Tapestry-worker, 154
Teutonic Order of Knights, 122
Theseus, Duke, 6, 21, 24, 96, 120, 121, 141, 142, 196, 201, 203, 208, 209, 210, 212, 215, 217, 218, 224
Thomas, 10, 39
Tournament, 142, 244, 245, 251
Tower, 3, 4, 6, 7, 8, 24, 68
Town-house, 9, 12, 13, 17, 18, 22, 29, 50, 248

Trees, 19, 50, 55, 58, 61, 63, 65, 68, 69, 82, 88, 89, 250
Troilus, 28, 31, 40, 84, 85, 94, 99, 180, 196, 237, 242
Troilus and Criseyde, 9, 39, 45, 52, 83, 232, 237
Trumpets, 209, 215, 217, 237, 244, 246
Tryst, 86
Tunic, 37, 39, 149, 157, 163, 168, 182

Ushers, 124, 125, 126

Velvet, 42
Venison, 116
Violente, 100
Violets, 56, 60, 76, 77, 78, 88, 89
Viollet-le-Duc, 3

Wall, 3, 4, 8, 11, 12, 23, 26, 29, 32, 33, 49, 51, 57, 61, 66, 68, 88, 89, 249
Walter, 11, 19, 26, 82, 96, 121, 141, 205
Wand, 128

Wardrobe, 12
Wattles, 19
Weaver, 154
Wedding Feast. See Marriage Feast
Westminster Hall, 24, 100
Widow, 18, 20, 28, 65, 82, 103, 104, 132, 136, 180, 224
Wife of Bath, 65, 138, 177, 179, 181, 186, 190, 221, 225, 245, 253
Wills, 27, 38, 149
Wimple, 178, 181, 182, 183, 185, 190, 253
Windows, 12, 17, 18, 45, 51, 68, 169, 249
Wine, 95, 96, 101, 104, 105, 109, 129, 133, 134, 135, 136, 137, 245
Wool, 20
Wrestling, 192, 227-230, 245, 253

Xerxes, 230

Ydlenesse, 172, 173
Yeoman, 154, 168
Ywaine and Gawin, 8